BENEDETTO CROCE

BENEDETTO CROCE

ESSAYS ON LITERATURE AND LITERARY CRITICISM

Annotated and Translated from the Italian
with an Introduction by

M. E. Moss

STATE UNIVERSITY OF NEW YORK PRESS

Published by
State University of New York Press, Albany

© 1990 State University of New York

For information, address State University of New York Press,
State University Plaza, Albany, NY 12246

Library of Congress Cataloging-in-Publication Data

Croce, Benedetto, 1866–1952.
  [Essays. Selections. English]
  Benedetto Croce: Essays on Literature and Literary Criticism /
annotated and translated from the Italian, with an introduction by
M. E. Moss.
      p. cm.   68586
  Bibliography: p.
  Includes index.
  ISBN 0–7914–0200–2. — ISBN 0–7914–0201–0 (pbk.)
  1. Literature—Aesthetics.   2. Aesthetics, Modern.   I. Moss, M. E.
II. Title.
PN49.C69   1990
801′.93—dc20   89–4627
                                                       CIP

10 9 8 7 6 5 4 3 2 1

To A. F. R.

CONTENTS

PREFACE

Many years ago when I began to study the philosophy of Benedetto Croce, my professors in Italy told me that the vital part of his thought lay not in his philosophic views but instead in his literary criticism. In these writings that distinguished the aesthetic from the non-aesthetic, the poetic from the non-poetic, occurred some of Croce's most valuable contributions. I would agree that his flexible and open approach to literary criticism is indeed refreshing and at times even inspired. His essays are pungent, full of apt images and have a summary quality. All this in addition to their philosophic principles.

My selection of the essays that follow has been governed by a wish to indicate the range and variety of Croce's literary criticism and yet to include pieces that treat topics familiar to the well-educated reader of English. Croce's discussions assume that one is to some extent acquainted with the works cited, and with the critical commentary about them. These essays, as for example "Poe's Essays on Poetry," also well reveal Croce's mature theory of art along with his principles of literary criticism as put into practice.

After I had selected and translated Croce's articles into English, it seemed best to arrange the writings in chronological order as to their subjects. This arrangement gave a sense of coherence to the great variety of topics Croce treated, since his themes ranged from ancient Greek epics to Poe's essays. My listing also followed one of Croce's own methods of arrangement, which was roughly chronological rather than in terms of ideologies, genres, or trends.

Many of the essays include long passages cited in a language that is not modern Italian. Whenever such passages are in Latin, German, or Renaissance Italian I provide an English translation in the notes. In some instances I use older, more literal translations, rather than recent or poetic ones, because they include passages, phrases, and words discussed by Croce, but omitted in other renderings. In every case the reader should understand that in his critique Croce was referring to the sound, that is, to the balance, rhythm, and music of the original work, which cannot be exactly duplicated in translation. For this reason I put the English in the notes instead of simply substituting the translation for the original text.

The essays are preceded by a discussion of the evolution of his aesthetics which includes illustrations from the literary critiques that follow. There is no doubt that for him literary criticism and aesthetic theory were inextricably linked. And although according to the Crocean logic, theory preceded praxis, in fact historically the reverse was the case. In 1893, the first stimulus from praxis to theory derived from Croce's early work as historian, when he realized the need for guiding principles in the organization of his research. Subsequently, in 1908, the first development in his concept of art as particular and complex intuition to one of art as lyrical came about as much as a result of his early review of Italian writers for *La critica* as from Giulio Levi's philosophical critique of Croce's 1902 *Estetica*. Working with the melody, balance and harmonious tones of the italian language must have reinforced and deepened Croce's concept of art. And his study of the "cosmic poets," such as Dante, Shakespeare, Corneille, and Goethe led in 1918 to his further characterization of aesthetic intuition as cosmic totality.

ACKNOWLEDGMENTS

Kind individuals who have played a part in the preparation of this book were in Italy, Professor Guido Calogero and his wife, Maria Comandini, Professor Raffaello Franchini, and Dr. Ernesto Paolozzi. In America, Professor A. R. Caponigri encouraged me to proceed with this project; Professor Giovanni Gullace reviewed the manuscript and its bibliography; Dr. John Steadman, Dr. Albert Travis, and Dr. Daniel J. Donno suggested translations for Greek, Latin, Renaissance Italian, and German passages. Dr. Andrew Rolle, Mrs. Corinna Marsh, and Mr. Morris Glaser helped to edit style and content. Dr. John Steadman, Dr. Elizabeth S. Donno, and Dr. Lillian D. Bloom helped to answer questions on translation and theories of literary criticism. I would also like to acknowledge the patience, courtesy, and careful attention to detail shown by the staff of the State University of New York Press. Mrs. Noelle Jackson typed various drafts and Mrs. Frances Rolle prepared the index of this work. None of these persons is responsible for any of its shortcomings.

Special thanks to Dr. Daniel J. Donno for carefully reviewing all aspects of the book and especially the translations. His criticisms and suggestions have greatly improved the over-all quality and accuracy of this work.

The libraries at the University of California at Los Angeles, The Claremont colleges, Occidental College, Harvard College, and the Huntington Library have made available some of the sources on which the introduction is based.

Signora Alda Croce kindly gave permission to translate her father's essays into Italian.

INTRODUCTION

Few philosophers and historians have sustained the strong, enduring interest in literary criticism that Benedetto Croce (1866–1952) demonstrated during his long life.[1] What were the salient factors in Croce's background which stimulated his great enjoyment of literature and criticism?[2] Croce's father, Pasquale, administered his family's estates, a task which his son, Alfonso, Croce's younger brother, would assume after the tragedy that left both adolescents orphans. Their mother, Luisa Sipari, probably introduced Croce to literature as well as to history and encouraged his love of learning. In his *Contributo alla critica di me stesso*[3] (*Benedetto Croce: An Autobiography*), Croce recalled that at an early age he avidly read historical romances, especially the novels of Sir Walter Scott. Accompanied by his mother, Croce also enjoyed visiting the ancient monuments and old churches of Naples.

Later, when Croce was a student at the *Liceo Genovese* in Naples, he attempted to imitate the combative attitudes of Giosuè Carducci "in a contempt for the frivolous and self-indulgent manners of the fashionable world."[4] At the same time Croce grew disenchanted with what he considered the romantic decadence of Gabriele D'Annunzio's work. Croce would write that, although they were contemporaries and from the same region of Italy, spiritually speaking he and D'Annunzio belonged to different "races" and "religions."[5]

During his student days at the *Liceo,* Croce also studied the theories of Francesco De Sanctis (1817–1883), whose ideas became a source of his principles of literary criticism. De Sanctis, influenced by the aesthetics of Giambattista Vico (1668–1744), developed a concept of art as autonomous *vis-à-vis* other disciplines, such as philosophy and the empirical sciences. Croce, concurring with De Sanctis on this point, adopted Vico's position that poetry and language issued from the same fundamental activity of the human imagination.[6] Despite the fact that some years would pass before Croce completely assimilated Vico's writings, even as a youth Croce felt his influence, albeit indirectly, via De Sanctis's ideas. Nevertheless, only gradually and much later in Croce's career would he fully understand De Sanctis's thesis that the essence of art expressed pure and spontaneous aesthetic form. Thus in his "Intorno ai saggi del Poe sulla poesia"[7] ("Poe's Essays on Poetry") we will read Croce's acknowledgment that De Sanctis had "explained art as 'form,' form not at all the dress of content, but rather content itself transfigured; however only after long and persevering work (this too mostly Italian) did this principle come to constitute a *doctrinal corpus* as part of a philosophy of the spirit."[8]

In 1902, Croce published his first major description of the nature of aesthetic expression, entitled *Estetica come scienza dell'espressione e linguistica generale*[9] (*Aesthetic as Science of Expression and General Linguistic*). In opposition to the utilitarian and behavioristic accounts that had dominated late nineteenth century philosophies of art, Croce's *Estetica* argued that intuition was a noetic yet emotive and clear expression of the human spirit, not a turbid, obscure vibration of one's brain. This was a conception of the intuitional process with its images that he was to reaffirm subsequently. When evaluating Homer's *Iliad,* for instance, Croce wrote that "he gave implicit and tacit notice that poetry is light and clarity (*claritas*); and though it may also be difficult, it must always be profoundly clear."[10]

The *Estetica* argued, moreover, that in comparison with other forms of cognition, such as conceptual, scientific, or even historical, intuitional knowledge was the more fundamental. Concepts such as space and time, reality and unreality, truth and error, for instance, were not present in pure aesthetic representation. What then were these expressions of the human spirit that remained implicitly and explicitly present in our every thought, as well as during the most simple moment of cognitive awareness? Intuitions amounted to unique impressions-expressions of particular feelings. They formed the subject matter of literary criticism, and were to be sharply differentiated from the general laws and universals of empirical and abstract sciences.

The *Estetica* also postulated that whatever spirit did not manifest, represented a limit and a *sine qua non* for cognition. Intuition became distinguished as form from the "flux or wave of sensation, or from psychic matter; and . . . this taking possession, is expression."[11] Croce's distinction between intuition as form and primitive sensation as content had also occurred in Vico's criticism of Plato's philosophy for confining poetry "within the baser part of the soul, the animal spirits" because "poetry precedes intellect, but follows sense."[12] Subsequently Croce would maintain that within intuition one did not separate form from content. He came to ascribe his dualistic conception of intuition to a residue of Kantianism and naturalism that had appeared even earlier in his *Tesi fondamentali di un'Estetica come scienza dell'espressione e linguistica generale,*[13] 1900 (Fundamental Theses of an Aesthetic as Science of Expression and General Linguistic).

Croce's later concept of the organic unity between form and content was illustrated, among other places, in his "L'arte dello Shakespeare," ("Shakespeare's Art"), where he wrote: "In art, form and content cannot be disconnected and considered separately. Accordingly nothing that is said of Shakespearean form (provided that it point to something real and that has been well observed) escapes these two alternatives: either to repeat with application to Shakespeare the exposition of the characteristics, indeed of the unique characteristic of all poetry; or to provide under the name 'formal characteristics' more or less completely, nothing other than the characteristics of Shakespearean sentiment or sentiments."[14] Croce's attempt to capture what was unique in art occurred, among other places, in his essay "Il sentimento shakespeariano"[15] ("Shakespeare's Poetic Sentiment"). Here Croce focused his attention on a concise image of William Shakespeare's work in order to gain a notion of what was special to his inspiration. And in "Carattere e unità della poesia di Dante"[16] ("The Character and Unity of Dante's poetry"), Croce's task was to determine what was characteristic of the Dantesque spirit, so that the uniqueness of the *Commedia* would not vanish in generalities without precise references. The motif of Croce's subsequent writings shifted, however, from defining the special quality of the aesthetic object *qua* object to one of distinguishing between the presence and absence of art. The reader can perceive this change clearly in the differences between the two essays on Dante's work included in this volume—"The Character and Unity of Dante's Poetry"[17] and "The Concluding Canto of the *Commedia*."[18] Croce's shift in focus was heralded as early as the 1909 edition of the *Logica come scienza del concetto puro*[19] (*Logic as Science of the Pure Concept*) and the 1913 *Breviario di estetica*[20] (*Guide to Aesthetics*). It was consistently implemented in his 1923 *Poesia e non-poesia*[21] (*European Literature in the Nineteenth Century*). Croce's altered emphasis amounted to a gradual change in interest, however, and not to a contradiction of his theory of literary criticism.

I have described Croce's early conception of intuition, generally, as the emotive form of expression required for all types of knowledge. Let me indicate more precisely how ordinary intuition was to be distinguished from intuition as art. The latter represented a markedly more complex expression than a commonplace one. Croce proposed that intuitional objects, such as a shade of blue or a musical note, were much more simple than the complicated and occasionally difficult expressions of art. The quantitative complexity of such an object, however, did not bring with it a qualitative demarcation from non-art; since even a relatively simple intuition might be as perfect *sui generis* as an artist's complex imagery. According to Croce:

> The intuition of the simplest popular love-song, which says the same thing, or very nearly, as any declaration of love that issues at every moment from the lips of thousands of ordinary men, may be intensively perfect in its pure simplicity, although it be extensively so much more limited than the complex intuition of a love-song by Leopardi.[22]

Thus, degrees of complexity helped critics to differentiate between ordinary intuition and art. Nevertheless, we must add organic unity to Croce's 1902 description of defining qualities. For him, every genuine work of art consisted of a synthesis or an interconnection of "qualia" (Croce himself did not use this term) that formed a unified aesthetic object. The relations among the qualia were felt as necessary and not merely fortuitous connections. In his "Omero: interpretazione moderna di taluni giudizî antichi,"[23] ("Homer: A Modern Interpretation of some Classical Judgments"), Croce asserted that "Poetry, certainly, is not to be sought in its structure, but beyond it; not in the walls that serve to support it, but in the organism that grows and flourishes there."[24]

Another example of the internal relations among intuitional expressions that form genuine art, lies in Croce's critique of Shakespeare's work in which he proposed that any of Shakespeare's plays could be evaluated by explaining the aesthetic coherence of the performance. "One could, for example, show the robust and potent unity of the movingly tragic representation in *Macbeth*, which breaks forth and flows like a single lyric outburst, with full agreement of all its various tones, wherein the single scenes seem strophes."[25]

What was to provide the organic unity of art? Its presence required a dominant image or particular sentiment that was uniquely characteristic of the aesthetic expression under consideration. In his "Terenzio"[26] ("Terence"), Croce enjoined the reader to extract the dominant sentiment from Terence's plays, which lay in human good will. Croce's "Character and Unity of Dante's Poetry" noted that what characterized the Dantesque spirit represented the true unity of the poem as well.

Thus, Croce's early aesthetic theory affirmed that complex unified intuition formed art objects. For him, what we would ordinarily refer to as a "work of art" which would include for example, the canvas, colors, and brush strokes of Claude Monet's *Water Lilies,* did not form a part of this aesthetic creation *qua* aesthetic. Instead, art consisted entirely of the complex intuitional expression or image, stimulated in our consciousness by the physical canvas with its colors, forms and their interrelations. By this claim Croce did not mean to deny that the physical, tangible aspects of an artifact influenced aesthetic creation or response. Nevertheless during the intuitional apprehension of art as art, all material stimuli became completely transformed into a fundamentally diverse aesthetic expression of consciousness.

In his evaluation of Dante's poetry, Croce gave us the "marks" of a genuine artist. We were to discover these characteristics within the range and depth of human feelings: in Dante's soul there was a "richness and variety of emotions that reached from the most violent or the most sublime to the sweet and tender, and extended to the joking and playful . . . beyond being a poet he was specifically an artist."[27]

Insofar as art did require the organic synthesis of its images, some unsuccessful expressions were characterized by disunity or incoherence among their representations. At times, non-art displayed disconnected series of single intuitions. An illustration of such flawed art was given in Croce's critique of Shakespeare's work, where he claimed that among the many examples of the mechanical combining of images,

> . . . the adventures of Gloucester and his sons inserted among those between Lear and his daughters are not completely satisfying, either because they introduce an overly realistic element into the fable of the play, or because they form a multilateral parallelism . . . that perhaps owes its origins to the need for theatrical variation, complication, and suspension, rather than to the moral intention of giving emphasis to the horror of ingratitude.[28]

In other cases an artifact may be perfectly "coherent," but in a rather mechanical and unaesthetic sense. Croce bluntly stated in his essay "Dante: l'ultimo canto della 'Commedia'" ("Dante: The Concluding Canto of the *Commedia*") that "poetry, as I know it, is not measured in meters or (as the Abbé Galiani said of a sonnet, whose verses were typographically all of the same length, but all wrong), with 'string.'"[29]

These passages suggest how Croce differentiated between the *immaginazione* that loosely associated images and the creatively functioning *fantasia*, a distinction not present in the first English translation of the 1902 *Estetica*. For the *immaginazione* (imagination), unlike the *fantasia* (creative fancy), mixed and combined single elements in a loose and arbitrary fashion—much as the grains in a heap of sand are mingled with one another. Croce's concepts of the rearranging process of imagination and creative fancy were akin to Coleridge's "fancy" which worked with fixities and definites, as well as to the transforming activity of "aesthetic imagination" requisite for metaphor and art. An art critic was, thus, also an artist. Upon stimulation by an artifact, he reproduced, or rather created, a work of art (complex aesthetic image) in his *fantasia*.

Croce considered a "mistaken" work, furthermore, as one in which a personality appears, not unified, but very disoriented and incoherent. Virgil's ambiguous representation of Aeneas, as hero, deceiver, and destroyer, is not a consistent one. The great warrior of the Trojan war should not have participated in a passionate affair, yet repaid Dido's love with abandonment, and her devotion with despair and death. It would have sufficed if he had "stuck to heroic deeds and left Dido in peace. To have made him enter into this relationship has been undoubtedly an artistic error."[30] Other examples of such error or disunity appear in Shakespeare's history plays, which "remain fragmentary and are not rounded off in poems animated by a single breath of passion; and some, especially the first part of *Henry VI* are dry and anecdotally disconnected; others, like *Henry IV* and *Henry V,* permit purposes of patriotic edification to shine through and are weighted down by purely informative scenes."[31]

Some cases of non-art might not amount to intuition at all, but to another type of expression—for instance, conceptual or practical in the sense of didactic. In the essay "Lucrezio e Virgilio. Il 'De rerum natura' e i 'Georgica,'"[32] ("Lucretius and Virgil: *De Rerum Natura* and the *Georgics*"), Croce gave excellent illustrations of this point. One could not determine, *a priori,* whether an expression might be intuition, art, or indeed another altogether diverse creation of the human spirit. He thought a critic should reproduce as well as possible, within the limitations of historical circumstance, the original representation. He next must categorize it as art or non-art. If the latter, the critic could then determine whether the expression be ordinary intuition, concept, or a form of practical (volitional) and not cognitive (theoretical) activity.

Perhaps today when dissonance along with discord and even disintegration are applauded, Croce's use of the concept of organic unity for determining the presence of art could appear overly simple. Thus Pablo Picasso's *Guernica,* for instance, expresses a deliberate incongruity and sharp juxtaposition of images, which apparently violate at least the "coherence of nature." Here, however, obvious incoherence serves lyrical expression and thereby becomes, aesthetically, an essential ingredient in the organic unity of the artist's intuition. In other cases, a poem that corresponds to psychological reality, such as one about a heroic warrior who betrays the love of a noble woman, may prove offensive to one's sense of aesthetic coherence. In short, artistic consistency for Croce, appears to be *sui generis,* and thus it fundamentally differs from natural (correspondence with nature), psychological, or logical consistency: *sui generis* and probably much more complex than other types of coherence, since an aesthetic object would also include in its organic synthesis, the hopes, expectations, wishes, and ideals of the artist-critic. Moreover, at times an artifact may be perfectly "coherent," but in a rather mechanical and unaesthetic sense, as for example in the case of *The Last Supper,* by Salvador Dalí, or some of T. S. Eliot's verses in *The Waste Land.*

Even if our difficulties with Croce's criterion of aesthetic coherence could be resolved, at least from within the framework of his doctrine, other problems arising from the use of "quantitative complexity" for defining art still remain. Although "complexity" does indeed characterize some art, it does not apply to all art. The aesthetic quality of Dante's poetry, for example, in part lies in the rich complexity of its imagery. The opposite, however, would be true for a Calder sculpture, or an abstract painting by Piet Mondrian. Yet one would be reluctant to exclude these objects from the realm of art on the ground of simplicity alone. In fact, Croce's initial description of art in terms of complexity and organic unity would eventually satisfy neither himself nor his critics, and the determination of lyricality among art's defining qualities came about to better distinguish art from ordinary intuition.[33] Croce himself confirmed that "the conversion of my first concept of intuition into the further concept of pure or lyrical intuition was not due to an inference from the first, which taken by itself satisfied me and remained inert, but to suggestions arising from the actual practice of literary criticism, as I wrote my notes on modern Italian literature and reflected directly upon works of art and tried to harmonize my former thoughts with the new thoughts that thus arose."[34] Art as pure intuition, Croce concluded, was also essentially lyrical: "l'intuizione pura è essenzialmente liricità." Croce gave us phenomenological descriptions of lyrical quality. It lay in "the life, the movement, the emotion, the fire, the feeling of the artist; only these qualities give us the supreme criterion for distinguishing works of true art from false, the successful from the mistaken. When emotion and feelings are present, much is forgiven; when these are lacking, nothing can compensate for them."[35]

According to Crocean aesthetics, the critic was to distinguish pure art from false, and from other forms of spirit, by the feeling, the emotion, and the warmth of the artist. As an illustration, Lucretius's *De Rerum Natura* originated from a painful, indeed irrational ground. At times this didactic poem even evokes strongly emotional passages. These occur in the praises of Epicurus elevated from the depths of the poet's heart, and in descriptions of "the desperate insatiability of carnal love that inflames and rages," and of the woman whom only the illusion of love idealizes and renders beautiful. Lucretius's art makes Juvenal's famous satire seem like a superficial disdain, over-blown and dilettantish, not because it is more irrational than the former, but because it lacks the awareness of pain expressed by Lucretius's extremely irrational description.[36]

How did Croce himself view the addition of lyricality to the defining qualities of his 1902 conception of art?[37] "Lyricality," he claimed, was simply a synonym for intuition, although it also represented a deepening of his understanding of aesthetic expression as feeling or emotion.[38] Indeed Croce's embellishment did not appear to be either an entirely new concept of art, or a contradiction of his earlier one. However, still another qualification of intuition, cosmic totality, was to follow lyricality. Its reconciliation with Croce's 1902 concept of art as the expression of particular images would prove far more difficult for many aestheticians than had his concept of "the lyrical."

In volume sixteen of *La critica*, 1918, Croce published "Il carattere di totalità della espressione artistica"[39] ("The Totality of Artistic Expression"). That essay further determined the Crocean concept of art by describing another of its important attributes—aesthetic universality. Croce did not elaborate his concept of the aesthetic universal before 1918. Nevertheless there had been suggestions of what was to come. The *Breviario di estetica*, 1913 (*Guide to Aesthetics* [1965]), for instance, proposed that a kind of "aesthetic universality" was intrinsic to the intuitional process, inasmuch as art consisted of an aesthetic *a priori* synthesis between feeling and image within intuition. Artistic representation expressed, moreover, the universe regarded *sub specie intuitionis*.[40]

There were, still earlier, somewhat ambiguous passages that acknowledged the eternality of art. These writings, however, may refer to its perennial occurrence as the result of the transcendental activity of human consciousness, rather than to art as an expression of the cosmos. Or they may reflect a remnant of some of the early influences upon Croce's views, that is the philosophies of Plato and Johann F. Herbart. Nevertheless, in the preface to the fifth and subsequent editions of the *Estetica* (1922), Croce claimed that the germs of his definition of art as lyrical and cosmic were present in the 1902 edition of that work. Perhaps he saw a suggestion of his concept of cosmic totality in the attribute of *estensiva*, which art, but not ordinary intuition, possessed. However as we have seen, this adjective implied mere *quantitative complexity*. It could thus include works of art that the category of cosmic art would exclude and *vice versa*. On the one hand, for example, James Joyce's *Ulysses* represents quite complicated aesthetic images. Still, it is not clear that its expression is universal in Croce's sense. On the other hand, Willa Cather's *My Antonia* gives comparatively simple images. Yet her novel may well express what Croce meant by "character of totality." However, the more important question here is not whether Croce's concept of cosmic totality was present as such in his 1902 work, but whether his elaboration of the aesthetic universal was consistent with his concept of art as the expression of a particular and unique object.

Upon reading these allusions to a concept that only subsequently was to be elaborated, one might wonder why the aesthetic universal had not been more fully developed before the publication of the 1918 essay. Indeed Croce himself acknowledged that other doctrines, developed prior to his own, had recognized the aesthetic universal, albeit unfortunately by linking it to philosophy and religion. He wrote thus that in general "the fact that the representation of art . . . encompasses everything and reflects the cosmos, has been noted many times."[41] And he credited specifically Wilhelm von Humboldt's 1797–1798 essay "Hermann und Dorothea" as having expounded the universal or cosmic character in artistic representation best of all its proponents.

An answer to this puzzle may lie in the fact that before 1910 Croce had been struggling against the dominance of the neopositivistic school in aesthetics. He was intent then upon stressing the particularity of intuition as art, when distinguished from the historical concrete universality of philosophy and the "absolute" universality of the abstract sciences. By 1918, however, Croce became engaged in a polemic against excesses quite different from the positivistic ones. A reaction against scientism had led to irrationalism in Italian literature; the leader of this neoromantic movement, as we have seen, was Gabriele D'Annunzio. Croce turned his attention accordingly toward the negative influences, as he saw them, that originated from the romantic reduction of art to merely individualistic or egoistic expression. The Italian philosopher-critic described his own perspective thus: "Now, however, after a century and a half of Romanticism, may it not perhaps be well that Aesthetics should throw light rather upon the cosmic or integral character of artistic truth, the purification from particular inclinations, immediate forms of feeling and passion, which this calls for?" Indeed for Croce, modern literature of the last century and a half had amounted to a series of confessions. Characteristic of its style was "an abundance of personal, particular, practical, and autobiographical outpourings."[42]

Along with Croce's debates with fashionable *literati,* his continuous work as critic of essays and their authors whom he was to describe as "poetici cosmici"—Dante, Ariosto, Corneille, Shakespeare, and Goethe, for instance—probably helped to inspire the elaboration of his concept of the aesthetic universal. If so, this elaboration of Croce's concept of art provides still another illustration of the dialectical movement between theory and practice that is the pervasive character in the evolution of Crocean aesthetics. Moreover, some critics, the American Joel Spingarn for one, had complained about the omission of the universal quality of art from Croce's commentaries. Spingarn probably felt that quantitative complexity did not suffice to differentiate the works of great writers from less distinguished ones.[43]

What did Croce wish to convey by the phrase "aesthetic universal?" He referred to it as both "carattere cosmico" (cosmic character) and "carattere di totalità" (character of totality). Inasmuch as he used these phrases interchangeably, it seems reasonable to assume that they possessed the same meaning. For Croce, the aesthetic universal did not represent an especially rich and intense lyrical motif that differed merely quantitatively from other themes.[44] Neither by "encompassing everything and reflecting the cosmos" did Croce mean that great literature, for instance, need amount to a treatise on metaphysics (although passages from Lucretius's *De Rerum Natura* and Dante's trilogy did qualify as aesthetically cosmic); nor was "character of totality" to imply that art became transformed somehow into all four fundamental expressions of consciousness—intuitional as well as conceptual, economic, and ethical. To quote Croce on this point:

> For Art is pure intuition or pure expression, not Schellingian intellectual intuition, not Hegelian logicism, not the judgement of historical reflection, but intuition wholly pure of concept and judgement. . . .
> And its character of totality can be understood without our having ever needed to issue forth from the limits of pure intuition, or to undertake readjustments or, still worse, eclectic additions.[45]

The autonomy of intuitional feelings was thus retained in relation to the other three forms of consciousness, when *they* became *transformed* into cosmic expression. And the unique quality of aesthetic expression as compared with ordinary intuition was intensified.

Later in his career, Croce would increasingly stress the interrelations among the various forms of human expression—aesthetic, conceptual, economic, and ethical—and thus the importance of the ethical intentions of the artist, to his aesthetic expression. In his *Defence of Poetry,* Croce metaphorically described expressions of mind as "paths" that "are not divergent nor even parallel, but join in a circle which is the rounded unity of the human spirit."[46] An individual, however, might remain "one-sided" and never experience all of his distinct capacities for aesthetic, philosophic, economic, and political or moral expression. These unfortunates are "dimidiati viri" (half-men). There is, for instance, the philosopher who does not carry out the practical obligations of his theory but "stands idle when he should be fulfilling his duties as a citizen and a soldier. There is the artistic genius who never effects the passage from the dreams of poetry to philosophic thought and consistent action."[47] This "stunting" of life leads to undesirable consequences. The immoral philosopher doubts his intellectual capacities; the poet degenerates into the stylist or purveyor of *belles-lettres.* Some critics have interpreted Croce's shift in emphasis from the autonomy of art to the interconnections among the forms of human expressions as a contradiction of his earlier theory. In my own opinion, however, Croce continued to hold that ethical volition became completely transformed into intuitional cognition during aesthetic expression. Other commentators, who have not understood Croce's conception of the unity of the activities of human spirit, have objected vigorously to Croce's so-called assertions of the artist's moral irresponsibility for his works, and of the complete separation of art from pleasure and philosophy as well as from morals.[48]

In short, for Croce aesthetic creation was particular, yet also concretely universal. Indeed, the feeling that formed the "essence of art," became individual and concrete only when it acquired "*totalità.*" This transformation occurred whenever a particular representation expressed the feelings of humanity. Croce judged Dante's *Paradiso* and Ariosto's *Orlando,* for instance, as masterpieces because they manifested specific images that fused into an organic unity and expressed the emotions—the hopes, fears and desires of humankind: "In every intonation of the poet, in every creature of his imagination, there lies human destiny—all the hopes, the illusions, the pains and joys, the greatness and the miseries, the entire drama of reality, which endures and thrives perpetually on itself, suffering and rejoicing."[49]

The essence of great art did not lie in its apparent subject matter, but in the depth and breadth of the artist's emotional expression that stimulated one's consciousness to move imaginatively beyond characteristics peculiar to culture and age. The emotive content of cosmic art exceeded thus the limitations of present space and time. Aesthetic universality occurred, for instance, in the works of such diverse poets as Ariosto and Shakespeare. Cosmic quality lay in their expression of "the constant yet varied rhythm, of the life that is born, expands, dies and is reborn, in order to grow and die once more."[50] When Croce wrote about the literary expression of Shakespeare, he recognized a " 'totality,' that is clearly synonymous with the lyrical character proper to all poetry."[51] This quality, however, failed to appear in the verses by Petrarca, in which one encounters something superfluous, indeed overly exquisite. Examples may be found in his opening invocation to "Chiare, fresche e dolci acque," where with phrases overly balanced, Petrarch asks his audience to heed his words.[52] In his "Nella stagion che 'l ciel rapido inclina," there is no effusion of pain at the loss of his beloved. One is left, instead, with a tissue of vague descriptions.[53]

The Crocean concept of art evolved thus from "intuition as complex feeling" to "lyrical expression" and to "cosmic universality." Croce himself wrote that these embellishments represented developments and not contradictions of the 1902 *Estetica.* With regard to his elaborations of the aesthetic universal, however, some commentators have not been as sanguine as Croce appeared to be. How are we to consider these developments from the point of view of both his aesthetics and the relations between the two theoretical forms of consciousness--intuitional and logical? Had Croce thereby denied a fundamental difference between aesthetic and logical activity? Do such alterations, if considered from within the framework of his doctrine, represent an attempt to bridge the gap of kind and nature between intuition and concept?[54]

Indeed, a doctrine of the logical nature of poetry—that is, of art as philosophy or religion—once prevailed in German idealism. Recently it has appeared in the aesthetics of such actual-idealists (the followers of Gentile) as Ugo Spirito. Nevertheless, Croce himself denied such an interpretation, and a careful reading of his works will not support it.[55] For Croce, intuitions could never possess logical universality. Genuine art reflected instead a kind of "emotive universality," which perennially allowed it to be recognized and felt as such. Croce's aesthetic universal thus evolved out of his experiences of the alogical qualities of art, to which the law of contradiction did not apply.

A second question is whether intuition itself can represent both the particular and the universal.[56] Some commentators have argued that early in Croce's career he had expounded a "positive" view that intuitional feeling is particular.[57] Afterwards Croce confusedly asserted that within aesthetic experience the individual and the cosmic indistinguishably unite. These critics have interpreted the attribution of the "universal and individual" to the object of expression as a "negative statement," contradicting Croce's earlier theories.

How can we answer these objections? Would Croce's aesthetics remain viable, for instance, if universality were predicated of the creative act, whereas the aesthetic image remained particular? Or was the artist-critic unable to separate *totalità* from art only when he judged it by reflective thought? Must aesthetic harmony, at best metaphorically describable as "cosmic," remain a particular feeling?[58]

Unfortunately these questions may imply that we can consider either the intuitional process or its images in abstraction from one another. In the Crocean aesthetics, however, such an abstractive process was not possible. Indeed, when only one of these factors becomes emphasized, Croce's views tend to be misinterpreted.[59] We would encounter further problems by phrasing the particular and universal qualities of art in terms of relations between object and subject.[60]

Traditionally, epistemological as well as metaphysical realists have used dualistic language when expounding their theories. Gnoseological idealists, however, tried to avoid such terminology in their descriptions of cognitions. They believed that during the act of knowing, an organic unity prevailed between consciousness and its "contents": neither became conceivable as separated from the other. In this respect Croce's doctrine did not differ from what his idealist predecessors had maintained. His essays, written prior to the *Estetica,* did discuss intuition and the "object" of art. His major works on aesthetics, however, generally avoided "subject-object" phrases. For Croce such thinking became an unfortunate by-product of various theories of nature that philosophers had expounded during the Renaissance. Logically speaking, an object was nothing other than spirit: *res* as *res* did not exist. Accordingly, it was to be conceived within consciousness—as a necessary moment, and as the most elementary form of the practical.[61] Such "objects" were the desires, feelings, and emotions of mind's "economic activity." They did not occur in the theoretic realm, and we should not attempt to find them there.

What was the source of "cosmic character"? "Form" conferred universality on the passionate content of art, and consisted of the rhythm, meter, color, and tones which one could not conceive apart from any object. In his essay of 1918, Croce asserted that "to give, then, artistic form to sentimental content is to give it simultaneously the imprint of totality, the breath of the cosmos; and in this sense, universality and artistic form are not two, but one."[62] The critic intuits the harmony of feelings, the work of art, as a fusion of the cosmic with the particular. He recognizes in this fusion a kind of aesthetic totality within both act and image.

Although there have been many criticisms of Croce's embellishments on his early conception of intuition as art as complex yet particular feeling, his elaborations did remain consistent with his overall view of the philosopher's basic task: to appropriate what was living in the history of thought, to discard what was false, and to transcend former falsehoods.[63] Croce at least remained satisfied that alterations in his concept of intuition amounted to enhancements and not contradictions of his conception of the aesthetic object.

Our outline of the Crocean conception of the art-object is now complete. Let us take a closer look at judgments about it. For Croce, evaluations of the reality and quality of art were to be stated in subject-predicate form. In such judgments, sometimes referred to as "individual," the subject was represented by what he called intuition-as-representation or representation (intuition that implied historical existence) and the predicate was expressed by the concrete-universal or pure concept "art." On the one hand, representation consisted of the re-creation of the aesthetic object by the creative fancy of the critic and provided criticism with a subjective quality; and on the other, the concrete-universal "art" supplied the objective aspect of judgment. The fundamental problem present in criticism was one of determining the reality and the quality of the art-object. When addressing the critical process, Croce wrote,

The critic is not *artifex additus artifici*, but *philosophus additus artifici*. His work is not achieved until the aesthetic image becomes preserved and simultaneously transcended. The critic's task pertains to thought, which, as we have seen, overcomes and clarifies the creative imagination with new light. Thought transforming intuition into perception, qualifies the real, and thereby distinguishes reality from unreality.[64]

Croce held that aesthetic judgment required that the critic re-create as well as possible the artist's expression as recorded in the artifact. However, as we should recall, the particularity of the art-object meant that its expression was unique. Given the non-repeatability of the intuitional subject of judgment, then, the artist's synthesis of image with feeling could never be precisely replicated, even by the artist. It was instead the synthetic *a priori activity* of imagination, or intuitional *process* that created art, which remained identical within both artist and critic. Similarity, not identity, of particular image and feeling became insured by placing oneself imaginatively in like circumstances. And for Croce this situation sufficed for the formulation of critique. After all if aesthetic expression were entirely unique, it would defy comparison and description as well. But how would we verify judgments about art? Croce, like other epistemic idealists, denied the existence of an object independent of consciousness. For these philosophers, there was no object to which a judgment might correspond. They espoused a coherence theory according to which a judgment was true, if it was consistent with a group of judgments held to be true. There are problems inherent in the application of a coherence theory of verifiability. I have discussed these difficulties elsewhere,[65] and space will not permit their treatment here, except to raise the questions: Are we satisfied with the criterion of coherence for evaluating true judgment? Or does verifiability, and indeed judgment itself, presuppose an object that remains external to and independent of consciousness?[66]

Critical judgments were more or less true, according to Croce's privative conception of value. It was impossible that any such judgment be completely false, since the universal nature of its predicate, art, meant that it was always present implicitly or explicitly in every aspect of experience. For Croce, on the one hand, whoever denied the absolute character of aesthetic judgment, also negated the autonomy and value of art, since without objective value aesthetic concepts would have amounted to descriptions of what were merely pleasing. On the other hand, whoever neglected its subjective aspect failed to recognize that the subject of a true judgment derived from the interests and needs of the artist-critic. Croce concluded that one could not separate, although one could distinguish, the subjective from the objective qualities present in true judgment (just as they could not be demarcated within the expression of the concrete-universal itself). Such ideas and the questions that they raised, which were implicit in the 1902 *Estetica,* anticipated and provided viable solutions to problems discussed subsequently by the deconstructionist school of literary criticism.

Although true judgments about the presence and quality of art formed what might be described as the "core" of critique, it was not exhausted by such evaluations. Indeed much of critique consisted of classificatory statements, which for Croce were neither true nor false. These volitional expressions of human practical spirit were what he named "pseudojudgments." They expressed a relation between a representation (subject) and pseudoconcept (predicate).[67]

Pseudoconcepts, which Croce described alternatively as empirical class names, are what contemporary logic usually refers to as class terms. Unlike the concrete-universal, the denotation of the empirical concept was limited to merely some particulars. An empirical concept—"comedy" for example—referred to instances of the genus "literature" but was not immanent in every aspect of reality, as Croce would have put it. The classes denoted by these empirical pseudoconcepts could be exhausted, thus, by a single intuition or representation, e.g., the class whose member was a mutation; and such classes invariably were completed by a finite number of objects.

One of the most important characteristics that empirical pseudoconcepts possessed, one that distinguished them from concrete-universals or pure concepts such as art, was "exclusiveness"—a quality which contemporary logic also attributes to empirical terms. The class of all comedies, for example, might exclude the class of all tragedies. Both the extension and intension of such classes were limited, although Croce allowed that they were not necessarily mutually exclusive. Literature, for instance, included didactic poetry.

Pseudoconcepts, according to Croce, depended on concrete-universals for their expression. What did he mean by his claim? The Crocean relationship between concrete-universal and empirical concept did not appear to be one of deduction, in the sense that, for example, the characteristics of a triangle could be deduced from its definition. Moreover, Croce himself denied that their order of dependency represented simple temporal priority. Nor was it one of "family resemblance" as in the case of a biological genus and species. Rather the pure concept "art" resulted from a *theoretic* activity of mind; whereas "tragedy," a pseudoconcept, issued from *practical* intent. In other words, to say that a pure concept was a necessary prerequisite for a pseudoconcept meant that a philosophical analysis of the acts of the human spirit would show that will was rational, that is, it required thought for its expression. *Praxis* was analyzable in terms of *theoria,* whereas the reverse did not hold.

Empirical pseudoconcepts were expressed via pseudojudgments that were akin to "nominal definitions." They classified objects and were formulated for the sake of expediency. To illustrate: the critic catalogued works of art in terms of genres in order to communicate feelings and thoughts about them. Croce described pseudojudgments as commands in which no determination as to value was involved. Frequently they stated the means one used to achieve a sought-after goal. A literary critic classified aesthetic expression in order better to communicate his opinion about it.

Empirical statements could also be called "judgments of classification." Croce warned us, however, that ordering objects in terms of types did not yield knowledge. For this reason, empirical judgments were not to function as logical ones, although at times they were made to do so. Examples occur in judgments about the correct length of a play, such as those offered recently about Jonathan Miller's rendition of Eugene O'Neill's *Long*

Day's Journey into Night; or in judgments to the effect that tragedies cannot be written in an age of the non or anti-hero.

Every empirical judgment presupposed an individual one. In *"Hamlet* is a tragedy," for example, the empirical predicate merely suggested other class terms—"noble birth," "character," "fate"—but presupposed, phenomenologically speaking, the pure concepts "art" and "the lyrical." In short, the useful but arbitrary classification of *Hamlet* as a tragedy required, for Croce, the judgment that *Hamlet* was a work of art. In every empirical statement, subject and predicate were linked thus to representation and pure concept as expressed in individual judgment.

Probably as much of Croce's influence on criticism derives from his critique of the literary genres, in terms of his conception of the pseudoconcept, as from any other one source. Thus the "literary kind" that formerly had provided a permanent ideal for artistic creation became, in Crocean aesthetics, a variable notion, applied for practical and mnemonic purposes. Croce bluntly recommended analysis (in terms of the genres) of Shakespeare's art, for instance, only for those who did not spontaneously feel. Arbitrary classifications of types of aesthetic expression served a merely didactic purpose and perhaps also in softening "hard heads"—even those of educated men.[68]

By his revision of these standards Croce demonstrated his recognition of the tremendous variety of aesthetic expression. In the past, works that had not satisfied the criteria of "form" and "content" automatically met with derogatory judgment. As an illustration, Croce noted that for a long time the value of Shakespeare's art was contested or even negated. Tolstoy, for instance, complained that men did not speak in the mode of Shakespearean characters. Croce, however, countered that Tolstoy's personages and romances were more Shakespearean than "their great but scarcely reasonable and not at all critical author [had] thought." Even a sense of the classical had been denied to Shakespeare—also by those who esteemed him. By this term critics understood "a partial and antiquated idea . . . made to consist in certain external regularities." Shakespeare's work was nonetheless "classical" in the authentic sense of expression, which for Croce meant unforced and continuous expression.[69]

Fruitless arguments that aestheticians, critics, and artists had waged could now be resolved with Croce's new conception of the genre as pseudoconcept. These debates had been based on judgments that confused the arbitrariness of a class name, e.g. epic, tragedy, comedy, didactic poetry, with the universality of a concrete-universal such as art. The reader will see Croce's contribution to such critical discussions illustrated in his essay on Homer's work, entitled "Omero: interpretazione moderna di taluni giudizî antichi" (Homer: A Modern Interpretation of Some Classical Judgments). Here Croce treated Aristotle's question of whether "the epic" or "the tragedy'' was the better form of imitation. Croce resolved this dilemma (just as he had dealt with other problems based on definition of a genre), by translating it into relations between "the poetic" (art) and "the extra-poetic" (non-art). Poetry, he concluded, was to be sought not in its structure, nor in its passages, but in the emotive quality that infused an entire expression. Every true lyric represented the tragedy that was life itself.[70] Other difficulties arose with attempts to classify art in terms of its design. The structure of Virgil's *Georgics,* for instance, has prompted critics to declare the entire work "extra-poetic"; whereas for Croce, Virgil's detailed description of nature indeed amounted to poetry, even if it bordered on being didactic.[71]

Croce's conception of the "literary kinds" as merely empirical classes likewise answered the question of whether a contemporary tragedy could be written. For *literati* the answer to this query depended on the fulfillment of the Aristotelian requirement of a fall from noble birth. In Crocean terms, however, such disputes neglected the authentic task of the critic, which was not that of a "pork butcher" or "surgeon who hacks out pieces of flesh."[72] Instead of evaluating art in terms of inflexible, unchanging rules, one was to determine the presence of a lyrical and cosmic expression. By means of this comparatively elastic mode of evaluating aesthetic creation, Croce sought to liberate it from the dogmatic restraints which the standards of the classical "literary genres" had imposed. By way of illustration from the critiques that follow, Croce cited an 1801 essay by Chateaubriand as attributing *le génie* to Shakespeare, but as also denying him *l'art*—the observance of the *règles* and the genres, which were "nés de la nature même." Later, however, Chateaubriand recognized that he had made the mistake of measuring "Shakespeare avec la lunette classique." With that confession, according to Croce, the French critic had pointed out the fundamental error of judging a work of art, not with intrinsic criteria, but in terms of other artifacts taken as absolute models.[73] Crocean aesthetics thus would not permit an evaluation of George Bernard Shaw's *Candida* in terms of Menandrian comedy, or Arthur Miller's *Death of a Salesman* by using Sophocles' *Oedipus Rex* as representing the ideal form of tragedy.

One of the most important of the genres was literature itself. Although it was given full prominence with the publication of *La poesia: Introduzione alla critica e storia della poesia e della letteratura*[74] *(Poetry and Literature)* in 1936 when Croce was seventy years old, "literature" remained an arbitrary class name for him. In that work, however, it became characterized further as resembling poetry (art), yet as falling short of genuine lyrical and cosmic expression. His description of the task of the critic, then, was restated as one of distinguishing between literature and poetry. Nevertheless, this differentiation did not mark a departure from Croce's earlier concept of critique as determining the presence or absence of creative fancy, and instead reaffirmed it in different terms. With great detail, and well illustrated from his earlier critiques of the cosmic poets, such as Dante, Ariosto, and Goethe, *La Poesia* described the differences between authentic poetic expression and the forms of non-art, along with their inter-relationships. Various classifications used in criticism were represented via the pseudoconcepts, as for example, prosaic, literary, didactic and oratorical forms. In this way every practical distinction that had appeared in earlier works became reposed and elaborated through the application of an empirical method. Croce's position was clear: there is "good literature" and occasionally non-poetic verse may be necessary in genuine poetry. With this discussion of the status and function of the genres, my outline of Croce's principles of literary criticism is complete. But before we turn our attention to the essays that embody them, I would like briefly to describe the reception of Crocean aesthetics and literary criticism in the United States.

It has been noted many times that it is difficult, if not impossible, to precisely trace the influence of Croce's philosophy of art on our aestheticians and literary critics.[75] A detailed discussion of this topic, moreover, would not be appropriate here,[76] since the focus of my book is upon Croce's own work, and not upon the views of his critics—whether they be followers or detractors. Nevertheless, at least some early effects of Crocean aesthetics upon American thought can be highlighted, and a summary description should serve the reader by further illustrating the literary principles treated in the preceding pages.

Croce's major writings on aesthetics and literary criticism began to emerge in Europe by the beginning of the twentieth century. During the early decades, Croce's philosophy of art was introduced to the American public via academicians and literary critics. Unfortunately, however, translations into English of Croce's work became available only sporadically and usually years after the Italian originals had appeared. Thus a major factor that determined how widely and accurately Croce's theories were transmitted to *literati* in the United States was knowledge of the Italian language. Yet requirements for our graduate schools usually included ancient Greek, Latin, German, and French, or, more simply, German and French. So a widespread ignorance of Italian adversely affected and still somewhat hinders dissemination of Croce's thought.

Another factor that determined the early spread of Croce's influence was geographic distance. Moreover, cultural affinities linked the East coast, where the major centers of learning existed, more readily with British concepts than with continental ideas, especially Italian ones. As an illustration, I quote from a letter to the editor of *The Nation,* a periodical published in New York and one of the earliest, most important U.S. publications in which Croce's name appeared. The author, signed T. D. B., wrote on

April 17, 1908, from Ithaca, New York: "praise is lavished with greater or less discriminate generosity upon the literary work of nearly all contemporary writers save those of Italy. For this reason it gratifies an enthusiastic student of this relatively unexplored, almost despised field, to read in your issue of April 16 your reviewer's comment upon Benedetto Croce's new edition of De Sanctis's work on Petrarch."[77]

Ignorance of the Italian language and the history of European intellectual ideas, along with a somewhat insular mentality, encouraged by geographic and ethnic boundaries, were not the sole reasons why the Crocean philosophy of art so slowly penetrated U.S. intellectual thought. For decades, aesthetics itself was not usually taught on the undergraduate level and only infrequently in graduate schools. Religious fundamentalism, which held that all human expressions were moral ones, schools of Aristotelian thought that affirmed fixed genres and rules, pragmatism, Marxism, and more recently, analytic philosophies, have all been opposed to Croce's views—at least to the extent to which their proponents understood or more frequently misunderstood them. Let us now examine a few of the earliest introductions of Crocean aesthetics to literary and philosophic audiences, along with some serious misinterpretations that originated from them.

During the first two decades of the twentieth century, there were several prominent U.S. expositors of Croce's philosophy of art. One of the most sympathetic of these was Joel E. Spingarn, who has been described as perhaps the best informed American on the history of literary criticism at that time.[78] What were the special circumstances that prompted the friendship and eventual collaboration between Croce and Spingarn?

Spingarn's dissertation on literary criticism in the Renaissance was published in 1899 by Macmillan[79] and attracted a favorable response from Croce. Subsequently he helped to expand its text and wrote a preface to an Italian second edition published in 1905—an edition which Spingarn described as far superior to the first.[80] Although Spingarn remained one of Croce's greatest admirers, his references to Crocean philosophy, at times ambiguous and misleading, reinforced fundamental misinterpretations of Croce's concepts, some of which have persisted to the present day. The late Professor Gian Orsini once pointed out that the identification of criticism with mere re-expression has been falsely attributed to Croce via Spingarn's introduction. I would now like to suggest other errors which can be ascribed to Spingarn as well.

In *The Nation* of November 15, 1900, he remarked that:

The Neopolitan scholar, Benedetto Croce, well known for his researches upon the Spanish influence in Italy, as well as for his contributions to critical theory, has performed a pious task in reprinting Baumgarten's "Meditationes philosophicae de nonnullis ad poëma

pertinentibus" (Naples, 1900), which has never been republished
since its first appearance in 1735 . . . his "Tesi fondamentali di
un'Estetica" (Naples, 1900) is a fragment of a prospective history of
aesthetics with special reference to Italy. This work is another illustration of the modern tendency to seek the assistance of analytic psychology in the explanation of aesthetic phenomena, and may
accordingly be compared with a work as Santayana's "Sense of
Beauty."[81]

Spingarn never clarified what he meant by "analytic psychology";
nor how Croce's aesthetic could be compared with Santayana's theory of
art. Croce himself was careful to distinguish his description of the activities
of consciousness as speculative (non-empirical) psychology, and in the
United States, Freudian psychoanalytic theory came to be identified as analytic psychology. Furthermore, although Santayana defined beauty in a
variety of ways, its association with pleasure objectified, sharply differentiated his philosophy from Crocean theory. Thus in the *Journal of Comparative Literature*[82] and in the *Philosophical Review*,[83] Santayana severely
criticized Croce's *Estetica come scienza della espressione e linguistica
generale*.[84] His critiques, however, were based on misinterpretations so serious that Croce himself wondered if Santayana had even read his book.
In the July 18, 1901 issue of the *Nation*, Spingarn reviewed Croce's
essay "Giambattista Vico, primo scopritore della scienza estetica," stating:

The essay is not without deficiencies, and its briefness alone will not
account for some of the more hasty generalizations. But it is always
suggestive, and particularly so when connecting critical theory with
the wider fields of aesthetic science. Their relation is not unlike that
which ethics bears to metaphysics, and other literary critics and aestheticians are more and more prone to forget this.[85]

From this statement, one might infer incorrectly as indeed some American
critics would, that the foundation of Crocean aesthetics was metaphysical,
instead of epistemic.[86] More important, however, was the point that literary
criticism implied an aesthetic science. It became one of the fundamental
tenets of what Spingarn would describe as the "New Criticism" in his 1910
public lecture at Columbia University.[87]
In the September 25, 1902 issue of *The Nation*, Spingarn reviewed
Croce's *Estetica*. Here he asserted that for Croce, the genres should be dis-
missed as "wholly unreal and unscientific."[88] This simplistic, misleading
interpretation was never corrected by Spingarn. It led to unwarranted criticisms which still occur today.[89] Furthermore, according to the critic,
Croce had failed to recognize the universal quality of art. Earlier, I de-

scribed the evolution of Croce's theory of aesthetic expression and some reactions to his early conception of art as particular only. Ironically, however, the fact that Croce later held that art was both a particular and universal intuitional expression failed to penetrate the minds of some aestheticians and literary critics. In the *Verbal Icon,* 1954, by W. K. Wimsatt, Jr., and M. Beardsley, for instance, one reads that "the main drift of Croce's aesthetic, in being against conceptualization, is radically against the universal."[90] And in their *Literary Criticism: A Short History,* 1957, the authors W. K. Wimsatt Jr. and Cleanthe Brooks noted that Croce had added the quality of lyricality to the defining characteristics of art, but never mentioned the aesthetic universal.[91]

Spingarn's talk, entitled "The New Criticism" delivered at Columbia in 1910 (six years after John Dewey had joined its faculty) became a most important if not the first introduction of Crocean aesthetics to an American audience.[92] By this time, as we have seen, Croce's concept of art as lyrical intuition had emerged, his distinctions between the activities of *theoria* and *praxis* had been clarified, along with his conception of criticism as judgment, and the useful, even necessary, function of pseudoconcepts, such as the literary genres. Finally, Croce's problematic approach to history had been well established in his critical monographs. With these developments in mind, let us consider the text of Spingarn's presentation.

The Columbia Professor noted that the Balfour "Romanes Lecture," delivered a year earlier, amounted to the first formal introduction of Croce to the English-speaking world.[93] What kind of introduction was it? How did its contents relate to Spingarn's address? Balfour himself stated that his ill-prepared delivery was sharply criticized for its lack of clarity. Members of the audience described it as full of confusion, ambiguity, and rarely intelligible. In the published text itself, Balfour did not even mention Croce by name. Nevertheless, in a long review of Douglas Ainslie's translation of the *Estetica,* which appeared in *The Athenaeum,* the unsigned author wrote that "Mr. Balfour in his recent Romanes Lecture spoke with enthusiasm of Sg. Croce."[94] Balfour, thus, chose to omit sources from the published version, much as years later his countryman, the Oxford philosopher R. G. Collingwood, would elect to do in his *The Principles of Art.*

Balfour, like Croce, claimed that the attempt to limit aesthetic expression by rules was futile. Contrary to Crocean aesthetics, however, Balfour also asserted that aesthetic judgments were entirely intuitive. Although in his preface Balfour acknowledged that "pleasure is but a poor and ambiguous name for what is valuable in aesthetic feeling," his critical question, "Does this work of art convey aesthetic pleasure?" may have prompted incorrect associations of Crocean aesthetics with hedonism. Finally, for Balfour mystical references to first and final causes should be added to any theory of art.[95] Such a proposal amounted to a conception of aesthetics which Croce consistently opposed. Spingarn, who alluded to Balfour's talk simply as Croce's official introduction to the English speaking world,[96] would have rendered Croce a greater service if he had clarified the great differences between their views.

Spingarn's own lecture on "The New Criticism" began with an historical account of the origins of the theory of art as expression:

> [It was]the Germans who first realized that art has performed its function when it has expressed itself; it was they who first conceived of Criticism as the study of expression. "There is a destructive and a creative or constructive criticism," said Goethe; the first measures and tests literature according to mechanical standards, the second answers the fundamental questions: "What has the writer proposed to himself to do? And how far has he succeeded in carrying out his own plan?" Carlyle, in his essay on Goethe, almost uses Goethe's own words, when he says that the critic's first and foremost duty is to make plain to himself "What the poet's aim really and truly was, how the task he had to do stood before his eye, and how far, with such materials as were afforded him, he has fulfilled it."[97]

One of the better-known U.S. critics who seized on Spingarn's references to Goethe and Carlyle was Henry Mencken,[98] who in his book *Prejudices* labeled them as the "Spingarn-Croce-Carlyle-Goethe theory." There Mencken noted that Spingarn's views ran counter to the largest and most influential groups of campus critics who held that art possessed moral value and must be judged according to fixed rules. To quote Mencken on Spingarn:

> What he offers is a doctrine borrowed from the Italian, Benedetto Croce, and by Croce filched from Goethe—a doctrine that it is the critic's first and only duty, as Carlyle once put it, to find out "What the poet's aim really and truly was. . . . " Every sonnet, every drama, every novel is *sui generis* . . . it must be judged by its own inherent intentions.[99]

According to Mencken, Spingarn claimed too much for his own views. Contrary to Spingarn, the critic cannot recreate the work of art in his imagination; and beauty does not occur *in vacuo*, it has social, political and moral implications.[100]

In an essay entitled "A New Manifesto," Spingarn replied to Mencken's harsh charges. His response also referred to theatre critic George Jean Nathan, who in his volume, *Critic and the Theatre*, had mentioned the "Goethe-Carlyle theory" and to Pierre Loving, who in his review of *The*

Drama in Transition, had described the Croce-Spingarn theory as a patent offshoot of what had been espoused by Goethe and Carlyle. Spingarn put it this way:

> Alas, there is no "Croce-Spingarn-Goethe-Carlyle theory," or if there is . . . it owes no direct debt to Goethe or Carlyle.[101]

Spingarn granted that such fame as Croce's theory had acquired in America was in some measure due to Mencken's journalistic trumpetings. Yet, he asked, what has become of Croce's ideas when infused with Mencken's vigorous personality? "And can any man who explains poetic inspiration by 'the chemical content of the digestive tract' be said to have 'passed through' Croce?"[102]

Despite a warning against possible misinterpretation, added to the reprinted essay in which Goethe and Carlyle were quoted, the critic Burton Rascoe asserted that the idea of "intention" is the basis of the whole Crocean system, and challenged Spingarn to state what Shakespeare "intended" at the moment when he sat down to write "The Phoenix and the Turtle." To this, Spingarn responded that nothing could be more wholly un-Crocean than to judge an artist by his intentions, in the literal sense, as distinguished from his achievements.[103]

Although these controversies took place during the early decades of this century, as late as 1954 two of our most prominent aestheticians acknowledged that "Croce had attacked emotive geneticism throughout his career," but then added that "the main drive of the *Aesthetic* is surely toward a kind of cognitive intentionalism."[104]

Unlike other American critics, Spingarn himself had long before enrolled himself under the Italian philosopher's banner. Spingarn's 1910 lecture issued a series of disclaimers, which supposedly he shared with Croce. "We have done with" all the old Rules, the literary kinds, all moral judgment of art as art, etc. The American critic concluded that taste must reproduce a work of art so that understanding and critique can take place; and at that moment aesthetic judgment becomes nothing more nor less than the creative act itself.[105]

Unfortunately the rhetorical tone of Spingarn's assertions suggested that the issues he raised had been settled to everyone's satisfaction. Many years later, his misleading tone would be repeated in John Dewey's response to Croce, regarding the influences on Dewey's aesthetic. Spingarn implied, moreover, that genres and rules were of no use whatsoever, an interpretation which reaffirmed what Spingarn had written in his 1902 review of Croce's *Estetica.* For the U.S. critic, judgment became identified with creative intuition, an error that echoed what Balfour had already proposed. This misinterpretation of Croce's philosophy became reinforced, moreover, by Spingarn's merger of genius with taste. Finally, he described aesthetic values as *sui generis*, which meant that art was to be judged by aesthetic criteria only—a claim that would prove offensive to American religious and moral fundamentalism, which held that all values possessed an ethical dimension.[106]

During the 1920's, Croce's work continued to be reviewed, sometimes favorably as by Raffaello Piccoli's "Italian letter" to *The Dial*,[107] and at other times very unfavorably as by the prominent literary critic Conrad Aiken for *The New Republic*.[108] Some Crocean views were affirmed by American thinkers who did not even realize their source. For instance, in the essay "The Doctrine of Literary Forms," Roy Hack noted as a source for his ideas Henry Newbolt's book on the theory of forms. Newbolt himself, however, had acknowledged his debt to Croce's critique of the genre.[109] Perhaps still another illustration of this phenomenon occurred in John Dewey's *Art as Experience*.[110]

Dewey published his *Art as Experience* in 1934. Not until the late 1940s, however, did he and Croce engage in a direct dialogue about similarities and differences between their aesthetics, Dewey argued that he had not been influenced by Croce, but had remained firmly opposed to all forms of Neo-Hegelian metaphysical idealism. Dewey's main source, instead, had been A. C. Barnes's writing on the plastic arts. Barnes was a self-made millionaire, collector and close friend of Dewey. Nevertheless Croce, in agreement with Stephen Pepper, one of Dewey's students, pointed out that the non-empirical, methodological and psychological assumptions of *Art as Experience* differed from the contents of Dewey's other works. Its conclusions instead resembled Crocean aesthetics in many respects.[111]

In my own opinion, Dewey's *Art as Experience*, unlike his other books, did not advocate application of experimental methods for a definition or an evaluation of art; not did it presuppose an empirical psychology in the Humean tradition. Dewey's critique of literary genres and fixed rules in art is consistent with both his instrumentalism and Croce's phenomenology of the human spirit. Yet other aspects of Dewey's philosophy of art, such as the affirmation that the "various arts," each with its special criteria of valuation, were in reality art, with a single set of defining characteristics, and his concepts of aesthetic autonomy and universality, would seem to follow from an idealist aesthetics rather than an empirical one. How can we account for this anomaly? Dewey's explanation that the non-cognitive nature of aesthetic experience allows it to be treated in a manner fundamentally different from all other human activities is not persuasive from an empiricist perspective. Pepper noted similarities between Dewey's aesthetics and the idealist views held by A. C. Bradley, F. H. Bradley, B. Bosanquet, and S. T. Coleridge.[112] I would suggest further that Dewey may have been influenced by Croce's aesthetics directly or indirectly through

Joel Spingarn's ideas. Although Dewey remained on the Columbia faculty long after Spingarn left, their tenures overlapped by more than six years. Dewey could have attended Spingarn's 1910 public lecture on the new criticism or at least read a copy of it. Both were prominent, outspoken activists while on the Columbia campus, and they shared a lifelong interest in social reform on a national level.

If Dewey had learned about Croce's theory of art from Spingarn or from his writings, why would he not acknowledge his source, instead of referring to their shared beliefs as generally accepted—a strange remark indeed, in consideration of the opposition which existed and still exists toward their ideas? Perhaps an answer lies in Dewey's approach to philosophy. Although trained in the "German method" when he took his Ph.D. at The Johns Hopkins University, Dewey never actually engaged in scholarly research. His pragmatic approach to philosophic concepts rarely acknowledged any sources whatsoever. Instead, Dewey applied his own version of empirical method to present-day problems. Although evidence of the Croce-Spingarn influence on Dewey's aesthetic is only circumstantial, this source would help to account for similarities between their views and the conclusions Dewey reached in his *Art as Experience,* so fundamentally different from his other writings.[113]

Generally speaking, American barriers to Crocean ideas have stemmed from ignorance of the Italian language, the sporadic appearance of too few translations, insufficient knowledge of European ideas, reliance on erroneous secondary sources, and a cultural bias against theory coupled with an insular mentality. Obstacles on the Italian side included the volume of Croce's work, which of necessity expressed the variations and nuances of his ever deepening consideration of philosophical and practical problems. The fact that Croce's literary critiques and historical monographs greatly outnumbered his theoretical writings, moreover, made his concepts less accessible than they otherwise would have been. This difficulty, I believe, would have been alleviated if Croce had published a revised and expanded version of his *Logica,* 1909. With a few notable exceptions, however, U.S. and Italian commentators alike have not sufficiently stressed the importance of that particular book for an understanding of Croce's theory of judgment and thus his literary criticism.[114] Finally, Croce's style, at times rhetorical, poetic, and diffuse, taken together with his vast erudition, have made translation of his work difficult—even for the reader reasonably fluent in Italian. Nevertheless, if translation is difficult, it is not impossible, even for an American. As one who has spent the last few decades on the study of Croce's ideas, I would say that my own attempts to understand them have proved indeed worthwhile.

1

Homer

A Modern Interpretation of Some Classical Judgments[1]

In the last chapter of the *Poetics,* Aristotle treats the question of whether the epic or tragic mimesis is superior.[2] He judges tragedy as superior since it is more condensed and better unified than are long and varied epic poems, from which one could extract several tragedies. Aristotle describes the epic, moreover, ύδαρή, as diluted poetry. There is a sense in which this conclusion, though based on an examination and comparison of two literary genres, may be justified. One can distinguish the non-poetic from the poetic motifs, and observe the greater range and importance of the non-poetic in the epic when compared with tragedy. Aristotle does differentiate between accidental pleasures deriving from a poetic work and what belongs to its intrinsic poetic end.

Whenever Aristotle and the other Greek writers treat the epic, they refer directly to the Homeric poems. We must allow (although for Aristotle the *Iliad* and the *Odyssey,* with respect to other poems, display almost perfect unity) that in the *Iliad* there exists a real dualism between structure and poetry; and this has provided one of the strongest incentives for the philological dissections and vain discussions involving the so-called "Homeric question." But variety and diversity characterize all composite works and may well be intentional for design. Now, to what if not to the non-poetic motifs and structure of the work, are we to ascribe the informative parts of the *Iliad,* such as, for example, the catalogue of ships? How else are we to account for numerous monotonous descriptions of battles and duels, which pleased the insatiable fanciers of warlike events and valor, who were also fond of hearing the names of persons, families, places, and countries they recalled? Again, how else can one explain the introduction of playful episodes—such as the contests, disputes, intrigues, threats, fears of the gods—which brought light relief to an audience intensely absorbed in astonishment and horror at the spectacle of so many battles, wounds, and deaths?

In this respect, the *Iliad* provided the model, sometimes simplified, sometimes complicated with elements from the *Odyssey,* for the epic poems of ancient and modern literature, from Virgil to Tasso and his imitators, and

also for more belated writers like Voltaire. At times the *Iliad,* without precisely or directly serving as a model, came to be reflected in other works
that satisfied similar varieties of interest.

Poetry, certainly, is not to be sought in its structure, but beyond it; not
in the walls that serve to support it, but in the organism that grows and
flourishes there. One cannot find poetry in the variations that interrupt it,
but in the melody that becomes interrupted and then resumed. Poetry does
not inhere in the tale but in the accent of the tale, in the lyricism that is
infused in it, and in the drama of the soul that every true lyric represents,
the lofty and severe drama, the tragedy which is life itself. Such poetry
abounds in the *Iliad.* The ancients, even when believing that the epic is
obviously inferior to tragedy, and especially the Homeric epic as opposed to
the work of other tragedians, expressed the judgment, only apparently contradictory, that Homer's work is "tragic." Plato thus (in the *Theaetetus* and
the *Republic*) calls the *Iliad* a "tragedy" and Homer "prince of tragedy."
The philosopher Polemon, in a statement preserved by Diogenes Laertius,
describes Homer as "an epic Sophocles," and "Sophocles a tragic
Homer." Nor was the bond between Homeric poetry and the development
of later tragedy ever overlooked.

The "serenity," "objectivity," and "humanity" extolled and attributed to Homer, amount to nothing other than this tragic sentiment of life,
which in him takes on its own particular tones and colors, but which essentially lies at the base of all genuine poetry. Homer is objective, because as
poet he is not partisan. He favors neither the Greeks nor the Trojans. Rather
to both sides Homer attributes courage and fear, impetuosity and mistrust,
ardor and bewilderment. He sees them equally at the mercy of fate and the
gods, "checked by the hard whip of Zeus."

Homer does not favor his own heroes, in whom he also sees the un-
heroic features, folly, rage, weakness, discouragement, vile thoughts, and
cowardly flights. None is without guilt. Pure and uncontaminated heroes,
all of a piece, are unknown to him. Nor is Homer obliged to pay special
tribute to the gods. He (as the author of the *Treatise on the Sublime* said)
can "make, by his own power, gods out of men and men out of gods."
Homer accepts the gods of popular religion as furnished with various capri-
cious powers, but not with better judgment or more good will than the men
beside or against whom they struggle. Inhumanity is a consequence of par-
tisanship, wherein men appear to one another not as fellow humans, but as
obstacles to overcome and forces to combat. The common tragedy therefore
is not perceived, but only the struggle of some against others, of what is
to our advantage and disadvantageous to others, or the just cause against
the unjust.

Homer does not take sides. He preserves heart and piety, and that
intelligence which originates from his heart. He listens and attends to his

feelings, even the most simple and humble. Achilles weeps and discloses his love for Briseis, who has been torn from him; and Briseis expresses the sadness and suffering of a wife, once free, now in servitude, but with the hope that the good Patroclus has inspired in her of a better lot. Agamemnon knows the defects of Menelaus yet feels tender solicitude and paternal concern for his younger brother. He acts unjustly toward Achilles and confesses his error to old Nestor. Hector reproaches while he remains indulgent toward Paris who, aware of his flaw, promises, with the humility of a weak shallow man, that he will strive to correct himself; yet he will neither correct his behavior nor, perhaps, even strive to do so. Helen, Helen of the long robe, goddess among women, accuses, despises, vilifies, and calls herself a "shameless bitch." Bowed under the weight of a fatal beauty, she becomes an instrument of evil and destruction in the hands of the gods. Her will power having failed, she loses her capacity for resistance and responsibility. Nevertheless the elect of mind and spirit—Priam and Hector above all—who on her account sustain the great tempest of war, do not condemn Helen. In their hearts they have forgiven her. They treat her with a kind of religious reverence, and protect her with chivalrous devotion. This feeling of humanity culminates with two great scenes, both poetic masterpieces: Hector's taking leave of Andromache and the encounter between Priam and Achilles, where the two look at one another with wonder and admiration, and share their tears.

Even in the cruelest episodes of the *Iliad,* as in the killing of young Lycaon by Achilles's hand, this feeling of humanity, of tragic humanity surfaces. There is in Achilles an admixture of the brute-human—cruel, lacerating, and sneering—and of the man who judges himself and life and submits himself to life's law, accepting his fate and his death. Achilles feels hatred, vengeance, and rage at not being able to inflict on the enemy something worse than death, which he too will soon undergo. These emotions become transformed into horrid and cruel sarcasm, directed at the youth who pleaded with Achilles to spare him. Mocking and calling Lycaon "friend" and "dear" (φίλος) Achilles extorts (as if he wishes to persuade) Lycaon to resign himself to death: after all the youth's death is such a little thing (but for Lycaon that little thing amounts to the infinity of life!) when compared with that of those who have been and will be killed, including the present bestower of death. He could spare him but does not and like the youth, will himself, fall dead. At these words Lycaon, as if bewitched, remains motionless, and Achilles butchers him, heaping insults upon the body of the fallen one, with cries and thoughts of savored but unsated revenge. In this fierce scene, pity for the youth and for Achilles, a different kind of pity finds breath as the latter is observed in his beastliness, in that spasm of fury, in that fatal race toward his own and the other's destruction.

Objective and yet not indifferent, Homer is a tragedian, neither pessimistic, nor desolate, nor desperate, for what dominates his sentiment and
concludes it is the idea of the heroic will. Homer's heroes know that they
must dry their tears quickly and resume their part in life, because destiny
made for man a spirit capable of suffering. Zeus presses them to battle from
youth to extreme old age until one by one they die. Like Achilles they
prefer the short life of labor and war to the long one of idleness and peace,
with victory followed shortly by their death. Homer proposes and seeks no
renunciation, no desertion of life, no escape, no retreat into a world without struggle, into a world beyond. Homer, nonetheless, knows a world beyond, one that is included within the world itself, and that is fame, glory,
the song of the poets, one's name upon the lips of men and women, a
remembrance in their hearts, all that those great ones about to die—Hector
and Achilles—see as arising from their bleeding and pain: a new life
springing from the attained peace of the tomb, the immortality to which
man ever aspires and which is the presupposition of his unwearying pursuit
of toil. Heroism and immortality are integral to the tragic sentiment of
Homer and elevate it to the serenity of poetry. It is customary to celebrate
Homer as the teacher of the Greek peoples, but he should be called the
teacher of all mankind, to whom, in that first outstanding poetic creation
seen by the world, he gave through the power of poetry a true, ethical, and
religious vision of life, as in his poem itself he gave implicit and tacit notice
that poetry is light and clarity (*claritas*); and though it may also be difficult, it must always be profoundly clear.

If, as it seems to be, many conjectures about the *Iliad* fall away when
we distinguish between structure and poetry, there is still another problem
to which critics and historians have often returned, that is one of the difference that is to be seen between the *Iliad* and the *Odyssey*. This one, I am
inclined to believe, is illuminated by another criterion established by modern aesthetics but known also to antiquity, and that is the distinction between poetry and literature, or more particularly between unfettered and
refined poetry, between genuine lyrical or tragic poetry and merely agree-
able, charming poetry. We must deem the latter (one must act courageously
against traditional prejudices in judgments and words) as not truly genuine—or rather not fundamentally poetry at all—regardless of the delicate
touches, even poetic ones, which such would-be poetry may contain and
adapt. This judgment too on the distinctive character of the *Odyssey* and
Iliad is found among the ancient critics, and I feel certain that this judgment is what substantially or unconsciously the author of the *Treatise on the
Sublime*, the pseudo-Longinus, leads us to. Due to inadequate aesthetic distinctions, however, he expresses the difference diversely or rather metaphorically by introducing an opposition between virility and old age, high noon
and sunset.

There is no reason why the *Odyssey* should have been the work of an old man rather than an adult or even a youth, of a man tired and declining rather than one in his prime. The true difference between the two works lies in another observation by the same Greek critic: in the *Odyssey,* the drama of the *Iliad* yields to narrative; and a love of myths, a delight in story-telling, and in talk pour forth. The *Iliad* has no equal—in vigor, consistency of sublimity, fullness of passions, force of oratory, and richness of imagery; and occasionally, it inclines to depictions of ordinary life in the manner of comedy. Only in our times has there been anyone—as for instance the Homerist Drerup—who has argued for the poetic superiority of the *Odyssey.* He writes that the *Odyssey*—with its fantastic portrayals full of color, with its eternally youthful celebration of conjugal fidelity, of final reunion after long separation—touches our modern feeling more closely than the bloody series of battles in the *Iliad.* Drerup finds the *Iliad* grave and heavy and relieved only by the leave-taking of Hector and the conversation between Achilles and Priam.

In general, however, even modern criticism judges the *Odyssey* poetically inferior to the *Iliad,* observing that the former is more rationally thought out and better ordered than the latter. The *Odyssey* is less archaic, more modern, that is, more reflective, and its art is more learned and refined, its style less plastic. The colors in the *Odyssey* are relatively muted. It offers not so much a poetry of the heroic and tragic as of the intimate and domestic. A saner more expert morality presides in it, and one even feels a certain moralizing didacticism. The gods are regarded with greater respect, and its narrative resembles fable and romance, rather than epic and tragedy. Indeed the characters of the *Odyssey,* Ulysses no less than Penelope and all the others including the delicate Nausicaa, are not rich in intensity and profundity, and demonstrate no need of such, for this poem strikes a tone that differs from that of the *Iliad* and pursues other ends.

These observations lead one to a conclusion that analysis could easily document: the difference between the two poems does not lie in a greater or lesser degree of poetry, but in their diverse natures. The *Odyssey* is indeed a work of art, yet not intrinsically of impetuous poetry. The *Iliad* stands at the head of all great modern poetry. The *Odyssey* instead—an exquisite example—stands at the head of the literature of voyages and adventures, of long separations and dispersals, of longed for and achieved recoveries, of whatever excites and amuses the imagination without overly engaging spirit and mind. However, even this fact, as I have noted, did not escape the solid judgment of the ancient stewards of art and poetry.

2

Terence[1]

The Roman critics criticized Terence for being weak, that is, for lacking the "force" or "strength of a writer of comedies." This is said in some famous verses attributed to Caesar;[2] and this perhaps is the reason why the grammarian Volcatius Sedigitus ranked Terence merely sixth in a scale of poets writing in this genre, whereas he placed Caecilius first and Plautus second. The author of those verses attributed to Caesar deplored the fact that because Terence had not added (*adiuncta*) comic force[3] to his exquisite or delicate (*lenibus*) writing (*scriptis*), he had been unesteemed (*despectus*), and considered unequal to the Greeks, remaining a quasi-Menander (*dimidiatus Menander*). The author, out of love and sympathy for Terence, sighed, "Atque utinam!" and, moreover, lamented, "Unum hoc maceror et doleo tibi deesse, Terenti!" How can one love a poet and yet feel that he lacks something substantial? Is not what we admire in a poet "the essential," the soul, the poetry, which either is or is not present? Did not that "purus sermo," that "lenitas" of his speech amount to his very own poetry? Was it not required for its appropriate and necessary tone? What if what was lacking was not, indeed, something essential, but a supplement, something to add ("adiungere"), something that need not be? Why then lament that a non-essential "something" did not exist in him? Why call one's beloved poet a "half-man" ("uomo a mezzo"), almost a castrated one?[4]

Of the many critics who have referred to these verses, it does not seem to me that anyone has raised these reasonable questions. If someone had done so, perhaps he would have found only this response which is grounded in the nature of the matter: the author of these verses was caught up in the theory of the *genres tranchés*, of the clearly defined poetic genres, according to which comedy is not comedy unless it is comic and induces laughter. In the clash between this theory that he accepted and his own sentiment, he did, indeed, suffer; but he could not resolve to sacrifice either the theory for the sentiment or fully the sentiment for the theory; and this resulted in his verses being composed of internally inconsistent judgments. In like manner Francesco De Sanctis felt the force of Machiavelli's *Mandragola*. Yet since Machiavelli did not invest his plot and characters with an atmosphere of intimate gaiety, but seemed to feel a kind of repugnance for them and held them at arm's length, De Sanctis concluded that

Mandragola had not succeeded artistically, because it was not a comedy. And what if it were a tragedy? (I have discussed this question elsewhere.[5]) What harm would there be? By the same token there would be nothing amiss if Terence's work were not comedy but something different. Nor should such a thought seem strange in the light of the present-day stress upon the relationships between Euripidean tragedy and the New Comedy. Some literary histories compare Terence's with the "bourgeois" comedy of the sixteenth century[6]—a comparison already made by our own Italian writer Signorelli who, discussing *Hecyra,* found it "a perfect model for tender comedy, which requires a poet of quite sensitive and delicate heart, a genre that among writers beyond the Alps has degenerated into an implausible and quite defective *comédie larmoyante.*"[7] Perhaps, however, we should avoid these anachronistic comparisons as much as possible, lest we infect, as in this case, the Roman poet's spontaneous and naive sentiment (a sentiment which, as Roman, was also somewhat severe) with the *sensiblerie* of the Enlightenment.

Deeper shadows have fallen on Terence in the criticism and historiography of the nineteenth century, chiefly the one that has gravely darkened all comedy (and in general all Roman poetry), including Renaissance comedy and other Italian art forms of the Renaissance: namely the charge that it lacks originality, because it is so clearly modeled on Greek comedy—as if the art of a later period did not always rest in some respect on what had come before! Those nineteenth-century critics and historians did not fundamentally deny this fact. They wished, however, that the Roman poets had taken their inspiration from the Atellan mimes ("genus delectationis italica severitate temperatum," as Valerius Maximus called it) or from other home-grown products; and that respectively those Italians of the Renaissance should have derived their model from the religious plays, so full of profane and comic elements, and from the popular farces. Roman and Italian authors would thus have acted in accordance with the romantic theory of the organic and autochthonous development of literature as of everything else. This theory seemed to explain facts neatly by claiming that they were born according to plan; and woe to them if they had behaved otherwise, committing sins against nature, for which they now had to render account and pay the appropriate penalty.

Someone should have gone directly to Plautus and Terence and told them not to read Menander, Diphilus, or Apollodorus and not to allow themselves to be seduced. He should have spoken similarly to Bibbiena and Machiavelli, and advised them not to read the two Romans. The former should have paid attention to the Macci, Pappi, Bucconi, and the Dossenni,[8] and the latter to the strolling players and actors of the sacred guilds. These authors would have shrugged their shoulders at such bizarre advice: to throw away the works that resounded in their minds, hearts, and sense of art, and to be thrust forcibly into the company of popular and common mimes, whom they so far surpassed as to have forgotten their existence. This false idea of originality calls for an art that bears no relation to precedent—an entirely national or provincial art—and is now encountered rarely in modern literary criticism and its historiography. Such a conception, however, does persist or at least lingers on in critiques of ancient literature. Here it seems that critics have not benefited from the results of long, and by now superseded discussions of originality, for example, of French tragedy with respect to Greek, and so on.[9]

The other shadow that has been thrown upon Terence's work lies in the suspicion that the pleasure which he provides and the reputation he enjoys, derive from our ignorance of the Greek originals, which he more or less freely translated. If one day, our ignorance is remedied by knowing those originals, our pleasure will vanish and his usurped reputation will fall. Let us suppose for the sake of talking that Terence's dramas are no more than very beautiful translations (one would at least concede that they are "very beautiful") rendered exquisitely into the pure Latin language. Why should the discovery of the originals cause these translations to be devalued? We know of the Greek text of Homer. This does not lessen our admiration for Vincenzo Monti's Italian *Iliad,* beautiful in itself besides serving as a mediator for those who cannot understand much of the Greek.

To the Germans the English text of Shakespeare is known, yet Schlegel's German translation remains a classic. We know that beautiful translations are not born into the world without some poetic spirit, which is disposed toward the work and contributes its own warmth to it.[10] Why should the supposition that Terence's comedies are translations and in a sense representations of lost Greek comedies render them weak and devalued? August Wilhelm Schlegel with his mean-spirited and Romantic preconception regarding everything Roman and Italian, touched upon Plautus and Terence with disdainful brevity (in his lectures on dramatic poetry), "because they were not creative artists."[11] Instead he talked at length on Greek comedy, thus refusing to speak of the two authors who are alive in their works, in order to discuss those writers whose works did not exist (in his time, we possessed a great deal less of them than we do now). But the follies of such critics, who very often when speaking of art, forget to speak of art, are innumerable; and one almost blushes in recalling and confuting them.

Another of these follies strikes at Terence himself, claiming that the plays that go under his name are very probably not his, that they were written by his friends and protectors, Scipio or Laelius, or were the fruit of a collaboration with one of these authors. Antiquity, too, had its "Baconians," or whatever those persons should be called, who attribute Shakespeare's dramas to the least poetic lord of his time, in order to strip them from "sweet William," a poor actor. In antiquity too there were those who thought to tear away Apollo's laurel wreath from the African, the slave, the freedman; and those who were wise to secret information whispered that these honors belonged to other illustrious personages who, disdainful or embarrassed at making a public appearance as writers for the theatre, had someone to appear for them. It does not seem very likely to one who knows about style that there was collaboration in the composition of Terence's comedies, but even granting this, and also granting the substitution of the author's name, what significance would this have in any judgment about his poetry?[12] Are we trying to assign points to Terence in an examination or competition, so that it becomes necessary to be certain that the work submitted was actually done by Terence? In making judgments professor-critics only with difficulty abandon their practice of giving examinations and judging competitions. This account for their mistrust and disapproval of Terence.

As may be seen I have put forward as hypotheses the worst complaints that critics have devised or can devise (that these plays are translations and not written by Terrence). I have also shown that such judgments count for nothing among those who enjoy and consider the works in themselves as works of poetry. I would not have one suppose, however, that I believe Terence's dramas are simple translations from the original Greek. True, Terence himself declares that he has taken this or that comedy from Menander or from some other Greek. The ancient stage directions confirm this and identify the other playwright as Apollodorus. Taking plots of Greek comedies and preserving Greece as the setting for the drama were techniques approved and inculcated in the Roman theatre. Indeed, to judge from the defense that Terence himself put forward, it was considered improper to put two or more of these well-known scenes together,[13] although once a plot was adopted, much liberty was allowed for unacknowledged alterations, variations, additional scenes, and characters.[14] What is really important to us, however, is not the plot but its embellishments; not the argument or the tale but its inner poetic fluidity. This point was understood in subsequent centuries of European literature, when the word "imitation," connoted both "humble" and "lofty" (a significance which only romanticism deprived it of), meaning precisely this acceptance of traditional plots to serve as a frame for one's own embellishment or the creation of beauty.

Still later, literary scholars unprepared in art criticism, if not downright deaf to poetry, gave great and primary importance to the canvas, and step by step they ended up adorning its composition with the scientific-sounding although scientifically improper term, "technique," so that today, instead of searching out the poetry, they pronounce judgment on the good or bad technique of the works and act as if they were craftsmen or (since here we speak of the theatre) expert stage-managers and actor-managers, who know how to maintain theatrical continuity and obtain effects. It was inevitable that once through papyrus discoveries, some of Menander's longer fragments and a good part of one of his comedies had come to light, these literary scholars should quickly judge and pronounce that Menander's technique is superior to that of Terence, who by comparison seems almost a bungler.[15] Whether true or not (and here too I sense the work of prejudice), the canvas *per se* or technique in poetry has secondary importance. Here I will repeat, and especially in reference to Terence, a truth so simple that it cannot find access to the hard brains of literary scholars. It was asserted by Michel de Montaigne who felt most kindly toward the Roman comic poet and called him, "admirable à rapresenter au vif les mouvements de l'âme et la condition de nos mœurs." Montaigne disliked anyone whose interest lay in plot, incidental events, accidents, complications, diversions:

> Il en va de mon aucteur tout au contraire: les perfections et beaultez de sa façon de dire nous font perdre l'appetit de son subject; sa gentilesse et sa mignardise nous retiennent partout; il est partout si plaisant, "liquidus puroque simillimus amni," et nous remplit tant l'âme de ses graces que nous en oublions celles de sa fable.[16]

We forget the tale, or rather, we remain indifferent to it, indifferent that the customary servant (Mr. do it-all, Mr. think-of-everything) concocts his customary clever devices for procuring money for the young master and deceives the old man; indifferent to the fact that the young master's sweetheart turns out to be the daughter of the old man's friend and that marriage crowns the comedy; and indifferent to all other such things. Our eye follows something that rises above the narrative, detaches itself, and hovers above it.

It is unlikely that Terence's plays are mere, albeit free, translations of Greek plays, and that in them we have of the original work only whatever is poetic, always issuing from the personality of the artist-translator-diminisher and making possible his work, or at most, some felicitous alterations of particulars.[17] Yet the scholars will not even grant him these: for where the sources show that a given character or scene was introduced by Terence, they reply that these are too beautiful or too skillful to be "flour from Terence's sack," and that the ancient commentator erred, or did not mean to say what he said, or that the text has been interpolated; and so these parts are also by Menander, or by some other Greek playwright, whom the commentator has been unable to identify.[18]

I may be mistaken, but this interpretation seems to argue in a vicious circle. However that may be, the fact remains that Terence and Plautus had before them approximately the same models. Yet, what a difference in their temperaments and respective works![19] In Terence's plays, there is a unity of sentiment, an even, coherent personality, a purity and artistic nobility, a reluctance to leave his sphere and to wander or to break into that of others; whereas translators, usually versatile, display this versatility in their varied artistic sensibility and virtuosity. Why did Terence write only "sex comoedias"? Very probably because "son verre n'était pas grand, mais il buvait dans son verre." The tale tiresomely repeated in so many books, might be taken as a joke about his scanty literary output (had it not originated from a corrupt reading of a passage in Suetonius). It recounts that Terence, having published his six comedies, made a little trip to Greece where he translated and adapted no fewer than one hundred and eight of Menander's comedies and loaded them on a ship that foundered; whereupon he died of heartbreak at the loss of his baggage and the "novas fabulas." Could it not be that the relation between Terence and Menander, instead of being what the modern literary scholars think, is that other which seems to be suggested in a well-known passage of Saint Jerome, who knew and loved both authors; and, being asked by someone concerning the way to pursue his studies, assigned Homer and Virgil, Menander and Terence as the four authors he was to keep before him in matters of poetry.[20] Did he, thus, believe that the former pair stood in approximately the same relationship to one another as that between Menander and Terence (putting aside, as Francesco Petrarca[21] once remarked, the "altitudo stili" of the two epic poems)?

Actually, that little more, if not much, of Menander's writing we possess today does not at all confirm that Terence was nothing more than an elegant and fine translator, but rather seems to accentuate the different features of the two authors. The Greek presents himself as lively, spirited, smiling, very charming and clever—even affectionate and touching in some of his characters: Glycera and the soldier of the *Perikeiromene,* for example, and Abrotonon and Charisius of the *Epitrepontes.* Terence, on the other hand, shows himself to be fundamentally humane, moved by emotion, and therefore little disposed to mirth and laughter.[22] Perhaps further discoveries of Menander's dramas (providing us with a more complete knowledge of his personality) will link the two authors more closely to each other. At this time, however, we should not venture beyond what we already know, since Terence himself has told us, he took some plots from Menander.[23] The copious literature, continually growing, committed to discovering all the scenes Terence took from Menander, along with the modifications and adaptations he introduced, remains entirely conjectural and sterile. To be frank, such attempts seem a true scholarly madness. If *tantus amor* inspires us to study such matters (as if the excess of writing offered us for the consideration of other poets were not already enough—an excess which nevertheless has proved of little use in interpreting their poetry), well then, let us await the discovery of other papyri and, meanwhile, let us be patient.

Still less from these new comparisons does Menander's superiority over Terence—as of a true poet over a man of letters or of a creator over a clever technician—emerge. Nor can we take seriously the game-playing that the literary scholars, converting themselves into philosophers (or rather perverting themselves into bad philosophers) have now taken up with great zeal and delight: to suppose that in poetic works, certain moral, or political, or other concepts are debated, these being the "problems" as they are emphatically called. By such means, a German scholar[24] demonstrated how much difference there is between an "artistic genius" like Menander and a "merely able playwright"[25] like Terence, or rather (since even this merit was denied him) like his model, Apollodorus of Carystus. In the *Epitrepontes,* Menander, it appears, had proposed the great moral problem of chastity, incumbent on men no less than women before matrimony; and Terence-Apollodorus disregarded this most grave and lofty problem for the petty pleasure of changing the plot and resolving a "technical problem."[26] Our Italian Pasquali[27] has hastily followed in the German's track by locating Menander's greatness in his self-revelation in the *Epitrepontes* as a "thinker preoccupied with the problems of social ethics"[28] and specifically one (the problem of prenuptial male chastity) which is "eminently modern, Kantian or Ibsenian;"[29] and though "Menander did not resolve it"—how could he have resolved it? Not even today (Pasquali lamentingly admits) has it been solved[30]—he could have developed it, in the manner in which Ibsen would have done, which Pasquali divines and delineates.[31]

In fact, this alleged problem, at best, does not belong to Kant, the philosopher, but to the Kant of the casuistical exercises. Nor does it occur, as a predisposition, in Ibsen's world. (Nora of the *A Doll's House* is not relevant here.) One finds it instead, in the abstract, insipid moralism of Björnson, whose play on this argument, (*The Glove,* 1883), Pasquali should at least have recalled for his purpose, whatever it may be. It would be superfluous to demonstrate once again that the existence of the conceptual problem (moral, political, and so forth) does not confirm the existence but indeed the absence of poetry;[32] and in Menanderian comedy, not only is such a problem not enunciated, even the material situation cited by the German scholar and his Italian follower does not arise. Charisius reproaches himself for an act totally unconnected with the one of not saving the flower of his virginity for his bride.[33]

These confutations of the distorted judgments that critics pile up around Terence's art I have made in homage to truth and logic, just as my earlier objections and reservations concerning the claim that he was a simple translator were inspired by methodical doubt and critical caution. Nevertheless, I repeat: I would readily concede—however improbable the hypothesis may be—that the six comedies attributed to Terence are nothing other than translations of Greek comedies. But what is truly important is something else. Translations or not, those six comedies standing before us speak to us and reveal the soul of a poet who has his own accent, his own music, and his own prevailing feeling. The reader of poetry asks the critic only to remove obstacles and to aid him in the enjoyment of poetry. Other questions, even when well founded and resolvable, falling outside and being extraneous to the poetic work, do not satisfy the reader's demand. Indeed they turn their shoulders to him, and if not downright annoying, remain indifferent.

After so many irrelevant discourses, I think it is time to take up the only pertinent one; after having tarried so long among his philosophers, to tarry a while with Terence himself and to learn that "dominant sentiment" from him, which by chance is a very dear and precious thing: human goodness. This goodness, specifically speaking, is well aware of human weakness, but more willingly seeks out and observes the spontaneous manifestations and strengthening of finer emotions; and with these, it limits, corrects, and overcomes less noble and less pure ones.

In this regard, the first example that offers itself, being so striking, is in his treatment of the impudent prostitute, the "meretrix mala" of the other comic writers, who in his presentation, cannot to be totally and profoundly wicked. But one way or another she always reveals some readiness to do good and generous work, an attraction and aspiration to virtue, and some humility about the condition in which she finds herself. One would say that Terence will not admit to fundamental malice in man, and he finds it repugnant to exclude any human creature from the circle of humanity.

Let us begin with the youthful Chrysis, who migrates from Andros to Athens, spurred on by her need and her family's indifference. She has neither thought nor disposition to dishonest conduct, and at first she lives a hard life, spinning and weaving for a living. Later she is subjected to the dangers of youth, of beauty, of the absence of familial and social restraints and supports, and yielding to the seductions of pleasure, she slides, by degrees, into the condition of a prostitute. Yet while in that situation, she arouses feelings of friendship and affectionate devotion. When she unexpectedly takes ill and sees that she is near death she summons a young man who had been like a brother to her, and recommends to his trust and honor, a young girl who had been as close to her as a younger sister. She puts the girl's hand into that of the youth as husband, friend, brother, father, everything, in short, that represents moral institutions and relations. Weeping, the young man, who had not been one of her lovers, accompanies her bier. His father, pleased by his son's feeling, the signs of a sensitive heart, also participates in the sad ceremony.

Bacchis, of the *Hecyra,* is loved ardently by the young Pamphilus, who unwillingly takes a wife in obedience to his father. But he does not touch his bride, firmly intending to restore her as a virgin to her parents, and he continues his relation with his lover. No longer entirely in possession of him, Bacchis becomes ill-tempered and overbearing so that in contrast the humility and sweetness of his wife touches Pamphilus's heart. Little by little, he transfers his love from his lover to his wife and ends up abandoning Bacchis. But at the most agonizing and desperate point of the drama, his parents, not knowing how to explain what has happened between Pamphilus and his wife, suspect that he is still in the power of his former lover. Pamphilus's father sets out to question her and if need be to threaten her. But she takes no joy in the grief into which Pamphilus, his wife and their relatives have been plunged, and has no thought of revenge toward the youth who has abandoned her, or toward the one who has been the cause. She quickly declares the truth—that the youth no longer comes to her house. When the father asks her to repeat her testimony to the women of his family, she feels a mixture of pride and timidity at the thought of showing what she is to a wife who must regard her with hostility, and in an honest house that for her amounts to a reproof and places her in an inferior position. She knows that no one else in her circumstances would endure it. But her good-heartedness and natural honesty conquer. She goes. Fortune wills that in her encounter she provide a proof even better than her testimony, one which cuts the knot and alleviates the painful discord that was tormenting the young couple. How great then is Bacchis's joy!

> Quantam obtuli adventu meo laetitiam Pamphilo hodie!
> Quot commodas res attuli! Quot autem ademi curas!
> Gnatum ei restituo, paene qui harum ipsiusque opera periit:
> uxorem, quam nunquam ratus posthac se habiturum, reddo:
> qua re suspectus suo patri et Phidippo fuit, exolui . . . [34]

Bacchis rejoices, congratulates herself that fate has chosen her to dispel so many sorrows, to spread such joy in a family which had not expected this from her. Here a distinguished scholar, one of those who cannot admire any poet without pulling down another, and who cannot praise a poetic personage unless he vilifies another, proposes that Bacchis was "ben inferior" (quite inferior) to Abrotonon of the *Epitrepontes*—a work which Terence must have had before him—because Bacchis "is too self-satisfied to talk about her generosity, flaunting deliberately an excessive modesty," particularly in the verses just quoted; whereas Abrotonon, "who feeling she has served as an object of ridicule, rather than exalt herself, intends to act after minutely preparing a plan and does not talk overly about herself."[35]

Let us put aside the misstatements of fact, for if Abrotonon quickly becomes displeasing to Charisius after so many protestations of love, after long attachment, Bacchis is abandoned by Pamphilus; and if Bacchis is pleased with what she has done, but neither seeks nor expects reward, Abrotonon aims to obtain the prize of freedom. Nor can anyone show where

Bacchis "exhibits excessive modesty" and also "speaks too much of her generosity": that self-satisfaction which she wears somewhat like a halo, becomes her well. The poet has not claimed to depict a woman of exquisite refinement and austere perfection. But setting this aside, the two characters are poetically entirely different. Abrotonon is a poor wrench, a little *cocotte* who is down on her luck, and she does not know how Charisius has come to take up with her. She laments comically that Charisius does not even want her near him at dinner and indeed has kept her in prenuptial purity for three days. She is also a good creature who, solicitously and hastily, attempts to discover whether the exposed child is the son of Charisius, and, who is his mother—all this with gracious words and acts, as well as shrewdness. What has this to do with Bacchis? She does not wish to be like the other courtesans with their cold and rough egoism, with their hatred and repayment of evil for evil to anyone who has left them and no longer serves their convenience. What Bacchis accomplishes need not be judged by moralizing, lordly scholars, because it is already well judged, understood and felt by young Pamphilus himself in his touching expression of gratitude and tenderness, when she comes before him, after her saving action, with a simple greeting:

O Bacchis, mea Bacchis, servatrix mea![36]

Pamphilus calls her "his" Bacchis, not in the same sense as before, but "his" as she has now become in his heart, the old affection being at once revived and purified into one of new new quality and savor. The words they now exchange are not of two former lovers, but of two beings who have been transported to another plane. He still finds in her the gentleness that had made her enchanting in her appearance, in her words, in everything; and she finds in the youth, the manner and spirit that made him the most lovable man in the world. Bacchis wants him to be happy in his new situation and affectionately recommends that he care for his wife, who is indeed worthy of him. She advises him: "Recte amasti, Pamphile, uxorem tuam,"[37] the wife whom she has just seen for the first time and who appears "perliberales," most kind. These two former lovers disengage from their common past and reunite on a higher present.

A similar inclination toward good deeds is found in Bacchis's girlfriend, Philotis. Though amazed and outraged by Pamphilus's abandonment of her friend, she is not persuaded by the hag, who admonishes her to take warning from the event and to have no pity for any man, but to exploit, mutilate, and tear all of them to pieces, without exception when they come into her hands. Philotis asks: "Eximium neminen habeam?"[38] No one at all? And when the hag presses her arguments further, she renews her objection:

"Tamen pol eandem iniuriumst esse omnibus,"[39] as if to say, such a bad goal should not and cannot be!

The other Bacchis (the character in the *Heauton Timorumenos*) is a fully active, ostentatiously avid courtesan, who attends to her own gain. Nevertheless she feels the need to explain to the young girl, Antiphila, on her way to meet her spouse, that she does not behave as she does out of wickedness, but because she cannot do otherwise. She is a prisoner of the logic of her situation. "Nam expedit bonas esse vobis; nos quibuscum est res, non sinunt."[40] It cause lies in masculine egoism, which seeks nothing besides voluptuous beauty and turns its back on it when it fades.

Thais (of the *Eunuchus*), whose name in Italian (thanks to Dante) has become synonymous with the most despicable sort of woman, is in Terence simply one who follows the iron logic of the life upon which she has entered, and plans and provides for future adversities; but she is not a wicked woman. In her way, she feels affection for the young Phaedria. If she courts the soldier, it is because she expects his young slave as a gift and she hopes to return her to her parents, thereby gaining some good will to ease her loneliness in the city. When this happens and she is received "in clientelam et fidem" in the home of Laches, I still remember the annotator of the Terence I read in school (that of Monsignor Bindi) was scandalized by this breach of custom and could only excuse Terence by citing the "corruptness of those pagan times." The good Monsignor Bindi had already transformed Phaedria and Thraso into two suitors "for the hand of Thais," which subsequently Phaedria had the good fortune to win! Nevertheless Bindi understood and enjoyed his Terence far more sensibly than do many modern scholars.

In the light of this treatment of the courtesan, I am amazed that the above-praised scholars have missed the opportunity to credit, not indeed Terence, that "santo pequeño," no, but rather Menander for having discovered and explored the "problem" of the "rehabilitation" of the fallen woman and thus for having anticipated a theme of the French Romantics. Yet some have already glimpsed this point; and it may be hoped that they will insist on it with their usual intuitive grasp of broad themes and sensitive interpretation of particulars. Lafaye says that Terentius-Apollodorus "semble avoir voulu, comme les romantiques, rajeunir les types traditionnels en leur prêtant des sentiments contraires à l'idée que l'on s'en faisait généralement: de là la bonne courtisane, fine, sensible, désinteressée."[41] According to this critique, Terence sought the unconventional because of his love of novelty—not therefore as a Romantic but at best as a Baroque figure. For the Romantics were drawn toward their paradoxical characterizations by a spirit of revolt against society and its conventions or laws. But neither the spirit of rebellion nor a Baroque love of the strange and bizarre guided the frank and sensitive Terence.

A sense of naturalness, indulgence, and fundamental goodness occurs in other scenes and characters of Terence. In the writings of Giovanni Boccaccio (the great connoisseur of the paths by which natural love can break through all obstacles, employing all the subtlest tricks in order to triumph, avoiding all those precautions that get in its way), there is nothing as suffused with moral nobility as the first scene of the *Andria*. The father has sagely determined that the best way of preventing the young Pamphilus from entangling himself in mischief is to allow him his freedom; and observing his actions—his youthful diversions, his passion for horses and the hunt, his interest in philosophy and in disputations, his dealings with his friends—he is pleased to see that his son is always temperate, tactful, and popular with everyone. He also sees that Pamphilus goes to Chrysis's house, where he converses and dines, with restraint and without scorching himself in love's fires. And inwardly congratulating himself on that, he rejoices for himself and his son; and as was pointed out before, when he sees his son in grief for the death of that woman, this too seems beautiful to him. He approves and joins him, respectful of his son's tears and sadness. But then among the women at the funeral, he notices one whom he does not know: a beautiful young girl, modest and gracious. He learns that she is the dead woman's sister. He is amazed; a veil falls instantly from his mind. The unveiling of the illusion with which he had soothed himself has, in its very feeling of astonishment mingled with the seriousness of the discovery, a flash of the comic. Tut tut—so that is what it's all about, is it?

> Attat, hoc illud est,
> hinc illae lacrumae, haec illast misericordia![42]

The love that binds the two young people becomes quickly evident to him without anyone declaring it, without leaving any hope for doubt, when the weeping girl comes dangerously close to the flames of the pyre. Pamphilus, terrified,

> adcurrit: mediam mulierem complectitur:
> "Mea Glycerium," inquit, "quid agis? quor te is perditum?"
> Tum illa, ut consuetum facile amorem cerneres,
> reiecit se in eum flens quam familiariter.[43]

These four verses form a picture, a poetry of disconsolate grief, of watchful, affectionate solicitude, of a lost and abandoned woman who seeks and finds refuge in the protection of the man she loves.[44] The youth deserves this trusting devotion. He feels the responsibility which awaits him in sheltering the girl who has given herself to him. If he were obedient to the marriage vows imposed by his father, if he were to throw her aside, he would not only cast her into utter despair, but also expose her to the danger of being corrupted in a corrupt world. Through his fault the treasure of that sweet ingenuous spirit would be lost:

> Hem, egone istuc conari queam?
> egon propter me illam decipi miseram sinam,
> quae mihi suom animum atque omnem vitam credidit,
> quam ego animo egregie caram pro uxore habuerim?
> bene et pudice eius doctum atque eductum sinam
> coactum egestate ingenium inmutarier?[45]

The promise that he has made to the dying Chrysis is sacred to him, and he will not release her hand from his—the hand he gripped as he swore his oath.

The passionate tone of the young Phaedria (in the *Eunuchus*) is quite different: a passion devoid of ethical elements, entirely palpable and sensual, rapacious and violent, fiercely tenacious, notwithstanding the woman's attacks and his efforts to extricate himself. One can say that Phaedria and Thais stand on the same level. Along with advising him, Parmeno dictates the rule of conduct which Phaedria's situation requires:

> Quid agas? nisi ut te redimas captum quam queas
> minumo: si nequeas paululo, at quanti queas:
> et ne te adflictes . . . [46]

Thais wishes to make a compromise between her preference for him and her needs and objectives, which require that she also satisfy the rich soldier, who had been her friend. In her words there is a resignation that is tinged with melancholy:

> Ne crucia te, obsecro, anime mi, Phaedria.
> Non pol, quo quemquam plus amem aut plus diligam,
> eo feci: sed ita erat res, faciundum fuit.[47]

Phaedria ultimately resigns himself for the sake of not breaking with the woman. He only begs and insists that their separation not last longer than two days. During this time he goes to his villa, but he can remain there no more than an hour or so, and returns to the city to wander in the area where Thais is staying. Here again Parmeno is compelled to meditate philosophically on how curiously poor humanity is made. He sees no remedy:

> Di boni, quid hoc morbist? adeon homines immutarier
> ex amore, ut non cognoscas eundem esse! Hoc nemo fuit
> minus ineptus, magis severus quisquam, nec magis continens . . . [48]

In short, Phaedria is not a blind and brutal slave of the senses, but a man, one who, having fallen into a net, struggles and becomes more tightly enmeshed. For now intoxication holds him, which one day will pass.

With the same heart (I speak of heart, because I believe that neither for Terence, nor for Menander, nor for any other poet, does praise for knowing how to reproduce the "immediate reality of daily life" and "contending against nature and conquering it" have any relevance), with the same heart then, the dramatist depicts the suffering figure of old Menedemus (in the *Heauton Timorumenos*), the father who cannot forgive himself for having—by his extreme strictness—allowed his son to become a soldier. Menedemus works furiously in the country and fearfully avoids the enjoyment of any pleasure or comfort that would seem stolen from the son who, because of his behavior, has been thrown into the fatigue and harshness of military life.

In the *Adelphoe*, the opposing methods of education, enacted by the two fathers, do not serve (as some moralistic exegetes say) to develop the thesis that one should avoid extremes; but are themselves ways of reflecting, with astonished eyes, on different human actions and their unforeseeable consequences. Actually, Terence does not know how to compare the two methods. He does not take sides; nor does he propose a pedagogic synthesis. Demea, who had seen his rigorous method defeated in its results, turns to practicing the method which previously he had opposed and fought. But he does this spitefully, furiously, like one who seeks ruin, carrying it to its worst extreme, exceeding in great measure the laxness his brother practiced, punishing him by forcing him to new laxness and by embarrassing him for the concessions he makes, one after another until his head spins. By so doing Demea wishes to prove that the praise and favor, which until now have befallen his brother, are not "ex aequo et bono," but come solely from catering to the interests and passions of others. War-weary, he drops the reins on his horse's neck and spurs him on a rapid and disorderly course. But, not for this does he lose faith that his method was a sound one, and that it ought to be taken up again. Nor on the other hand, does his indulgent brother become dissatisfied with his own method, or can he be persuaded to disown it. Here we are not treating of a "problem" or a pedagogical thesis, but of conflicting emotions, diverse temperaments, and those changes of circumstance that seem to challenge every pedagogical theory.

If these two father-brothers are different, the two mothers of the *Hecyra*, in two diverse situations, in two necessarily different roles, are alike in their sacrifice and their maternal humility—the one with regard to her daughter, the other with regard to her son. It is strange that this spontaneous agreement between maternal souls and the harmony they establish, should be called a "duplication" and be attacked, always because of that before-hand conviction that Terence everywhere and in all things ought to be inferior to the great Menander.[49] Even poor Philumena, it seems, is inferior to the Pamphila of the *Epitrepontes*—Philumena, that violated innocent who confides the shame she has suffered only to her mother, but conceals it from her husband and father. The honesty of these Terentian maidens and brides is represented with equal delicacy and simplicity.

In concluding these brief examples of the tone that Terence adopts in treating of human emotions, I would like to mention the parasite of the *Eunuchus*. He is entirely different from the rigid caricatures that we find in other comic writings (Ergasilus, for instance, in Plautus's *Captivi*), and he is as entertaining as a Casanova when he states his rule of life: fools are in the world solely for the benefit of intelligent men. Since there exist in the world soldier-types like Thraso, who thrive on boasts and who wish to pass for brave, wise, wily, and spirited, why not a "Gnatho" at his side, to amuse Thraso and, by so doing, provide for himself? To correct Thraso or to change him would not be possible; a soil so fertile could only be left uncultivated, unharvested, or be abandoned to the industry of others, and that would be a shame. Gnatho, thus, backs up the glorious boasts of his companion with assents, consents, aphorisms, validations, and embellishments on what was said. He laughs at the jokes which Thraso thinks amusing. He listens patiently at the continual reiteration of the same stories of his deeds. He asks to have them repeated, as if he did not well remember all the details, and would be overjoyed to hear them again. But Thraso is a poor fellow too, who (in spite of being wronged and deceived) cannot renounce Thais, but crawls back to her subdued and then, as usual, wraps himself in memories of his heroic peers: "Qui minus quam Hercules servivit Omphalae?" Gnatho approves: "Exemplum placet."[50] As a man who understands and knows how to manage the things of the world, Gnatho's master work is achieved when he gets the warrior, and himself as well, accepted into the new society that has formed around Phaedria and Thais, on the prudent counsel that the expenditure which Thais requires is too heavy to be sustained by one man, and that since a partner is needed for this reason, no one is more convenient than this rich, spendthrift fool, who is already in hand.

Even Thraso and Gnatho are not wicked men. They exist as low-lifes and get on as well as they can. True, Pasquali protests that Terence spoils Menander's delicate representation of Thais (in a lost comedy, so that no one can really say now he presented her:[51] yet another demonstration of the great and peculiar imagination of the literary scholars). Presumably he spoiled the representation with this last scene "so unworthy of that gentle creature (Thais)," which, "if perhaps it did not offend most of the spectators, must have offended more refined readers including Terence's contemporaries" and amounts to a contradiction "not only logical or psychological but artistic as well."[52] But if Dante exhibited violent contempt for poor Thais, it appears that Pasquali has allowed himself to be seduced by her enticements, and, as in a lover's dream, forgets what she is in her simple reality, in the words of Phaedria and Parmeno, and in her conversations with them. On the other hand, he reveals a scholarly moral intransigence unsuited for embracing the emotions, their gradations, complications, and contaminations, which real life and poetry contain. Poetry will not suffer such narrowness and prudery. Whatever the unknown Thais may be like in that unknown comedy by Menander, in Terence's work she suits very well as she is, and as she is, she arouses human understanding and compassion.

Such are the motifs of Terence's poetry that occur time and again in his comedies, among which the prize is usually given to Terence's *Eunuchus*, a play that is certainly is full of life and an abundance of the comic elements with, here and there, some farce that is lacking or very rare in the others. But perhaps with sounder judgment the prize should go to the *Hecyra*, which is followed by the *Eunuchus*, the *Andria*, the *Adelphoe*, the *Heauton Timorumenos*, and lesser than these, because it has more of the simple comedy of intrigue, the *Phormio*.

Antiquity[53] admired Terence for the moving goodness with which he represented human life and for an almost Christian charity which occasionally is felt in him, not indeed solely for his beautiful Latin. In the Middle Ages, he was one of the most frequently read of the Roman writers and was as dear to Petrarca as he later was to Montaigne, to Erasmus as to Carlo Borromeo; dear for his gentleness, and the brilliant clarity of his art, as though he were the Virgil of Roman comedy. Later, familiarity with his writings diminished. His drama fell heir to the lot of all Latin literature, and his decline was accelerated by the low regard accorded him by scholars. Nevertheless, whoever reopens his volume of Terence will draw from it an ever living gratification which will transcend time.

3

Lucretius and Virgil[1]

I

The *De Rerum Natura*

Lucretius' *De Rerum Natura* and Virgil's *Georgics* have often been compared and contraposed with a two-fold and antithetical contraposition: for if the latter has usually been regarded as the more truly poetic, there have been some who have preferred the poetic robustness of Lucretius and, in this regard, have raised doubts about the value and vigor of the *Georgics*. Perhaps it would be useful to take up this comparison and its terms, so as to define them in a more precise manner.

Giambattista Vico, one of the major founders and representatives of modern criticism, substantially denied the poetic quality of the *De Rerum Natura*, acknowledging it in the *Georgics*. He judged Lucretius' poem thus: "with the exception of the poetic introductions to his books and a few well known digressions—as for example, in the sensitive inimitable description of the tender heifer who has lost its mother,[2] and in the incomparable passage describing the pestilence of Athens—the rest treats matters of physics in a style no different from that taught in a Latin school of natural philosophy." The *Georgics* instead treats rustic craft "poetically."[3]

Yet if the intent and tenor of Lucretius' poem is didactic, it is also powerfully impassioned. The passionate or sentimental element is never disassociated from scientific exposition, which in its expressive concreteness does not proceed from intellect alone, but from the entire man. This is why the style of individual scientists, which ideally one would replace with a so-called impersonal scientific one which, though it be called impersonal, will always reveal a personal coloration to anyone possessing a fine ear. But the impassioned element becomes stronger and more evident if, from areas where abstract or merely classificatory sciences are treated—areas where this element is restricted by the zeal to be scientifically exact and so by the explicit and implicit polemic and the mocking of imprecision—we pass to areas of philosophical or historical inquiry concerning men's affairs, the inquiry that is always aroused by some need to act and whose expression is taken up and pursued by the mind impassioned with a fullness of humanity. The more the pathos is ignited in the preparation, development, and conclusion of the inquiry, the more the work reverberates with passion,—here effusive, there compressed. This is the case in Lucretius' poem born from so much pain, from so much struggle for redemption, so much yearning for serenity, so much joy at its achievement, so much gratitude and devotion toward his teacher, saint Epicurus, who brought it about:

> Tu, pater, es rerum inventor, tu patria nobis
> suppeditas praecepta, tuisque ex, inclute, chartis,
> floriferis ut apes in saltibus omnia libant,
> omnia nos itidem depascimur aurea dicta,
> aurea, perpetua semper dignissima vita.
> Nam simul ac ratio tua coepit vociferari
> naturam rerum, divina mente coorta,
> diffugiunt animi terrores, moenia mundi
> discedunt, totum video per inane geri res.
> Apparet divum numen sedesque quietae,
> quas neque concutiunt venti nec nubila nimbis
> aspergunt neque nix acri concreta pruina
> cana cadens violat semperque innubilus aether
> integit et large diffuso lumine ridet.[4]

(III, 9–22)

These praises of Epicurus, recurring throughout the poem, are almost prayers, acts of thanksgiving elevated from the depths of the poet's heart. He speaks of the "quaedam divina voluptas," and of the conjoined sacred awe that he experienced at the unveiling of the mystery; and of the feeling of achieved security that gives him joy even in seeing those other men who, by comparison with what he has won and in confirmation of it, foolishly only weary themselves quarreling over false truths:

> Sed nil dulcius est, bene quam munita tenere
> edita doctrina sapientum templa serena.[5]

(II, 7–8)

The insatiability, the desperate insatiability of carnal love that inflames and rages but does not achieve penetration, the intimate union and fusion, sought vainly in mingling and embracing bodies, makes Lucretius' description of sexual embrace truly terrible:

> Adfigunt avide corpus iunguntque salivas
> oris et inspirant pressantes dentibus ora:

nequiquam, quoniam nil inde abradere possunt
nec penetrare et abire in corpus corpore toto;
nam facere interdum velle et certare videntur.
Usque adeo cupide in Veneris compagibus haerent,
membra voluptatis dum vi labefacta liquescunt.
Tandem ubi se erupit nervis conlecta cupido,
parva fit ardoris violenti pausa parumper;
inde redit rabies eadem et furor ille revisit,
cum sibi quid cupiant ipsi contingere quaerunt,
nec reperire malum id possunt quae machina vincat.
Usque adeo incerti tabescunt volnere caeco.[6]

(IV, 1100–1112)

We can believe that the philosopher who analyses and describes thus, must have suffered the same attraction and the horror of that avid, that vain, that sad effort to conquer the impossible. Equally, in another pitiless description of the ugliness of the woman, idealized and made beautiful only by love's illusion, one feels the quivering disgust and horror of someone who has torn himself away and been released from that stupid and base fantasy, of a sick man become cured; or of a convalescent who, shuddering at the thought of becoming ill again, provides himself with a memento, which keeps true reality always before his eyes, the only one on which he can rely to affirm that he is free, master of himself and of things. By comparison, Juvenal's famous satire on women seems a mere irritation expressing a superficial disdain, both self-willed and dilettantish, not because it is more irrational, but because it lacks that grounding in pain that occurs in Lucretius' description, which is most irrational.

The passion that enriches and accompanies science and philosophy does not find fulfillment in what is usually called prose rhythm, the rhythm in which philosophers have written nearly all of their most highly moving pages, and so it rises to the rhythm and meter of verse; not merely for extrinsic or mnemonic reasons, as is the case in many parts of that science in metrical form that we find in medieval literature, but for the most essential reasons. Hence it flowers with poetic images that rise and become one with the rhythm and meter. We know that Nietzsche, recognizing this tendency, exclaims in the *Birth of Tragedy* that the matters he is treating should not be expressed discursively, but in song. Other philosophers rose from prose to meter (like Bruno and Campanella in Italy and also Giacomo Leopardi, in some of his poems, or in passages of poems, that are philosophical professions of belief). In this regard, however, the greatest poet of all is still the Roman Lucretius.

This form of verse, and of the poetic images conjoined to it, rising spontaneously from his thought and from the passion of his thought, is what frequently prompts us to acclaim him a poet and to consider the *De Rerum Natura* a lyric, either an interlacing or series of lyrics; because not to everyone and not always is there a clear and precise distinction between passionate and poetic expression, between enslaved passion and free floating contemplation, between verbal sincerity and the creation of beauty, between lyricism and lyric. It is the former qualities, understood in their genuine and best sense, and not the latter ones that reign in the Lucretian poem. This is the reasoning that has imposed itself on Marchesi, and when comparing Lucretius with Virgil, has caused him justly to deny Lucretius "poetic breath and contemplative unconstraint," even though he attributes the origin of this attitude solely to his being a "thinker and obstinate investigator of natural causes" and to his "feeling the things of the world physically." Therefore "however much he immerses himself in the seeds of cosmic life and ascends to the heavens and spaces of the firmament," he retains a certain "narrowness" with respect to the poetic law that "permits a man not only to re-evoke the universe but to recreate it."[7]

This didactic and passionate limitation may be noted in Lucretius in varying degrees, even in those passages that are generally singled out as splendid, rare exceptions of pure and complete poetry. The famous description of Iphianassa's sacrifice supports the thesis that "too often it is that very Religion which has brought forth criminal and impious deeds" ("saepius illa religio peperit scelerosa atque impia facta") and is emphasized by expressions of horror, repugnance, condemnation "foully defiled by blood" ("turparunt sanguine foede"), by the sorrowful astonishment at the men who acquiesced in this deed, and yet were "chosen leaders of the Danai, chieftains of the host" ("ductores Danaum delecti, prima virorum"), by the unsparing horror of details about the presence of Iphianassa's father and of the priests who, out of respect for him, conceal the knife ("et hunc propter ferrum celare ministros"), and of the virgin, who, beseeching the king as her father, is seized by the priests and led "tremebunda" to the altar, not for the nuptials that she anticipated, but to be "casta inceste" slaughtered in an expiatory rite. The description concludes with the no less famous exclamation, "So potent was Religion in persuading to evil deeds"[8] ("Tantum religio potuit suadere malorum"). This—for Lucretius the text of an anti-religious polemic—was later taken up as the text for an historical evaluation by Vico, who judged that those events horrible to us, such as "Agamemnon's unhappy vow regarding his pious daughter Iphianassa," did not come about through "the imposture of others, but through their own credulity"; and he recognized in them the counsel of Providence: "that so greatly wished us to domesticate the offspring of Polyphemus and lead them to the humanity of an Aristides, a Socrates, a Laelius, and a Scipio Africanus."[9] Iphianassa has her avenger in Lucretius, but her poets are properly Euripides, Racine, and Goethe.

Magnificent and loftily poetic is Lucretius' picture of the young calf's mother who anxiously searches everywhere for traces of her offspring, taken away and slaughtered before the altar of the god. Nothing draws away her attention and nothing distracts her. No other living being of her own species appeals to her, because she wants only her own kin, her child whom she knows well and can distinguish from all others. This picture moved the austere Vico, so tender-hearted (even though, parenthetically speaking, this did not spare him from his incorrigibly inexact references which, as may have been noted amount to a reversal of Lucretius's description[10]):

> Nam saepe ante deum vitulus delubra decora
> turicremas propter mactatus concidit aras,
> sanguinis expirans calidum de pectore flumen;
> at mater viridis saltus orbata peragrans
> noscit humi pedibus vestigia pressa bisulcis,
> omnia convisens oculis loca, si queat usquam
> conspicere amissum fetum, completque querellis
> frondiferum nemus adsistens et crebra revisit
> ad stabulum, desiderio perfixa iuvenci,
> nec tenerae salices atque herbae rore vigentes
> fluminaque ulla queunt summis labentia ripis
> obloctare animum subitamque avertere curam,
> nec vitulorum aliae species per pabula laeta
> derivare queunt animum curaque levare:
> usque adeo quiddam proprium notumque requirit.[11]
>
> (II, 352–365)

This admirable representation, heartrending in its simplicity, which gathers emotion with every small act of the poor mother, seems to suffer with her. It is permeated with an immense pity and animated by an implicit disdain for the fierce deity who inflicts tortures on all his creatures. Its object, however, is to illustrate by an example the thesis both men and animals recognize one another by their appearance, offspring run to mother and mother to offspring. The description (with "nam" and "saepe") is attached to this declared thesis, and lively as the representation of the actions and of their minute details is (almost losing itself in them), it does not lose sight of its function as an example ("usque adeo . . . "). This function (as Marchesi would rightly say) makes for a certain narrowness and presents an obstacle to its fusing and coming fully to rest in that particular-universal that properly belongs to poetry. It is a lyric, but enclosed if not really constricted, by limits; and it is not allowed full freedom of movement.

Perhaps only one passage of open, unconditional poetry (without "nam" and "saepe") occurs in Lucretius's poem. It is in the prologue, where Venus having been invoked and her function in the universe acknowledged, the poetry kindled into flame by that imagery, continues in the verses that we all know by heart:

> Te, dea, te fugiunt venti, te nubila caeli
> adventumque tuum, tibi suavis, daedala tellus
> summittit flores, tibi rident aequora ponti
> placatumque nitet diffuso lumine caelum;
> nam simul ac species patefactast verna diei
> et reserata viget genitabilis aura favoni,
> aëriae primum volucres te, diva, tuumque
> significant initum perculsae corda tua vi;
> inde ferae pecudes persultant pabula laeta
> et rapidos tranant amnis: ita capta lepore
> te sequitur cupide quo quamque inducere pergis;
> denique per maria ac montis fluviosque rapacis
> frondiferasque domos avium camposque virentis
> omnibus incutiens blandum per pectora amorem
> efficis ut cupide generatim saecla propagent . . . [12]
>
> (I, 6–20)

How could he ever abandon himself to this truly lyrical enthusiasm, to this enraptured contemplation of beauty, so dissonant from the tone of his poem, so little in conformity with the concept of the gods that he expresses and demonstrates? There are critics who have thought that if Lucretius been able to correct and polish his work, he would have removed, corrected, or tempered this poetic evocation; and editors have enclosed it within parentheses, parentheses of poetry. But more curiously, following these verses and those other no less poetic ones that portray Venus with Mars, we read still others that contain a doctrinal declaration, almost a protest. Here Lucretius seems to say something like "Do not pay attention to what I have sung with such fanciful rapture, for this is poetry, poetic falsehood, but the truth is otherwise:

> Omnis enim per se divum natura necessest
> immortali aevo cara cum pace fruatur
> semota ab nostris rebus seiunctaque longe;
> nam privata dolore omni, privata periclis,
> ipsa suis pollens opibus nihil indiga nostri,
> nec bene promeritis capitur nec tangitur ira. [13]

Michele Marullo, one of the first critics of the text of the *De Rerum Natura*, expunged these lines forthwith, so much did they seem to jar with the wonderful prologue and appear to him unworthy of Lucretius. Today, the prevailing opinion is that these lines are the interpolations of some reader (who, by referring to another passage, wished to catch Lucretius in a contradiction);[14] but others have conjectured that a lacuna precedes them which contained or must have contained Lucretius' explanation that the Venus whom he has poeticized was intended as an allegory and that literally speaking, the gods do not operate in human affairs.[15] All such conjectures lead, nevertheless, to the same conclusion: the prologue issues from the feeling and concept of the poem—regardless of whether it be the readers who notice it or the poet himself who is inclined to remove it in homage to doctrinal coherence, or to discredit it with prosaic declarations.

II

The *Georgics*

In the *Georgics,* a didactic motif is also accompanied by a non-didactic one, but both motifs differ greatly from those of the *De Rerum Natura* and in their relationship to one another. In the Virgilian poem the non-didactic motif is not passion but poetry; and the didactic does not stand on its own for the instructional objective it has in view, but as support for the poetry.

Yet one would not deny that Virgil, as a farmer or farmer's son, was an enthusiastic expert in rural matters. He was also a student of the relevant literature. Nor can one deny that his advice and precepts are useful and even today are, as some devoted agronomists claim, good to follow. One may also concede to those who hold the belief, although not solidly grounded, that beyond a theoretical end Virgil had a moral one, such as to stress work as the law of life, and to make us feel the joy of it, or a political one, that of cooperating in the encouragement of land cultivation in Italy, particularly after the breakdowns of a devastating civil war. But the fact is that whether as an instructional tool or a medium for popular rhetoric, the poem turned out too beautiful and thus ineffective for such ends, as is said to have been the case with that very learned and most beautiful lady who taught law at Bologna, and whose looks would have enchanted and distracted her students—and perhaps love's very smile would have flowered on her own face—had she not (according to legend) taken the precaution of lecturing from behind a curtain. But Virgil did not take this precaution with his work, the most charming, sweet, harmonious sounds and rhythms that have ever been sung.

But, on the other hand, the poem's foundation and design, which remain didactic, have aroused distrust, and have led some, notably in the romantic period, to place it outside the realm of true and proper poetry. I suppose that the German author of a dissertation (Hamberg, 1830), which I

have not seen, argued and voiced just such a condemnation. Its title expresses a clear plan: *Virgilii Georgica tantum abest ut sint poëma omnibus
numeris absolutum ut potius sint poëma verae genuinaeque poësi omnino
repugnans.*[16] Nevertheless, we have no difficulty in locating poetry wherever it happens to be or lies hidden even within the structure of a didactic
poem. Indeed, for this very reason we should not weary ourselves by exag-
geratedly claiming that the *Georgics* by their nature constitute a purely lyrical composition, from top to bottom, that sings the Virgilian ideal of the
simple, pure life amid the busy tasks of the field. It suffices that there is
poetry, not scattered here and there with a free hand, but profuse everywhere, even if it happens to border on a didactic poetry. This "enborder-
ing" poetry that for the skill with which the entire poem is fashioned, for
its union of reflection and inspiration, and for its demeanor—not of a rush-
ing river, but of a quiet stream or placid pond—ought to be called Alex-
andrine—not, however, because it imitates the genre elaborated by the
Alexandrians (for even this element of his composition should be called
new and original)—but precisely for its character as here described. The
Virgil inspired by pathos, singer of great misfortunes, tragic passions, and
bittersweet emotions, the author of the *Aeneid*, has more ties with the author of the *Bucolics* than with the author of the *Georgics*. Even the episode
of Orpheus and Eurydice adopts an ornamental and decorative style rather
than a tragic one; and certainly as all who judge it agree, it is exquisite, an
adjective that points to its excellence and also to its limitations.

     The *Georgics* is poetry inspired by the life of plants and animals, by
the life of nature—nature in this case that is not an image or metaphor for
human feelings and aspirations, as in those landscapes that express "states
of soul;" nor is it the accomplice of sensuous pleasure and wantonness as
the decadents would have it. On the other hand, it is not the object that the
scientist considers in devising its laws. Rather it is simply an order of beings, with whom it is a pleasure to cultivate relations, to observe in their
mode of living, to follow in their movements, to accompany in their adventures. With those beings, those natural phenomena, those plants, those animals, we engage in the life of all things. Our lives are interwoven with
theirs. We exchange with them, and our actions exert their influence on
them. But we are also separated from these beings, because their life is not
of humankind and does not enter into our problems. We do not invest it
with love and hate; it does not trouble, agitate, or hurt us.

     This is the sort of affection that moves us to care for plants, birds,
pigeons, or other small creatures that we domesticate; and when we talk
about and describe their habits, poetic words and expressions spring spontaneously to our lips, like those we read in books written by lovers of ag-
riculture, ornithology, and the like: "Not only in the didactic poems (a

writer of treatises on literary principles noted when referring to old Latin and Italian books on such matters), but also among good writers we find this gift of speaking allegorically (what he calls 'allegorical' we call 'imaginative' and 'poetic') although more sparingly used. Where did this style originate if not from the great charm of Latin and Italian writers on rustic affairs from Varro to Columella, down to Davanzati and Soderini? Pietro Crescenzi, for instance, says that the 'plum' desires 'mainly warm air and is happy in pleasant places.' Pier Vettori writes that 'one should treat the tender plants of the olive tree well in every way and caress them as much as possible insofar as they merit it,' and he wants 'to see them staring at each other in the field, all noble and pleasing as though they enjoyed their own and the countryside's loveliness.' Davanzati notes that 'the soil's humors run entirely to the new sweet vine-shoot, while the old vine shrinks.' "[17]

Of such impressions and representations the supreme poet is Virgil, who gathered and reproduced them with an art both ornamental and sober; and he enclosed them in the interstices of his precepts, arranging them as it were, in an earnest and elegant frame. Thus one understands the need and function of the didactic expedient to which he had recourse, or of the alliance he pressed between didacticism and poetry. Since lyrical representations of the life of nature could not find their center in a drama or tragedy, and would have followed one another like loose pearls, it was fitting to bind them in a piece of jewelry or necklace and make use of a material diverse from their own.

A few examples of these bonds and this art suffice to reawaken the music that the poetry of the *Georgics* leaves in the soul. These verses contain a guiding principle and introduce it with a rhetorical "quid dicam?":

> Quid dicam, iacto qui semine comminus arva
> insequitur, cumulosque ruit male pinguis harenae,
> deinde satis fluvium inducit rivosque sequentis
> et, cum exustus ager morientibus aestuat herbis,
> ecce supercilio clivosi tramitis undam
> elicit? Illa cadens raucum per levia murmur
> saxa ciet scatebrisque arentia temperat arva.[18]

What was in the poet's fancy and has passed into ours, resounding in our own ear, is the water that falls from the brow of the hill-side channel onto the slope of the scorched field—grieving for its dying plants—and produces a hoarse murmur among the rocks as its rivulets alleviate the suffering of the arid land.

Virgil retraces the history of the origin of various instruments and arts:

>tum ferri rigor, atque argutae lamina serrae
>(nam primi cuneis scindebant fissile lignum),
>tum variae venere artes . . . [19]

These epithets of the "ferri rigor" and "arguta serra" are entirely poetic.

>Alternis idem tonsas cessare novalis,
>et segnem patiere situ durescere campum,
>aut ibi flava seres mutato sidere farra,
>unde prius laetum siliqua quassante legumen,
>aut tenuis fetus viciae tristisque lupini
>sustuleris fragilis calamos silvamque sonantem.
>Urit enim lini campum seges, urit avenae,
>urunt Lethaeo perfusa papavera somno.[20]

The bean, happy for its brandished pods, the poppies steeped in Lethean slumber, and the sad lupin are the characters and actors that with their *modus vivendi,* drive the farming instructions into a secondary role and cause us almost to forget them.

>Saepe exiguus mus
>sub terris posuitque domos atque horrea fecit,
>aut oculis capti fodere cubilia talpae,
>inventusque cavis bufo et quae plurima terrae
>monstra ferunt, populatque ingentem farris acervom
>curculio atque inopi metuens formica senectae.[21]

Animals and insects that damage the harvests are thus denounced as enemies of the farmer, who hates them, but here they are composed into a group of "persons," variously engaged, who assiduously attend to their needs and provide for their comfort, in spite of the avaricious farmer, being more persistent and clever than he.

And elsewhere there are the rooks who, the rain having ceased:

>Tum liquidas corvi presso ter gutture voces
>aut quater ingeminant et saepe cubilibus altis
>nescio qua praeter solitum dulcedine laeti
>inter se in foliis strepitant; iuvat imbribus actis
>progeniem parvam dulcisque revisere nidos:[22]

The rooks are regarded as human in their family life; as the equals of the peasants who are similarly viewed in their existence; as equal to yet detached from us; and as natural in the evening at home with the women attending to the domestic chores:

> Et quidam seros hiberni ad luminis ignes
> pervigilat ferroque faces inspicat acuto.
> Interea longum cantu solata laborem
> arguto coniunx percurrit pectine telas
> aut dulcis musti Volcano decoquit umorem
> et foliis undam trepidi despumat aheni.[23]

Viewed, not as poetic work but as a literary and cultural one (which in truth is not our concern here), the *Georgics* is an archetype; because it and not indeed the poems of Empedocles and the other Greek philosophers and scientists, nor yet those of Lucretius and the other Romans, furnished the schema for the didactic poem of artistic character, which was adopted innumerable times, most notably from the Renaissance to the end of the eighteenth century. One need open any treatise on literary principles to find the recipe for the genre: "In order to succeed, the didactic poem should first of all not be dictated by cold reflection but indeed by a live feeling for the true and the beautiful. Secondly, it should take as its subject not some matter that is alien to the grace of the poetry, one that is abstruse and unknown to the general reader. Thirdly, it should deploy its material in a certain natural order, yet not as rigorously as in a treatise. Fourthly and finally, following the dictates of imagination, it should tarry over things that are more disposed to poetic ornamentation and frequently embellish them with episodes that are all the more necessary in this genre of poetry, because they serve, not merely for variety, as in the epic, but also to review and re-examine the material."[24]

Perhaps never again did that schema encounter the good fortune of being filled out by a poet who was the equal of its inventor. Nevertheless, among later poems, the didactic element held a place more or less as a pretext—not indeed a pretext for poetry but instead only for beautiful literature.

4

Virgil

Aeneas Facing Dido[1]

There have been many and continually recurring declarations of antipathy, repugnance, disapproval, and condemnation directed at Aeneas for his conduct toward the Carthaginian queen. On this subject there exists a true and genuine anti-Aeneas literature, which some inquisitive person might collect and compose into a brief description.[2] A similar psychological reaction occurs toward other more or less odious characters in poems, dramas, and romances—the hard Creon, the perfidious Iago, the treacherous Bireno, whom no gentle soul would wish to resemble; though one would incline toward martyred Antigone, slandered Desdemona, abandoned Olympia, and perhaps even impetuous, but generous Othello in spontaneous sympathy and feel an affectionate rapport with them. Nor does this come about, as is sometimes believed, through a morbid romanticizing, but through healthy feeling and a similar judgment, induced by genuine humanity.

If it is entirely natural that this should be the case with the Trojan hero, it is—for reasons I shall cite below—not strange, but assuredly inadmissible—for reasons I shall state immediately—that condemnations of Aeneas the man should be transformed into censures of Virgil the poet. Thus among the commentators and critics, we read that Virgil has represented Aeneas with much less poetic force than Dido: she is alive and concrete, he is abstract, cold, stylized, monochromatic, primitive, and archaic. By highlighting and shading, Virgil should have delineated him as more moved, more tender, more anguished, more sensitive in the presence of the woman who loved him, and as suffering more intensely in leaving her; and he should not have made him talk, as he does talk, like a rationalizing, subtilizing, cavilling lawyer for his own cause, one who at some points even becomes crude and brutal; nor should he have had him take to "hidden ways" and attempted deceptions. At times, when reading these censures, we almost expect the commentators and critics themselves to suggest the groans that Virgil should have made break forth from the breast of Aeneas, the wailing lamentations he should have had placed on his lips. We must thank them for not attempting these corrections and for not furnishing such poetic supplements.

Indeed their doing so would have been equal to misusing the emotional and moral revulsion aroused by Creon, Iago, and Bireno to criticize the art of Sophocles, Shakespeare, and Ariosto, or to blaming a painter for applying shadow or a spot of black where it was necessary for the harmony of his painting. In the fourth and sixth books of the *Aeneid,* Aeneas is figured very well as he is in relation to Dido and exactly as Virgil wanted him to be, petty, unpleasant, and contemptible. He wanted him so, not of course through critical awareness (which perhaps here made him search for and believe the opposite, and regard his hero as excused and justified) but through a more profound will aimed at actual poetic creation, and this is all that matters and concerns us. He wanted Aeneas as he is because of what inspired him, which in the Dido episode is love, love whose imperious force *omnia vincit,* that takes possession of an exquisite creature, a woman of great spirit and undefiled life and compels her to disregard every other bond, every other duty, to be obedient solely to a new duty, a new law that has imposed itself on her and that she has adopted as a religion, having become insensible to fame and glory, ready to humble herself in prayer for the sake of love, ready to die. In this kingdom of love Dido is the heroine. Aeneas is an impoverished man who, in love, is inferior to love, not a strong Hippolytus who enjoys the rigors of hunting and abhors Venus, but a weakling who has put his foot, he knows not how, in love's snare. As soon as other matters of a diverse nature, and of greater importance to him, present themselves and beckon, he thinks up ways to beat a hasty retreat, without much concern for anything else.

In poetry as in life, we hear cries of disdain and contempt for men of this kind in like situations. Perhaps Maria Mancini, when forced to leave the young Louis XIV and his court, did not speak the passionate words of scorn and disapproval legend has attributed to her: "Vous m'aimez, vous êtes roi, et je pars!"; but legend interpreted the logic of love. Here is a king capable of everything. Yet he does not feel obliged to place his omnipotence in the service of his love and to make it triumph over every prosaic obstacle! What a king! What a man! It takes Racine's Bérénice, enamored, but only to a certain point, a point determined by political interests whose higher claims she recognizes, to yield spontaneously in such a case, and resign herself. Emma Bovary cries in the face of the lover who coldly withdraws at her request for aid: "Mais moi, je t'aurais tout donné, j'aurais tout vendu, j'aurais travaillé de mes mains, j'aurais mendié sur les routes, pour un sourire, pour un regard, pour t'entendre dire merci!" Ibsen's women revealing their long torment, and rising above themselves, condemn in almost priestly language the man who has killed their soul: the artist who has sacrificed them for his art, or the practical man who has sacrificed them to his ambition. The women of Baudelaire obsessed with love, heap their most scornful invectives on the inept, the useless dreamer who would temper that sublime delirium with moral precepts, contaminating it with something different and extraneous; on the man who is unworthy of such profound suffering and

> n'échauffera jamais son corps paralytique
> à ce rouge soleil que l'on nomme l'amour.

In this lyrical expression one could say that inferiority in loving is given, not merely its representation, but directly, boldly, its theory as well.

Aeneas belongs with men of this kind, men who in the kingdom of love, correspond to those who in militias and armies are cowardly deserters. Virgil assuredly does not side against him; if anything, he seeks to defend him and to present him in a favorable light. But the poet who in Virgil is dominant, inexorably developing the logic of poetry, does not spare him. Instead he delineates the hero only in those acts and words that suit him. At the outset and during the course of Dido's love, Aeneas is passive. It is not he but the queen who "is wasted with fire unseen"[3] ("caeco carpitur igni")—the flame burns in her marrow and a voracious wound opens in her breast. While she lives entirely in her love for him, he allows himself to be loved with a love that a good deal of rest, comfort, and pleasure accompany, in the hospitable city after so many travels over land and sea. When Jove's command, or rather, the interrupted plan to seek Italy, obliges him to leave, beyond his quick decision he sees indistinctly in the things on which he is turning his back, not at all the pained features of his beloved, but scarcely, if at all, the *dulces terras* which he must soon leave. Given Aeneas's egoism, great to the point of guilelessness, and his preoccupation with the lofty undertaking that awaits completion, a conflict of passions not only has no place; it does not even present itself to his heart, wherein the conditions for such a conflict are lacking because he does not love and has never truly loved. His problem is solely how to break away; how to leave without endangering himself and his men and with the least annoyance; how to announce his resolve to Dido:

> Heu quid agat? Quo nunc reginam ambire furentem
> audeat adfatu? Quae prima exordia sumat?[4]

His meditation concentrates on this question:

> Atque animum nunc huc celerem, nunc dividit illuc,
> in partisque rapit varias perque omnia versat;[5]

The best way that he finds lies in concealing the preparations for departure and awaiting the opportune moment to communicate the situation to the

queen. The scheme does not fully succeed. For although he is prudent and
cautious, the queen quickly perceives her lover's mind:

> At regina dolos (quis fallere possit amantem?) praesensit . . . [6]

Thus he must face up to the discussion he had wished to avoid or postpone:
a discussion that, on Dido's side, amounts to desperate and vain recollections, reproaches and pleas that are imposing in their explosive emotion,
but on his side amounts to not replying, avoidance of her gaze, banal mut-
terings ("he will always remember her and the kindness he received"),
ill-mannered words ("Their relationship was not a marriage"), or stupid
ones ("why does she want to prevent him from reaching Italy, his son's
inheritance?").[7] He seems not to recognize that, besides Italy and his
son's inheritance, there is love in the world too, love that does not forgive
and that up to the present has stood beside him in its will to sacrifice and
that now stands before him in its terrible agony, its revolt against desolation
and the death that threatens it. It is as if a veil falls from the enamored
woman's eyes. She now sees what she had not seen before:

> Nam quid dissimulo aut quae me ad maiora reservo?
> Num fletu ingemuit nostro? num lumina flexit?
> num lacrimas victus dedit aut miseratus amantem est?[8]

He is capable solely of putting on the appearance, for convenience, of also
being saddened, of feeling a great love, of wanting and not knowing how to
comfort the sufferer and say kind words. Meanwhile he hastens his departure in order to be free of his embarrassment and annoyance:

> At pius Aeneas, quamquam lenire dolentem
> solando cupit et dictis avertere curas,
> multa gemens magnoque animo labefactus amore,
> iussa tamen divûm exequitur classemque revisit . . . [9]

So he perseveres, not for a moment deterred from his task: "steadfast
stands his will; the tears fall in vain. . . . [10] ("mens immota manet, lacri-
mae volvuntur inanes. . . . "); until he unfurls the sails for the voyage
which, at daybreak from the watch-tower of the house, the queen sees as
they move off into the distance, and in that distancing she perceives a sign
of her own death. She has nothing more to do on earth, which had been for
her so full of work and of hopes, where she had built a magnificent new
city, which for her has now become an uninhabitable desert:

Vixi et quem dederat cursum Fortuna peregi,
et nunc magna mei sub terras ibit imago . . . [11]

The Dido episode has been correctly analyzed many times, and recently, with great acuteness, in the Italian criticism of Fiore, Mocchino, Bignone, etc. It would be entirely superfluous to go over its poetic beauties and artistic perfection.[12] Even some very trifling blemish—as for instance, the way Virgil introduces and stresses Dido's regret to the man who wants to abandon her that not even a token of their love remains ("if in my hall a tiny Aeneas were playing. . . . "[13] ["si quis mihi parvulus aula—luderet Aeneas. . . . "])—has not escaped the sensitivity and acumen of some of these critics (Mocchino). For my purposes, it suffices to have clarified Virgil's representation of Aeneas, a man inferior to love,—a representation, artistically speaking, as excellent as that of the impassioned queen.

But this representation of Aeneas attains its highest point and seal with the magnificent scene of his encounter with Dido's ghost in the great forest, where his stature further diminishes and shrinks, and she, in her pain and scorn, becomes more majestic. He speaks to her. She does not look at him and remains silent. When he has finished speaking, she does not respond but turns her back, taking shelter near the shade of her first husband. Aeneas has never been so shabby, bungling, and awkward as in what he says to placate her and be reconciled with her. "Never had he thought that she would kill herself!" In effect he had measured her passion in terms of his own loveless soul. "He had abandoned her, not willingly, but by order of the gods!"[14] As if such an order could have had any force and weight for the enamored heart. "Qui donc devant l'amour ose parler d'enfer? . . . " Who here dares to speak of gods? Even Dido felt so in these matters, though she may have been unlike the crazy women who uttered this saying.

Talibus Aeneas ardentem et torva tuentem
lenibat dictis animum lacrimasque ciebat.
Illa solo fixos oculos aversa tenebat,
nec magis incepto voltum sermone movetur,
quam si dura silex aut stet Marpesia cautes.
Tandem corripuit sese atque inimica refugit
in nemus umbriferum, coniunx ubi pristinus illi
respondet curis aequatque Sychaeus amorem.[15]

Here is the constant love, the pure love, wherein only the wounded and embittered heart recovers some sweetness, the tremendous passion having been suffocated, the past not forgotten, but its torment transformed into the lassitude of melancholy.

I have mentioned that the censures of Virgil's handling of Aeneas in the Dido episode, though mistaken, have some justification, which should not be sought, however, in that perfectly harmonious passage. The discord, the dissonance, lies in the representation of Aeneas, the hero of the poem. He is the poem's protagonist who, after long travels and wars, leads and settles his Trojans in Italy, laying the foundation for Rome's greatness. Why should the hero ever have entered, as deceiver and destroyer, the love life of a most distinguished woman? Why should he have participated in a passionate affair and been the one who repaid love with abandonment, devotion with despair and death? Why should he have been allowed to cut so poor a figure as we have shown? Had he refrained from the intrigue of love, he would never have been unworthy of it, just as the peace-abiding bourgeois who has no stomach for weapons and combat and avoids them, is neither a coward nor a deserter. It would have sufficed (repeating the Venetian Zulietta's advice to Rousseau) "if he had stuck to mathematics and left women alone," that is, if he had stuck to heroic deeds and left Dido in peace. To have made him enter into this relationship was undoubtedly an artistic error. Nor was it possible to cover it over by attributing it to the alleged will of the gods, because if this will can justify or explain an action in life, it cannot cure an aesthetic error, just as it cannot make an unmetrical line of verse scan correctly, or ill-matched colors not clash.

Virgil tried as well as he could to overcome this error in his art. Perhaps even the last scene (discussed here) was intended to fulfill this purpose. But with what result? "En le mettant de nouveau en présence de Didon" writes a commentator,[16]

> il est probable que Virgile a voulu effacer l'impression désagréable que laisse au IV livre la dureté de son héros et lui prêter enfin les sentiments tendres que nous avons jusqu'ici vainement attendu de lui. Il s'y est assez mal pris, Enée se montrant aussi maladroit qu'au IV livre. Ce qui est certain, c'est qu'il s'est proposé, et ceci est assez piquant, de donner une contrepartie à la fameuse scène de rupture, c'est à dire en attribuant cette fois à Enée la tendresse, à Didon l'insensibilité inflexible.

The failure lies in Virgil's intent to restore some coherence to his poem's structure and to the hero who bears it. It certainly does not lie in the poetry which is most felicitous and sublime. Here (let us understand well) it is Aeneas who is "maladroit," and not the poet who has depicted him as he deserves to be, caught in a situation into which he has injected himself, to which he is unequal.

Nevertheless the artistic error we have noted, which Virgil did not rectify, is largely compensated for by this Dido episode, by this tragedy of love-passion, that Virgil's heart and fancy had conceived and that he did not know how to introduce into the poem he was writing except through that error, making use of his hero for the character he needed, for the antithesis of Dido and her inferior. Without this error the tragedy would perhaps have remained impeded, undeveloped, and been lost to us. The contradiction that confuses and confounds the character and mission of Aeneas does not have solely this great compensation. But in itself it counts for little, because the poetic reader can set it aside and in fact does put it aside; and while with the task assigned to Aeneas, the Dido narrative obtains its coherence and truth, the poetry of that story certainly does not annul the poetry of Aeneas during the last night of Troy, or during his meeting with King Evandro, in the wooded regions where Rome was fated to rise.

One must only refrain from wanting to shift the one Aeneas to the other or make the two fit perfectly together and, by excessive pointless subtlety, deny oneself enjoyment of the poetry. This kind of abstracting seems to be easier the more frequently it is commanded and needed in reading poetic works. To others, instead, it turns out not merely difficult, but downright illicit and sinful. They cannot bring themselves to undertake it; and so they hunt for agreement and unity where they do not exist and cannot be found. This, then, is the cause of so many useless disputes, so many labored and absurd critical interpretations, which pile up especially (I do not tire of repeating it) about Dante's *Commedia* and *Faust.*

5

The Character and Unity
of Dante's Poetry[1]

With this glance through the three canticles, I certainly do not mean to survey all of the poetry of the *Commedia* (who could ever propose such a task?), or to describe it in every part, but only to indicate the various and diversely shaped peaks of the immense mountain range, so that the character of Dante's poetic spirit in which I have located the true unity of the poem, will not ring hollow or vanish in generalities owing to a lack of precise and particular references in the reader's mind.

What, then, is this Dantesque spirit, the ethos and pathos of the *Commedia*, the "tonality" peculiar to it? This can be answered in a few simple words: a sentiment of the world founded upon a firm faith and a sure judgment, and animated by a robust will. Dante knows what reality is, and no perplexity impedes or divides and weakens his knowledge, in which there is only so much of mystery as must be reverently bowed to and which is intrinsic to the conception itself—the mystery of the creation, Providence, and divine will, which reveals itself solely in the vision of God, in heavenly beatitude. To Dante perhaps, at times even this mystery seemed to dissolve in those moments when he experienced or imagined mystical ecstasies. In his poetry, however, this mystical cognition was translated, and had to be translated into a negative mode as the story of experiencing ineffable things. Similarly, he knows how the various human emotions ought to be judged, and how to deal with them, and which actions to approve and execute, and which to condemn and repress, in order to direct life to a true and worthy end. His will does not waver and hesitate among discordant ideals; and it is not torn by desires pulling in opposite directions. The disagreements and conflicts that we can discover in his concepts and attitudes lie in the depths of things themselves; they will develop in history later on, but in him they remain in embryo, undeveloped, and do not belong to his compact and unitary consciousness, which expresses steady faith and unswerving conduct, sureness in thought and work.

But within this robust intellectual and moral framework, as we have said, stirs his sentiment of the world, the most varied and complex sentiment, of a spirit that has observed and experimented and meditated upon everything, that is a complete expert of human vices and virtues,—expert not in a summary, general, or second-hand manner, but through having lived those emotions in himself, in practical life and lively sympathy and imagination. The intellectual and ethical framework encloses and dominates this tumultuous material that is totally subjugated, as a powerful adversary might be subjugated and chained, who even when trodden under foot and chained tight, flexes his strong muscles and assumes a majestic form.

Various other definitions, which are infrequently found in critics and interpreters about the character of Dante's poetry, strive to assemble and determine nothing other than the spiritual attitude which we have so defined. How can one fail to see somehow what is so real, actual, and obvious? The truth always comes out, or reveals itself at least, in patches of illumination. But these formulas are forced to serve some end and do not work, because either they adopt inadequate concepts, or they have recourse to metaphors, or they lose themselves in abstractions and in catalogues of abstractions. It is commonly said, for instance, that Dante portrays not becoming, but what has become, not the present but the past. What is meant by this abstruse distinction, or what is the source of the observations that inspired it, if not precisely that in Dante, all the emotions are contained and subjected to a general thought and a steady will that transcends their particularities? But this dynamic representation of one force surpassing and dominating another is also, like all poetry, the representation of a becoming and not of what has become, of motion and not stasis. It is said that Dante is supremely objective; yet no poetry is ever objective, and Dante, as we know, is supremely subjective, always true to himself, always Dantesque; so that in this case, "objectivity" is evidently a vague metaphor designating the absence of confusion and discord in the poet's conception of the world, his clear thinking, his determined will, and therefore his sharply outlined delineations. It is commonly said that Dante characteristically abolishes temporal distance and diversity of manners, and places men and events of every epoch on the same level. This claim means that he measures worldly things of every time and every kind with one fixed rule, with a definite model of truth and goodness, and projects the transient upon the screen of the eternal.

The characteristics of Dante's form have been enumerated—intensity, precision, concision, and the like. Assuredly, whoever dominates strong passions with the force of will expresses something vigorous and intense; and since he fixes his attention on them and understands them, he is precise, and since he does not lose himself in their minutiae, he is concise; but to be satisfied with such enumerations of characteristics amounts to confining oneself to the extrinsic. It is common to call Dante "a poet-sculptor" and not "painter." Assuredly when by the sculptor's action and chisel, we understand the virile, vigorous, robust, bold gesture in contrast to leisurely painting with a "feather-like brush" (as Leonardo portrayed his art), Dante may well be called a sculptor and not a painter. I do not dispute the images that one may like to adopt—even if logically and critically they lack sense, just as the famous comparison of Dante with Michelangelo lacks sense. There is a well-known passage in the *Ottimo Comento:*

> Io scrittore, sentii dire a Dante che mai rima nol trasse a dir altro da quello ch'aveva in suo proponimento, ma ch'elli molte e spesse volte facea da vocaboli dire nelle sue rime altro che quello che erano appo gli altri dicitori usati di esprimere.[2]

Verba sequentur; and as Montaigne added, if they do not follow quickly, they are dragged along by force.

Even when one affirms that the character and unity of Dante's poetry remains entirely in the meter in which the poem is stressed, in the terzina— linked, enclosed, disciplined, vehement and yet calm—one is affirming and not affirming what is true; as is always the case in similar attempts to gather the essence of art in abstractly conceived forms, attempts that are now much in vogue, especially in the criticism of the figurative arts. Undoubtedly the Dante of the *Commedia* is born solely with the terzina, and only through this does he sustain the drama of his soul. And the terzina could not (as has sometimes been conjectured) have been intellectually and intentionally chosen as an allegory of the Trinity, because even if he had thought of this allegory, his thought this time would have had to superimpose itself upon or ally itself to the requirement of his soul, to the spontaneous impulse of his expressive fancy, which is all one with the terzina. But which terzina? Certainly not any terzina in general, but precisely the Dantesque terzina—kneaded out of his very own linguistic, syntatic, and stylistic material, beaten out with the inflection and accent, that he himself gave it, different from the terzina adopted by other poets. With this obvious consideration, it becomes clear that in this case the terzina is remembered not as in itself the determinant of this particular poetry, but insofar as it evokes the whole ethos and pathos of the *Commedia,* its intonation or tonality which is the spirit of Dante.

That Dante's spirit is an austere one is universally recognized and is implicit in the characteristics noted above, because anyone who restrains and dominates his passions must be austere and, as such, encloses within himself much experience of sorrow. But when the imagination depicts a Dante whose visage is perpetually contracted with disdain; or when critics speak, as they have of his "black temperament," of his "misanthropy," and of his "pessimism" it is perhaps useful to caution against exaggeration, to seek to retouch and soften some of the lines of that traditional and conventional portrait, as we have tried to do in the course of our exposition.

However Dante may have appeared to his contemporaries and passed on into legend, granting that his face was "thoughtful and melancholic," as Boccaccio writes, it is certain, because the poem itself proves it, that there was in his soul a richness and variety of interests that ranged from the present to antiquity, from the immediacy of living and suffering to the pleasure of erudite and scholastic recollections; a richness and variety of emotions that reached from the most violent or the most sublime to the sweet and tender, and extended to the joking and playful.

And he was a poet. With the eye of an exile in the lands of Italy, he did not regard political and moral matters solely politically and morally, but ranged over every sort of spectacle, enjoying spectacles, gazing at beautiful things with admiration and bowing with sympathy even before the lowly. And beyond being a poet he was specifically an artist. He always studied and theorized about it. He gloried in the "bello stile" and took joy in the word, the appropriate, suitable, sensuous word, which is the thought itself, generating its living body in a divine thrill of creation. In his spirit, therefore, there were far more varied sentiments and above all, far more happiness than is generally thought; even though those sentiments and that happiness were enclosed in an austere nature that tempered and harmonized them.

On the matter of Dante's ethos and pathos, and on the intellectual conception and the practical tendencies that conditioned him, controversy has frequently arisen no less in foreign countries than in Italy, about the "modernity" or "nonmodernity" of his spirit: put in more exact and clear terms, this amounts to asking if Dante can or cannot be the master and guide for us moderns, in our spiritual life, in our political and moral ideals, and in everything else. Now the truth is that all great men are masters of life, but no one can be so by himself, because each one is a moment of history; and the true master is all of history, and not only that which we re-create continually, but also, and above all, that which we create during every moment. Eternal in its poetic form, the *Commedia* is, in another respect, in its material, limited by the historical moment of its occurrence, whose particular physiognomy I have already briefly described. The consideration of this historical birth suffices to differentiate between what is truly present in Dante which was not there earlier, and what is not in him and could not be there, because it was formed later, and to remove from his portrait some shades and colors that were wrongly added to it.

The medieval, the harsh medieval spirit, both of the fierce ascetic and the proud and joyous warrior, is not found in Dante. Perhaps there is no other great poem like Dante's, as free of passion for war for war's sake, of the tumult that accompanies military battle, the risk, the force, the triumph, the adventure. The medieval epoch, the Carolingian cycle, is barely a distant rumble in the simile of a terzina. Instead of asceticism, one discovers firm faith reinforced by thought and doctrine; instead of war-like ardor, civil zeal. The latter and no longer the former belonged to his age, to the Italy of his time, or in any case, to his consciousness; and they formed the object of his continuous intense concern, of his human passion. Though I have often shown my distrust and repugnance toward ethnic characterizations of poets, nevertheless I shall say that if the name "teutonic," with which Dante has been decorated (not only by Germans, nor primarily by Germans) is understood symbolically as designating at times a mystic and ascetic impetus, and at times a bellicose one, Dante was not "teutonic," and ought to be denominated as Italian, Latin, or some such other contrary. In the very beautiful re-evocation that Giovanni Berchet made in the *Fantasie,* of the meeting between Italians and Germans for the peace negotiations at Constance, Dante would not stand among the "blond folk" and barons who, with iron helmets and mailed breasts, "signal a by-gone age," but in the group garbed in long, simple cloaks, "remarkable only for their black, shrewd brows."

For a different reason we should not overly liken Dante to Shakespeare—his first equal in the history of European poetry; because Shakespeare represents, and indeed is, another epoch of the human spirit, an epoch wherein Dante's conception of the world had been overturned. Upon the brightness that had illuminated even the need for mystery, fell a new shadow of mystery; and a perplexity of mind and soul, which Dante had not known or had quickly overcome, became the dominant note.[3] As for the Romantics who then followed, what is there to say? Their infinity is not his; their dream is not his dream; their style is not his "bello stile"; their "sentiment of nature" (that Jacob Grimm denied to Dante) is not his; and in general their sentiment of life is the opposite of his: the person who reads or declaims Dante as if he were a Romantic disfigures and betrays him. Here too, if "germanic" is taken as the symbol for "romantico," Dante, as he cannot be described as a medieval German, so he cannot be said to be a nineteenth century one. If he had known the heroes of Romanticism, the Werthers, the Obermans, the Renés and their pallid brood, he perhaps would have placed them in the "black slime" among the "slothful." And he must have known somewhat about this melancholic disposition of spirit which became enriched, complicated, extended, admired and attained its apothesis in the romantic period, but which belongs to all periods. Perhaps as a youth he himself suffered for a time from that malady and, like the Romantic heroes, through melancholy, sadness, and sloth, fell into dissipation: if this is the significance of the sonnet, which his friend Cavalcanti addressed to him, reproaching him for the "contemptible life" into which he had "settled," for the "debased soul" and the "tedious spirit" that had mastered him. In any case, he quickly recovered from this sense of being lost and put it among his other experiences, just as he had done with those raging amorous passions which his biographers describe and from which he created the Francesca episode. In the *Commedia,* there is no sentimentalism of any kind, but simply the joy, pain, pride, and courage of living, restrained by moral scruples, sustained and animated by high hope.

This, in quick strokes, is the image of Dante, the authentic image, drawn from his own writing. But one must never forget—and here concluding, it is useful to repeat—that this image which serves to differentiate Dante from other poets and to aid understanding and comprehension of his work, is (like every other representation), somewhat narrow and so to speak, prosaic, if it is not located and resolved in the amplitude of poetry, of the unique poetry, which is not shut up in any thing or group of particular things, but ranges always through the universe. Hence our rapture at Dante's rhythms and words, even the lightest and most transitory ones that come to us circumfused with enchantment—whether it be when, mythologizing, he speaks of the dawn as "the mistress of ancient Tithonus" leaving "the arms of her dear lover"; or when he calls the snow "white sister," and the like. This, which then is the essential, involves no other characteristic than the universal character itself of poetry; and in this regard Dante is no longer Dante, in his definite individuality, but is that voice, wondrous and stirring, exhaled by the human spirit in its perennial recreation of the world. At this point, all differences vanish, and only that eternal, sublime refrain resounds, that voice which has the same fundamental timbre in all great poets and artists, always new, always ancient, heard by us with ever renewed trepidation and joy: poetry with no adjective. At one time, to those who speak with this divine or rather, profoundly human accent, the name of Genius was given; and Dante was a Genius.

6

Dante

The Concluding Canto of the *Commedia*[1]

Dante—by now this point should be beyond dispute—had an idea of poetry that was different from our own,[2] considering what is for us the whole of poetry, as "fine dress" or "beautiful style" (the "decorative" as opposed to the "illustrative" element) and locating its substance elsewhere—in scientific concepts and moral ends: an idea that was his rule in composing his sacred poem. This, of course, does not mean that if he had held our idea of poetry, or a more correct one, he would have avoided obstacles and dangers, and would have been a freer and better poet, because ideas, right or wrong, remain extrinsic to actual poetic making, and both one and the other indifferently accompany strengths and weaknesses of this making. But without doubt, this does mean that we must examine his poetry not according to his idea which, together with the whole of medieval philosophy and aesthetics to which it was bound, has been criticized and has been superseded, but according to our own, which we hold true or more suitable than the other for our understanding.

Proceeding accordingly, we must distinguish in his poem the poetic tones from those that are not fundamentally poetic, a task that makes the inexperienced and the thoughtless cry out and opens the way for commonplace rhetoric, exalting the unity and wholeness of Dante's thought and depreciating the mutilations and cuts that are thought to be inflicted on him: almost as if the critic were a pork-butcher or surgeon who hacks out pieces of flesh, and not simply a discerning mind, as though it were permissible, indeed obligatory, to speak of Dante's work without discernment.

For instance, would one want to continue treating the concluding canto of the poem in the customary fashion? I do not see what taste it would serve; nor how much it would increase the delight that the canto produces for us; nor what advantage it would have for the precision and the logic of our concepts. I read in Del Lungo's essay on this canto:

> When did the ponderous intricacies of scholastic theology ever allow themselves so to be dominated as to produce poetry so appealing as in this final ascension, so admirable and dismaying, so engrossing and

penetrating, so confident in fear, so overcome in victory, so humble
in triumph as to seem defeat? Invocations, exclamations, protestations
that his words are inadequate to the theme, preamble and accompany
that supreme representation, which can finally be nothing more than
an adumbration of what in itself, notwithstanding all the power of
human speech, remains ineffable. But Dante confronts it, even though
his words must annihilate the final notes of the immortal canto in that
ineffability.[3]

I read this and I think that with all the respect I sincerely have for the late
Del Lungo's literary scholarship, this is not criticism but oratory.

I read Pistelli's essay and find at the very beginning of it a refutation—spiced with irony ("at least," he says, "according to antiquated aesthetics," the one that pleases him and that he is proud to own)—a
refutation of the distinction that I usually make between structure and poetry, because "the framework of a building has importance even for art,
although it does not as yet display the reliefs, mosaics, and pictures which
will later adorn it."[4] And I am compelled to remark that such words stand
midway between not understanding and not taking the trouble to understand
owing to the mind's being occupied by something else, that is by the intent
to contradict, and if possible, to mock the person contradicted, as one
whom the ignorant and indifferent, always quick to laugh, will ridicule.

Given the intent of Dante's poem, that its concluding canto is admirably developed is beyond question. Its assumption is the "visio divinae
essentiae," that yields the "perfecta beatitudo hominis," with which the
journey through the three kingdoms of the beyond must and does conclude.

Philosophically speaking, this kind of vision is inconceivable, posing
but not gratifying the contradictory need "to see" what one can merely
"think," and what humanity has always thought and always thinks and,
indeed we can say, what humanity has never done and does not do except
by thinking it, developing in all its thoughts the theme of the divine essence, of the *rerum natura,* of the eternal spirit. Philosophers who, not
content with thinking, have devised and placed above it an "intellectual
intuition" (precisely a "visio essentiae"), and with this term either have
defined the concreteness of thought (which, always in the same act is an
intuiting, rising upon intuition and permeating it) or, instead of ascending
higher as they try to do, have descended beneath the level of cognition.

The mystics who without thinking, reckon to gather this essence, either think without knowing it and without willing it, or gather mere impressions and impulses of feelings and sensations. Nor can poets conceive for
the obvious reason that they know neither ideas nor external things, but
only their own feeling. Wolfgang Goethe, when he thought about the kingdom of the Mothers, of the generating Ideas, ended by refusing to describe

Faust's journey there; and confined himself to expressing in negative form
the yearning toward that inaccessible and inexorable world, to which it is
vain to seek passage and to petition, and the aspect of the infinite expanse
stretching out from the entrance, lacks every relation to man and every
support:

> Nichts wirst du sehn in ewig leerer Ferne,
> Den Schritt nicht hören den du thust,
> Nichts Festes finden wo du ruhst.[5]

And although Faust, notwithstanding Mephistopheles' warning wants
"to seek 'the whole' in that nothingness," the object remains beyond his
reach. At the most, Mephistopheles sketches a scene with a new mythology,
suffused with fresh irony, in which beside the flaming caldron, the Mothers
toil at their work:

> Bei seinem Schein wirst du die Mütter sehn;
> Die einen sitzen, andre stehn und gehn,
> Wie's eben kommt. Gestaltung, Umgestaltung,
> Des ewigen Sinnes ewige Unterhaltung:
> Umschwebt von Bildern aller Kreatur,
> Sie sehn dich nicht, denn Schemen sehn sie nur.[6]

But if the vision of the divine essence is denied to man by philosophy
for no other reasons than logical impossibility, it is also denied to the Christian by his faith, which requires departure from this mortal life and ascen-
sion to the kingdom of the blessed, to Paradise. Desiring that the story of
his journey to the world beyond should not lack this final chapter and (because of a logical impossibility that faith reinforces with its prohibition)
being unable to expound an intuitive act—by its nature non-doctrinal—in
doctrinal terms, as he had done in the case of numerous philosophical and
theological concepts throughout his poem, Dante had one course only: to
relate how grace had granted him the vision of God and to declare the
impossibility of expressing it with words, insofar as they are adopted as
signs of concepts.

And this course runs through the concluding canto, with a mastery of
word and verse that has increased through the three canticles and here in
the *Paradiso* attains its greatest fluency and power. Saint Bernard prays to
the Virgin that God may grant beatific vision to his protégé. Beatrice and
the other blessed join in his prayer, and the Madonna, assenting, seeks this
grace. And Dante sees—with a vision that exceeds the limits of human
speech—something so immense and intense that memory cannot encom-
pass it. Nevertheless he hopes that he will be allowed to convey it and

make some part of it intelligible, or to give a faint idea of it; but attempting to do so, he repeats many times, in various ways that what he saw is ineffable, and he reports not what he saw but what he should have seen—the plan the execution of which is lost, the unity of all parts of the universe, substance, accidents, properties, and the universal form of this nexus. And when he wishes to relate something of what he saw directly, nothing less than the holy Trinity, that is, the loftiest theological and metaphysical thought, contemplated and measured with his eyes, in its place he describes three diversely colored circles and enclosing the same space, the second circle a reflection from the first and flashing a human likeness, and the third resembling fire; whereupon he quickly exclaims again that his speech falls feebly short of the concept revealed, and that, what he saw in sum was granted in the radiance of grace which only momentarily satisfied his mind's desire.

Now, when I join in the deserved admiration for this final representation of the great journey, for this last chapter of Dante's teaching, may I then be permitted to observe, tactfully, that what is being admired is didactic poetry, possessing a magnificent theme, a majestic movement, the loftiest intonation, but still didactic poetry employing the expedients of didactic poetry? And, having paid my tribute of admiration to this didactic poetry and setting it apart, may I be permitted to seek out the poetry that Dante, who was a great poet—this must not be forgotten, though literati and commentators seem to forget it too often—has also strewn throughout this canto? Or must we yield to the inexorable dilemma of drinking or drowning: to accept for poetry what is didactic poetry, or to give up the search for poetry in this canto, because all that is in it, possesses the same quality as what has been discussed and is indistinguishable from it?

Cosmo,[7] who recently discussed the concluding canto of the *Commedia*, with greater shrewdness and reflection than others--and with good reason, among other things, denied that Dante shows himself there as a mystic and follower of St. Bonaventura—has clearly recognized that the poetry of this canto is not in the representation of the beatific vision or in what Dante reports about it. Seeking where it really is, he places it "in the sentiment Dante brings to those concepts, which for him are the foundations on which his entire spiritual world is based," so that "if the reader does not succeed in seeing the truths Dante discovers, he sees and feels his spiritual struggle in attaining to them; and that is enough for the creation of poetry."

With this, it seems to me, we are placed upon the real ground of inquiry; because, what else can we ask or ought we to ask of a poet except that he express the motions of his soul, the fullness of his feeling and suffering and elevate them to the level of beauty?

But, where then, in this canto, does Dante truly express his sentiment? Not in the many terzine that extend over two-thirds or more of the canto, where he tries to speak, while protesting that he is unable to speak, because here clearly, he continues the line of his theological exposition, tying it to that point where theology must deny itself in the inscrutable and in the ineffable; and if we lose sight of this intent, according to which the inability to speak is necessary to the completion of his initiated goal, there is the chance that the theologian who he is and who wants to signal the limit of theological demonstration will take on the air of a professor who does not know the material of his lesson and seems to beat about the bush before his students, helping himself by phrases, gestures, and exclamations of astonishment. Where he truly and marvelously expresses his sentiment is very clear to the poetic reader, for whom three terzine in this canto stand out resplendently; and these alone, above all the rest, he remembers:

> Qual è colui che somniando vede,
> e dopo il sonno la passione impressa
> rimane, e l'altro alla mente non riede;
>   cotal son io, ché quasi tutta cessa
> mia visione, ed ancor mi distilla
> nel cuor lo dolce che nacque da essa.
>   Così la neve al sol si dissigilla,
> così al vento nelle foglie lievi
> si perdca la sentenzia di Sibilla.[8]

This is the lyric of the man who has been taken captive by a dream of singular joy and pleasure—contradictory, absurd, chaotic perhaps in the images that compose it—such that it has left no trace in intellectual memory, but has left a profound one in his sentiment of pleasure and well-being which still endures, the image that produced it having vanished: "Ed ancor mi distilla"—the last drops of joy that earlier had poured forth in a stream; "lo dolce"—that form of desire which, while diffusing itself gently in the organism, soothes it and harmonizes with it. Whatever the content of the dream was, the recollection of joy remains. This content has dispersed, dissolved like snow under the sun's rays, scattered (says Dante who, with an image of greater solemnity, elevates the mystery that had been revealcd to him and has escaped him again) like the replies that the Sibyl had written upon leaves scattered to the wind. It has dispersed; and yet it was once a real and possessed thing, like that lost paradise that man carries in the depths of his heart, which he longs for and cannot find, and knows that he cannot find anywhere. But just as soon as he seems to recall it and to glimpse some feature of it, the stimulus, though dimly, is renewed, and this recollection is made more intense:

La forma universal di questo nodo
credo ch'io vidi, perché piú di largo,
dicendo questo, mi sento ch'io godo.[9]

"So," I seem to hear the so-called Dantisti ask me sarcastically, "all of the marvelous final canto, viewed as poetry, for you comes down to three or four terzine and to the beauty of one simile?" To this I must reply that poetry, as I know it, is not measured in meters or (as the Abbé Galiani said of a sonnet, whose verses were typographically all of the same length, but all wrong) with "string"; because poetry, like the divine grace of which Dante speaks, is a radiance that strikes the mind. And with regard to the simile, I would add that poetry is always a comparison, a similitude expressing the supersensible through the sensible, the eternal in the transient, humanity in the individual, and precisely for this reason, similes can be rendered in prose and used for comparisons that clarify concepts in scientific prose. But this is not the occasion to outline a theory of poetic similes in passing, especially since everyone recalls that a large part of Dante's great poetry lies in the so-called "similes," true and completed lyrics.

There is in this canto another passage that pleases me very much; and it is not, as it happens, Saint Bernard's stylized prayer to the Virgin (which belongs, Cristoforo Landino commented, to the "deliberative genre"), but the conclusion of the prayer, where the venerable old Saint, who has taken Dante under his protection, praying to the Virgin on his behalf before the assembly of the blessed, draws her attention in the end, in the peroration, to the attitude of these blessed ones, who have joined in his prayer:

Vedi Beatrice con quanti beati
per li miei prieghi ti chiudon le mani.[10]

This is truly a scene from a Giotto fresco, with those blessed ones who, all together, raise their clasped hands, humble and simple in the fervor of desire. And the scene is completed in the figure of the Virgin, who, without speaking, assents with her eyes, which have visibly accompanied and approved the prayer, so consonant with her benign and pious heart:

Gli occhi da Dio diletti e venerati,
fissi nell'orator, ne dimostrâro
quanto i devoti prieghi le son grati.[11]

There follows the intercession of the Virgin with God; this moment too so much more intensely expressive, in that it is made still with the eyes alone, with those eyes, which look with unequaled clarity at the divine power and whose tacit look is quickly understood:

Indi all'eterno lume si drizzâro,
nel qual non si de' creder che s'invii
per creatura l'occhio tanto chiaro.[12]

And since grace is bestowed with that very act, Bernard, who cares for, aids, and guides his protégé as a tender father, now with a father's happiness at seeing goodness rain upon his own child, performs his last task, urging him to look toward God:

Bernardo m'accennava e sorrideva,
perch'io guardassi in suso . . . [13]

It is like a family festivity, in which all participate and all are variously busy about the beloved person who has obtained a long-desired and long-awaited happiness.

Dante's talent pours poetry forth even where it would be least expected. He wishes to say that a single moment suffices to submerge what he has seen in the abyss of forgetfulness, and he says it in a somewhat contorted way, with medieval display of mythological erudition:

Un punto solo m'è maggior letargo
che venticinque secoli all'impresa,
che fe' Nettuno ammirar l'ombra d'Argo.[14]

Yes, but what a vision unfolds before us in this last verse, of that ship "Argo," the first that was launched upon the waves and cleaved them, and that Neptune, sensing the shadow upon his transparency, turns to watch and marvel! It is the God who sees his own kingdom strangely violated, and it is not at all the ignorant shepherd who, in the fragment of Accius's tragedy, watches stupefied, "tanta moles" that "labitur fremibunda," noisily stir and rough up the waves;[15] or the Nereids who in the Catullian ode, flock about, "monstrum admirantes," in a spectacle of voluptuous nudity which inflames the sailors with love: a little picture of Alexandrian charm. And in what dramatic guise can one show the concentration of the mind in meditation and the inner fire that nourishes it and is increased by the meditation itself?

Cosí la mente mia tutta sospesa
mirava fissa, immobile e attenta,
e sempre nel mirar faceasi accesa.[16]

Of this kind are the delights, the illicit, the forbidden delights that one experiences who sacrilegiously reduces Dante to bits and pieces: pleasures that those who honor him whole and entire chastely and devoutly abstain from.

—A cui pace e vecchiezza il ciel consenta!—[17]

For my part, I can offer these critics only the good wish of this Leopardian verse. They merit both rewards, because I see that they are careful not to weary either brains or nerves.

7

Petrarca

I

The Dream of Love that survives Passion[1]

Tutta la mia fiorita e verde etade
passava; e' ntiepidir sentia già 'l foco
ch'arse il mio core; et era giunto al loco
ove scende la vita, ch'alfin cade.
    Già incominciava a prender securtade
la mia cara nemica a poco a poco
de' suoi sospetti, e rivolgeva in gioco
mie pene acerbe sua dolce onestade.
    Presso era il tempo dove Amor si scontra
con Castitate, et agli amanti è dato
sedersi insieme e dir che lor incontra.
    Morte ebbe invidia al mio felice stato,
anzi a la speme; e féglisi a l'incontra
a mezza via, come nemico armato.[2]

To this image of a green age that has ended and of the autumn and winter that have come upon him and his beloved, Francesco Petrarca had turned his thoughts more than once, during the travails of his long passion, briefly interrupting the feverish course of the present to contemplate and compare it to that very different future that presented itself to his imagination. He had first thought about it, when he was still strongly enmeshed in his insatiable desire, in the sonnet: "Se la mia vita" where, imagining the still young Laura as she would one day be, devastated by the years, it seemed to him that he would have the "boldness" ("baldanza") to tell her about his long travails, at an age by then "hostile to sweet desires"[3] ("contrario ai bei desiri"), and that this revelation would elicit from her "some little help of tardy sights"[4] ("alcun soccorso di tardi sospiri").

There is here, even if in a very delicate form, barely adumbrated in that "hostile" and "help" that is not help because "tardy," a hint of the regret and melancholy which she would have felt for so great an offering of love, left unharvested and allowed to come to nothing. This is elegiac fore-shadowing, and not indeed the expression of a "secret desire and a clever insinuation that Laura not wait too long in taking pity on him"[5] (As Car-ducci, even he, through excessive deference to the interpretation and judg-ment of Muratori, who in matters of love and poetry was not very expert, admitted into his commentary). One of the ways of falsifying a poem is to add to it what is or could be in the real situation from which it takes its stimulus, but which the poetic soul has not made his own or not said or does not wish to admit even to itself, and to transform the ingenuous poetic images into calculated means to an end.

But now that autumn was slowly advancing, the thought of her fading and of his entering an age in which desires soften, the emotions diminish in intensity, pain and pleasure become aware of their limits, and resignation comes more readily,—that thought assumed a different color and infused him with an unaccustomed sweetness. Life wanes, but sunset too has its beauty; even this brings something that youth does not have and compen-sates with its gifts for what elsewhere is lost. We do not then become empty, cold, without love, without the love that is the very pulse of life: if ardor is calmed, its warmth is still diffused in the soul. We still love at that age the person whom we first loved in the splendor of her beauty and in the ardor of our senses; the image that the heart suggested and the fancy cre-ated, frees itself from physical determinations, idealized, seen, as we say, with the eyes of love, and therefore it resists corporeal changes; it survives them; it retains fascination for as long as something of the beloved creature still remains, for as long as she still breathes on earth.

The enchantment is not broken, as happens through the exhaustion of a love as the result of another, or through the detachment of the soul that consecrates itself to holiness and heroism and, disdaining them, no longer feels earthly affections: it lives on and displays its old magic power, but in new conditions, because all of the sensible and animal that accompanies love, has given up its cupidity; it no longer oppresses with its weight, while on the other hand the superior faculties, moral and intellectual, have ac-quired freedom and vigor. Consequently we can regard and reflect upon the past without emotionally detaching ourself from it; we can, without con-cealing and feigning, tell what we truly felt and thought and desired; we can confess our own errors and follies; even smiling, we can recognize that reason has its rationale and that virtue has exercised its unbending power well; we can be indulgent toward ourself and others, employing the com-passion that man owes to man, employing it toward ourself as well as to-ward that other mortal creature whom we have made to suffer and who has suffered, the one whom, in the sweetness of a new aspect, we now gaze upon, as the one who has been our companion on the well traveled way of love and sorrow.

The two are like two persons convalescing from the same illness, an illness that is by chance the fever called life. They exchange their impressions, and compare them, and often the same word comes to the lips of each, and the one same amazement—painful and sweet—grips them. It is like lingering a few moments longer on the threshold, before the final departure. Meanwhile to the imagination it seems that in this way, after the harsh labors and wearisome commotions endured, love remains solid, having overcome its feral passion, having preserved the best that is in it, in its human nobility.

And this season of repose, which he sees announce itself on the horizon and drawing ever nearer, Francesco Petrarca laments, has been stolen from him by the death of his lady. The verses we have read speak of that hope, of the dying away of that flowering, green age, of the allaying of passionate torment, of life's slipping into decline that has for its end, the fall into the shadow of death and, simultaneously, they speak of the beloved lady who now puts aside her cautious pose of defensive shyness and returns his demonstrations of love with some keen and benign witticism, turning it respectably into a joke. And they, those verses, describe the arrival of the awaited moment of conciliation and sublimation, representing it in the encounter and engagement of Love with Chastity, which do not proceed here as two allegorical abstractions, but as two real currents of emotion, earlier divergent and opposed and now reconciled and confluent: the two lovers are no longer represented as one avoiding the other or separated from the other who is far away, the one humble and supplicant and the other aloof and haughty, but as sitting tranquilly, close to one another talking of their concerns, as if to seek advice and to reach an accord, after painful trials, in order to establish the rules for the brief future that remains.

This dream, so long cherished and become familiar, was so dear to the poet's heart, and so cruelly did he feel its wrench that he turned to it more than twice, in two other sonnets, erroneously considered exercises in the literary art of repeating identical things in different words but, as another critic[6] has clearly seen, were really born from the need to better determine and particularize his feelings regarding his vision of the calm he had promised himself, of the renunciation which was not renunciation but the passage to a new vital rhythm. In the quatrains and the first tercet of the second sonnet, he resumes the sadness of the lament against the death that had interrupted the already begun process, of the alleviation and assuagement:

> Tempo era omai da trovar pace o triegua
> di tanta guerra, et erane in via forse;
> se non ch'e' lieti passi indietro torse
> chi le disuguaglianze nostre adegua.

Ché, come nebbia al vento si dilegua,
cosí sua vita subito trascorse
quella che già co' begli occhi me scòrse;
et or conven che col pensèr la segua.
    Poco aveva a 'ndugiar, che gli anni e 'l pelo
cangiavano i costumi, onde sospetto
non fôra il ragionar del mio mal seco.[7]

The attempt to color the picture more vividly is in the last tercet:

Con che onesti sospiri l'avrei detto
le mie lunghe fatiche, ch'or dal cielo
vede, son certo, e duolsene ancor meco![8]

But this sonnet, which is certainly less felicitous than the first, did not satisfy him: and so he resumed the motif in the third, very much like the first, but which adds other touches to the scene of the two lovers, seated together conversing:

Tranquillo porto avea mostrato Amore
a la mia lunga e torbida tempesta,
fra gli anni de la età matura onesta,
che i vizî spoglia, e virtú veste e onore.
    Già traluceva a' begli occhi il mio core
e l'alta fede non piú lor molesta.
Ahi, Morte ria, come a schiantar se' presta
il frutto di molt'anni in sí poche ore!
    Pur, vivendo, veniasi ove deposto
in quelle caste orecchie avrei, parlando,
de' miei dolci pensier l'antiqua soma;
    et ella avrebbe a me forse risposto
qualche santa parola, sospirando,
cangiati i volti e l'una e l'altra coma.[9]

The last tercet is stupendous, with those words of deep feeling joined with the melancholy, with which Laura responds, and with that grouping of the two lovers, over whom the dry arid breath of time has passed, their faces faded, their hair grey, and yet still lovers.

Even the *Trionfo della Morte* resounds with this dear conversing that never really took place, where the poet repeats what Laura, visiting him in a dream, had revealed of her soul during her time on earth; and how the same flame that had burned in his breast had burned in hers, and, how she had "dread of its dangerous sparks" ("temenza delle pericolose sue

faville''). Consequently she had armed herself with cold reserve in order to
save their reputation and had been obliged from time to time to feign anger
when she further perceived his voracious desire; and to gaze on him and
greet him sweetly when she saw him sorrowful and despairing. "Teco era il
cor; a me gli occhi raccolsi." [My heart was with you; my eyes I hid.''])

This surely would have been the principal theme on which their conversing would have turned, if it could have taken place. But Laura, in the
Trionfo della Morte, is no longer the faded, greying Laura, the saint and
sinner, earthly and mortal; she has been transported to heaven; not to mention that the tercets of this poem, being unusually prolix, do not have the
beauty of the restrained sonnets.[10] The overcoming of passion in memory,
in regret, and in the goodness that reconsecrates love, remains in Petrarca's
poetry something longed for but not achieved, a state of soul imagined and
not lived.

And, if he had achieved it, if he had lived it, would this have been a
new period of his life, or merely a fleeting moment—but one of those moments that, through their intensity, become eternal? Would it have been a
new kind of loving relationship, or a farewell instead to a life that had
become invincible torment? Can a thrill of sweetness and sadness give way
to a placid habit like the drowsy company of two old lovers at rest or like
that tremulous idyll of Baucis and Philemon that De Sanctis recalls in this
connection,[11] and that does not seem to suit that vein of sorrow running
through all of this poet's imagination, with Laura's "holy word" ("santa
parola"), and with the "sigh" ("sospiro") that crowns it? Even with an
inopportune reference, the truth of a poem can be altered.

There is a novel in which some pages describe this condition of love
being overcome, of love emitting its last sparks: among the final pages of
the *Éducation sentimentale,* Madame Arnoux, after many years, revisits Frédéric, who had loved her and to whom, although returning his love, she had
not yielded. Unexpected, she enters his study, "à la nuit tombante," and he
receives her with joyous excitement. "Dans la pénombre du crépuscule il
n'apercevait que ses yeux sous la voilette de dentelle noire qui masquait sa
figure." For a long time they remain silent, smiling at one another. Then
questions begin; they recount what happened since they last saw each other;
they recall the details of their last meeting. Like Laura, she tells him that
she had feared being overwhelmed and carried off by passion: "J'avais
peur! Oui . . . peur de vous . . . peur de moi!" And she circles throughout
the room, looking at the furniture, knick-knacks, pictures, and then she
wants to take a short walk with him, on his arm; and walking, they talk of
their love and how strong it had been on both their parts—"Sans nous
appartenir pourtant," sighs Frédéric: "cela vaut peut-être mieux," she replies;—and in what way she had discovered that he loved her and how
much she had feared and enjoyed his passion and reserve. At these confi-

dences, "il ne regretta rien. Ses souffrances d'autrefois étaient payées." They re-enter. Madame Arnoux removes her hat: "la lampe, posée sur une console, éclaira ses cheveux blancs," and this for him is like a sharp blow on the chest. But he hides it, sitting at her knees, he takes her hands in his, and fervently utters all the sweet things that he had been unable to say before, and she listens to those words of adoration, addressed to the woman that she no longer is. In the intimacy of that conversation, in the contact of their bodies, his old desire takes possession of him—furious and raging. "Cependant il sentait quelque chose d'inexprimable, une répulsion et comme l'effroi d'un inceste." She was a woman, but he had elevated her to an ideal, and he could not "dégrader son idéal." He draws away from her, and begins to roll a cigarette. Eleven o'clock strikes: within a quarter of an hour she must leave. "Tous les deux ne trouvaient plus rien à se dire. Il y a un moment, dans les séparations, où la personne aimée n'est déjà plus avec nous." She rises and says farewell: "Je ne vous reverrai jamais. C'était ma dernière démarche de femme. Mon âme ne vous quittera pas. Que toutes les bénédictions du ciel soient sur vous!" Before leaving she asks for a pair of scissors, undoes her hair, cuts off a long lock. "Gardez-les! Adieu." From the window, Frédéric follows her with his eyes: he sees her call a carriage and depart. "Et ce fut tout."

I have related the main points, highlighting some details. But these pages of Flaubert can stand, in the world of beauty, beside the exquisite lyrics of Francesco Petrarca, and in their own way, they are a perfect lyric in the form of narrative. It pleases me to repeat this now when it is customary to disdain poet-narrators in the very act of going into raptures in our worship and admiration of the so-called pure lyric or quintessential lyric, usually an effort of poor, disintegrated sensual impressions, mixed together with abstract meanings. But the lyric is a delicate flower that unfolds in the sunlight of poetry only on that soil which is the human heart.

II

Canzone: "My Ancient Sweet Cruel Lord"[12]

It may or may not be correct to say that the design of the canzone "Quell'antiquo mio dolce empio signore" was discovered as already existing in provençal poetry.[13] In this case, the discovery has no importance because we are dealing with a design that is obvious and we would say, almost ingenuous: the poet and Love dispute one another, the first accusing and complaining, the second defending himself and reproaching the other, before the tribunal of Reason. It is important, instead, to understand why the personifications and metaphorical tribunal in this poem do not seem to be cold, impoverished devices, but affirm themselves as natural forms, fitting the poet's sentiment.

This time the sentiment is not passionate, a surge of aroused feeling, a flood of sorrow, or an outburst of amorous exaltation that would not bear personifications and metaphorical materializations, requiring direct, vehement forms. The poet has arrived at what might be called a moment of equanimity toward himself and toward the course of the events that has seized and thrust him forward in life,—at a moment of reflection, when he does not want to overpower and suppress one kind of emotion by means of its opposite, or to deny the one for the other; but the reality of both is impressed upon the soul. He feels their necessity and, however opposite they may be, both are seen as coexisting and both are justified, as the right and its wrong side: neither one being able to prevail except through the other; or to abolish the other, without also dissolving itself. Nothing remains, therefore, but to allow both to speak, each one telling at length what he has sought and wanted, each one supporting his complaint: this is the theme of this canzone.

The offended party, the slave, the oppressed one speaks, upon whom Love has inflicted all kinds of torments ever since taking possession of his youth. Love has taken him away from participating in pleasures and in the festival of life; he has prevented him from rising as high as perhaps he could; he has hunted him in a never-ending war; and he has made him forgetful of all other things, even of God.

> Questi m'ha fatto men amare Dio
> ch'io non dovea, e men curar me stesso:
> per una donna ho messo
> egualmente in non cale ogni pensèro.
> Di ciò m'e stato consiglier sol esso,
> sempre aguzzando il giovenil desio
> a l'empia cote ond'io
> sperai riposo al suo giogo aspro e fero.
> Misero! a che quel chiaro ingegno altèro,
> e l'altre doti a me date dal Cielo?
> Che vo cangiando 'l pelo,
> né cangiar posso l'ostinata voglia;
> cosí in tutto mi spoglia
> di libertà . . . [14]

And how greatly and fiercely overbearing this adversary has been, who has pursued him without respite wherever he has gone, always standing over him, in the hard, toilsome, and dangerous journeys through foreign countries; and he has deprived him of restful sleep and made him suffer through long vigils in which he futilely counted the hours!

> Poiché suo fui non ebbi ora tranquilla,
> né spero aver, e le mie notti il sonno
> sbandîro, e piú non ponno
> per erbe o per incanti a sé ritrarlo.
> Per inganno o per forza è fatto donno
> sovra miei spirti; e non sonò poi squilla
> ov'io sia in qualche villa,
> ch'io non l'udissi . . . [15]

He is an enemy who, having penetrated inside him, attacks and wounds him internally:

> ché legno vecchio mai non rose tarlo
> come questi il mio core, in cui s'annida.[16]

But Love—the hostile power, the destroyer, the cruel one—rejecting the accusations, recalls and establishes that only through his power was the plaintiff released from being a mediocre hack, from the assigned task of peddling words, of handling disputes in the forum; and only through him was the poet's intellect raised to a level which his own strength would never have attained. And, wishing to find for him a lady to love, he, Love, selected one who had no equal in the world:

> E sí dolce idïoma
> le diedi ed un cantar tanto soave,
> che pensier basso o grave
> non poté mai durar dinanzi a lei.[17]

And through that woman, the ingrate was made a poet, celebrated, famous, approved, and dear to the most distinguished people:

> Sí l'avea sotto l'ali mie condutto,
> ch'a donne e a cavalier piacea 'l suo dire;
> e sí alto salier
> il feci che tra' caldi ingegni ferve
> il suo nome, e de' suoi detti conserve
> si fanno con diletto in alcun loco;
> ch'or saría forse un roco
> mormorador di corti, un uom del vulgo . . . [18]

Through that woman he was kept from many dishonest acts; he abhorred baseness and cowardice; his feeling was refined: from her he achieved as much as he possessed of elegance and nobility. Still more, she—earthly creature with her pure beauty, with her rare virtues—became for him the ladder to ascend to God; that is, Love had given her to him as a support against his earthly frailty.

The love-tormented, the accuser, has followed his adversary's words intently, his commemoration and exaltation of the woman so long loved, of the woman who had been his; and, under the force of the images evoked, he is almost persuaded of the great good she had bestowed upon him, of the heights to which she alone had brought him. At this point he feels so seized by the infinite desire, by the empty yearning for the woman whom he has lost, that he forgets the earlier accusation and takes up another opposing one, one that is completely irrational and inconsistent with the preceding, but arises unexpectedly from the very words of his adversary who, exalting Laura, makes him feel all the immensity and sharp cruelty of the wrong that had been done to him.

> A questo un strido
> lagrimoso alzo e grido:
> "Ben me la dié, ma tosto la ritolse!"[19]

But the adversary pronounces a word to which there is no reply. It was not he who had taken her from him, but Laura was made for heaven and God had wanted her in heaven.

> Risponde: "Io no, ma Chi per sé la volse."[20]

The dispute which had been set in motion as an accusation and a defense, as a judicial process, is about to be transformed into a drama with its own development and its own catharsis of resignation, of elevation, and of serene resolution. But the drama flares up and is soon extinguished, with the resumption of the debate between the two contestants, about the love that is torment and death, and the love that is exaltation and life. And the two, having said all that each had wanted to say, turn now with the same motion, to the one who must judge, to the "queen, who keeps the divine part of our nature and reigns at its summit," to Reason. The lover speaks with a voice still trembling with the emotion that had assailed him just a moment before, and the other, self-assured, with words both bold and cutting. But Reason, who has listened to them silently until now, avoids pronouncing judgment:

> Alfin ambo conversi al giusto seggio,
> io con tremanti, ei con voci alte e crude,

> ciascun per sé conchiude:
> "Nobile donna, tua sentenza attendo."
> Ella allor sorridendo:
> "Piacemi aver vostre questioni udite;
> ma piú tempo bisogna a tanta lite."[21]

Why doesn't she pronounce the judgment? Why does she smile and dismiss it *ad graecas calendas?* Because in this matter there is no place for acquittal or condemnation; because the parties of wrong and right have already been transcended when, breaking out of the self-enclosed torment of the sentiment, which one moment is sorrowful and rebellious, and the next moment is ecstatic in the enchantment of beauty and in the joys of love, they begin to consider the two opposite orders of emotions,—those of suffering and those of joy, of evil and of good—setting them side by side, binding the one to the other, because the condition of happiness is the torment that has been suffered, of good evil, and *vice versa.* The passionate lover has ascended to that height where, even with his lashes still moist with tears, he looks at the past, he looks into his own heart, no longer wrapped in illusion nor strained in a vain effort to will the impossible—joy without sorrow, love without its anguish, peace without war; and he accepts the existence of these opposite forces which remain there, and nothing can take them from the world. This is the design of the canzone, simple, clear, almost schematic, and the plain form, discursive, particularizing opposing theses, terminated in a smile that is the smile of wisdom.

And this is poetry of wisdom, one poetic tone among others, that has no need of being affirmed and defended in its right to exist, because it is enough to the purpose, to recall Goethe in his Olympian period. But in order to avoid misunderstandings, it is useful to note that just as wisdom is not strictly criticism and philosophy, so, too, the poetry of wisdom rises not from a concept or judgment but, like all poetry, from a sentiment, and has nothing to do with didactic poetry that may be adorned with images or put into meter. Let us look at this Petrarchan canzone. Reason insofar as it is wisdom (meaning one's practical acceptance of the coinciding of opposites), is present in it, but not at all as philosophy and dialectic. For if the corresponding philosophical doctrine had been present in the poet, then the two orders of sentiments would not have been arrayed before his mind, the one against the other; the opposition would not have been developed; we would not have had the decision that not deciding it would leave the opposition intact and respect its existence.

In philosophy, problem and solution coincide; to formulate the first means to formulate the second, and the one is born only by dying in the other. In this canzone there is no problem because there is no solution. The poet lives the opposites and their dialectic, but he neither poses nor dominates them with thought. Sometimes the same man sings as poet of something that, striving to think it through as philosopher and failing to grasp its logic, he denies the reality of, though it quivers in his verses; or more frequently, he declares it unthinkable and mysterious and speaks as Jesus speaks of the world in Goethe's *Wandering Jew:* "die ich obgleich ich bei der Schöpfung war, im Ganzen noch nicht sonderlich verstehe."[22] And sometimes it also has happened—or at least once it did—that a philosopher who was also a poet, Tommaso Campanella, clearly recognized the truth of the bonding of opposites as supreme cosmic law; and in his poetry he represented the struggle between his firm philosophic conviction and his human suffering, between the quick spirit and the weary flesh;[23] that is, he re-immersed philosophy in the world of sentiments, sentiment against sentiment, thus obeying the demands of the poetry.

This canzone stand almost by itself in Petrarca's *Canzoniere* as the unique smile of indulgence and acceptance of life's passions, of life that is passion, on Francesco Petrarca's countenance.

8

Ludovico Ariosto

The Realization of Harmony[1]

The first change these[2] sentiments underwent as soon as they were touched by the Harmony[3] that sang in poet's breast, was the loss of their autonomy; in their submission to a single master, in their descent from whole to part, from motifs to occasions, from ends to instruments; in their dying for the benefit of a new life.

The magical force that accomplished this prodigy was the tone of expression, that light and easy tone, transmutable into a thousand, ever-charming modes, which the old critics called a "confidential air"[4] and specified among the other "properties" of the Ariostean "style." Not only does his entire style consist in this but, since style is nothing other than the expression of the poet and of his very soul, the whole of Ariosto with his harmonious singing, consists in this.

The work of devaluation and destruction, performed by the expressive tone, is palpable in the proems of the single cantos, in the argumentative digressions, in the interjected observations, in the resumptions, in the words chosen, in the phrasing and in the pauses and, above all, in the frequent comparisons that, while forming pictures, do not reinforce the emotion but divert it; and in the interruptions of the tales, occurring at times at their most dramatic point, with skillful transitions to other tales of a different and often contrary nature. Nonetheless what there is that is palpable, rhetorically isolatable, and analyzable is only a small part of the whole, of the impalpable, which flows like a thin fluid and will not allow itself to be grasped with scholastic devices but, being soul, is felt with the soul.

And this tone is the oft noted and designated, but never well defined, Ariostean *irony:* not well defined, because it has customarily been buried in a sort of joking or mocking, similar to or coinciding with what Ariosto sometimes used when contemplating chivalric figures and their adventures; and so the result has been to restrict and to materialize it at the same time. But what we should not lose sight of is that this irony does not invest one order of sentiments—for example the chivalric or the religious, sparing others—but it invests them all, and therefore is not an idle playfulness, but something much deeper, something purely artistic and poetic—the victory of the fundamental motif over all the others.

All the sentiments—the sublime and the playful, the tender and the strong, the effusions of heart and the cogitations of intellect, the discourses on love and the encomiastic catalogues of names, the descriptions of battles and the comic witticisms—all are equally reduced by irony and elevated in it. Upon the equal leveling of all, arises the marvelous Ariostean octave that has its own life: an octave which is not sufficiently defined by being called a "smiling" one, unless "smile" is understood in an ideal sense, precisely as the manifestation of a free and harmonious life, energetic and balanced, pulsating in veins rich with health-giving blood and calmed by this continuous pulsation. These octaves have the corporeality, now of flowering maidens and again of well-formed young men, supple-limbed in exercising their muscles and unpreoccupied with giving proof of their dexterity, because it is revealed in their every pose and gesture.

Olympia, after so many misfortunes, after a long and tempestuous sea voyage, lands with her lover on a wild deserted island:

> Il travaglio del mare e la paura,
> che tenuta alcun dí l'aveano desta;
> il ritrovarsi al lito ora sicura,
> lontana da rumor, ne la foresta;
> e che nessun pensier, nessuna cura,
> poi chi 'l suo amante ha seco, la molesta;
> fûr cagion ch'ebbe Olimpia sí gran sonno,
> che gli orsi e i ghiri aver maggior nol ponno.[5]

We have here a complete analysis precisely set forth of the causes of Olympia's deep slumber; but all this is clearly secondary to the intimate feeling expressed by the octave, which seems to delight in itself and actually takes pleasure in the resolution of a movement, of a becoming that achieves its consummation.

Bradamant and Marphisa, together, search in vain for King Agramant, to kill him:

> Come due belle e generose parde
> che fuor del lascio sien di pari uscite,
> poscia ch'i cervi o le capre gagliarde
> indarno aver si veggano seguite,
> vergognandosi quasi che fûr tarde,
> sdegnose se ne tornano e pentite;
> cosí tornâr le due donzelle, quando
> videro il Pagan salvo, sospirando.[6]

Same process, same result. But we observe the same process and result where really there seems to be nothing of intrinsic interest in the material, or rather there is only a conventional notion and a complementary phrase of courtly homage, or an attestation of esteem and friendship. To say of a beautiful damsel, "In her every act, she seems a goddess descended from heaven," is to say nothing uncommon; but Ariosto gives it such a turn and rhythm that we become witnesses to the appearance of the goddess with majestic pace; and to the amazement and to the reverent bowing of the bystanders and rivals; in short, to the development of a little drama:

> Julia Gonzaga, che dovunque il piede
> volge e dovunque i sereni occhi gira,
> non pur ogn'altra di beltà le cede,
> ma, come scesa dal ciel Dea, l'ammira . . . [7]

Rattling off a string of bare names for purposes of commemorative record and scarcely varying any of them with a poor play on words, is in itself something still less uncommon; but Ariosto arranges the names of contemporary painters as if they were on a Parnassus, exalting the greatest among them, and each of those bare names resounds in such a way (through mastery of accent and period) as to seem animated and full of sense:

> E quei che fûro a' nostri dí, o sono ora
> Leonardo, Andrea Mantegna, Gian Bellino,
> duo Dossi, e quel ch'a par sculpe e colora,
> Michel, piú che mortale, Angel divino . . . [8]

Ariosto's "pronouncements" were judged by De Sanctis as "commonplace" and not "original and profound observations," and by others as "banal" and "contradictory" besides. These are, nevertheless, Ariosto's pronouncements, and in the presence of these, we do not meditate, we sing:

> Oh gran contrasto in giovenil pensiero,
> desir di laude, ed impeto d'amore!
> Né, chi piú vaglia, ancor si trova il vero,
> che resta or questo or quel superïore . . . [9]

Even in the more daring places, where another would have entirely immersed himself in lascivious pleasures, he succeeds in at once both lowering and heightening the material; as in the tale of the adventure of Richardetto and Flordespine:

Non rumor di tamburi o suon di trombe
furon principio all'amoroso assalto;
ma baci, ch'imitavan le colombe,
davan segno or di gire, or di fare alto . . . [10]

Ariosto's irony, we would say, resembles the eye of God that watches
the movement of creation, of all creation, loving it all equally, in the good
and the bad, in the most grand and most minute, in man and in a grain of
sand, because he has made it all and heeds in it only its motion, its eternal
dialectic, its rhythm and harmony. With this, the passage from the common
acceptation of the word "irony" to the metaphysical meaning is completed,
the meaning it had among the Fichteans and the Romantics. We would
gladly explain the nature of Ariosto's inspiration in terms of their theory, if,
among these thinkers and *literati*, "irony" had not then become confused
with so-called humorism,[11] with the bizarre and extravagant or, in other
words, with attitudes that disturb and destroy art; whereas the critical definition we propose remains rigorously within the boundaries of art, just as
Ariosto does, never wandering into the humoristic and outlandish (an indication of weakness), and he uses irony like an artist, confident of his own
strength. And, by chance, this is the reason, or one of the reasons, why
Ariosto did not please the dissolute Romantics, who were inclined to prefer
Rabelais and even Carlo Gozzi.

To weaken all the orders of sentiment, to make them all equal in this
leveling down, to deprive things of their autonomy, of their own particular
soul amounts to transforming the world of spirit into the world of nature: an
unreal world that exists only to the extent that we so posit it. And in certain
respects "nature" becomes the entire world for Ariosto, a designed and
colored surface, resplendent but without substance. Hence that habit of seeing objects in their every detail, like a naturalist who observes minutiae and
describes them without losing himself in the unique detail which other artistic geniuses alone note and point out, without impassioned impatience
and consequent disdain. It may seem that the figure of St. John is drawn as
it is, in fun:

che 'l manto ha rosso e bianca la gonnella,
che l'un può al latte, l'altro al minio opporre;
i crini ha bianchi e bianca la mascella
di folta barba ch'al petto discorre . . . [12]

But basically Olympia's beauty is described in the same way, disregarding
the woman's chastity that would have seemed to require another kind of
representation or rather some use of veiling:

> Le bellezze d'Olimpia eran di quelle
> che son piú rare; e non la fronte sola,
> gli occhi, e le guance, e le chiome avea belle,
> la bocca, il naso, gli omeri e la gola . . . [13]

And with the same method even Medoro, whose courageous and devoted heart, whose youthful heroism seems to require a portrayal less attentive to the freshness of adolescence and more to the features that reveal courage and devotion:

> Medoro avea la guancia colorita,
> e bianca e grata ne la età novella . . . [14]

The great many likenesses among the characters and the situations in which they are found, with scenes offered from animal life or from natural phenomena, are, even these, the almost graspable, palpable part of this conversion of the human world into the world of nature. We will not resort to statistics, because a German philologist with irritating patience has already done so in a thick fascicle that makes us lose the desire to pause, even for a moment, over Ariosto's similes, comparisons, and metaphors.

This apparent naturalization, this objectivization which, as we have demonstrated, is at the same time also profoundly subjective, has led to the fallacious affirmation, already noted, concerning the indifference and coldness of observation, all poured into things, that constituted Ariosto's form. In this regard he has been given a companion, his contemporary, Machiavelli who, as it is usually said, investigated history and politics with a shrewd eye, described their processes, formulated their laws, and expressed his conclusions in his prose, characterized by like inexorable objectivity and scientific coldness. In a certain sense, but only in a very remote sense, it is true that both men, in different fields and for different ends, destroyed an anterior spiritual content (in Machiavelli, it was the medieval religious conception of history and politics) and naturalized it. But such a judgment on Machiavelli—who as a thinker, scrutinized the facts and clarified them with fresh, vigorous thought; and, as a writer, expressed his severe passion with apparent coldness—must be regarded as nothing more than a figure of speech. Similarly, to characterize Ariosto as naturalistic and objective is to utter nothing more than a metaphor, because Ariosto naturalized in order to spiritualize in a new manner, creating spiritual forms of Harmony.

On the other hand, and as a consequence of what we have been demonstrating, we must abandon the praises that have been given to Ariosto, now for his *epicità,* for the epic nobility and decorum that Galileo so greatly exalted in him, and, again for the force and the coherence to be admired in the character of his personages, according to the opinion of early critics, and new ones, and indeed recent ones. How could epic quality ever exist in the *Furioso,* when its author not only lacked the ethical sentiments of epic poetry, but the little, that one can somewhat dimly perceive he possessed by inheritance, was also dissolved in harmony and irony with all the rest? And how could there ever be true and proper characters in the poem, if, in art, the characters of the personages are nothing other than the very notes—varied, diverse, and contrasting—of the poet's soul, embodied in creatures who do indeed seem to live their own particular lives, though all actually live the same life, variously distributed, all sparks from the same central fire? It is a very poor critical prejudice to regard characters as living on their own, and as very nearly continuing to live outside of the works of art, of which they are parts and in which they are not at all unlike or separable from the strophes, the verses, and the words.

In the *Furioso,* there being no unfettered energy of passionate sentiments, there are no characters, only figures, shaped and colored, certainly, but without prominence and roundness, drawn with generic and typical, rather than individual, features. The knights are like one another and blend into one another, being differentiated by goodness and wickedness, their greater courtesy or rudeness, or by extrinsic and accidental attributes, or often by their names alone; the women likewise are differentiated, as amorous or perfidious, as virtuous and contented in one single love or as dissolute and perverse, and often by the different adventures in which they turn up and by the names that embellish them. The same applies to the external appearances of the tales and of the descriptions (typical and not individualized, or only slightly individualized, is Orlando's madness, which only for rhetorical satisfaction, some critics have likened to Lear's), and to the external appearances of objects, landscapes, palaces, gardens, and everything else. Even with regard to the coherence of the characters, understood broadly as conforming to a typical design, we would make certain reservations (that rightly have been made), because Ariosto's personages take many liberties with themselves, according to the situations they run into, or rather according to the services that the author requires of them.

Such reservations prove indispensable, for if the supposed objectively and coherently configured characters bring praise from those who discover them in Ariosto, they bring blame, equally unfounded, from others who seek them there and do not find them. Thus De Sanctis once found Ariosto's female characters inferior to Dante's, Shakespeare's, and Goethe's: an impossible comparison, because Angelica, Olympia, and Isabel certainly do not possess the passionate intensity of Francesca, Desdemona, and Margaret; but neither do the latter express the harmonious octaves in which those others extend, indulge themselves, and effectively consist; and, what is more important, neither the former nor the latter suffer from correlative defects, which are defects only in the light of a critical prejudice and are not real privations or poetic contradictions in themselves.

Even De Sanctis had occasion to accuse Ariosto of lacking a feeling for nature (almost a defect and privation); but the so-called feeling for nature (as, incidentally, he, the great master, himself taught), does not proceed from nature, rather from attitudes of the human spirit, from feelings of relief, of melancholy or of religious terror that man from time to time instills into nature, finding them there after placing them there; and these attitudes, in their particularity, were excluded as a result of Ariosto's fundamental attitude, and if by chance some hint of it had been introduced into the poem, if some sentimental note had resounded there, it would have been quickly felt as discordant and unsuitable.

To Lessing, another objectivist of criticism, Ariosto's depiction of Alcina's beauties seemed mistaken and exceeded the limits of poetry: to which De Sanctis retorted that the materiality condemned by Lessing, was, in this description, the secret of its poeticality, because the beauty of the witch Alcina, consisting of a fictitious disguise, called for a material description. Here we have an unjust censure and a reply that, though, indeed very ingenious, is perhaps not equally true, because as we have already seen, Ariosto always described in this way both the genuine beauties as well as the feigned ones, the Olympias as well as the Alcinas; and the correct reply seems already given: that in Ariosto it is vain to seek energetic features, live physiognomies obtained with two strokes of the brush, things that presuppose a way of feeling that he did not possess and, in every case, repressed. The "shyly smiling eyes" that are all Silvia, the "doux sourire amoureux et souffrant," that is the entire spiritual friend of the *Maison du berger,* belong not to Ariosto, but to Leopardi and De Vigny.

There are two ways in which we must not read the *Furioso.* The first is that with which we read a harmoniously proportioned book of high moral inspiration, like *I Promessi sposi,* that is, following in its various parts, the process of a serious human emotion that circulates in all the parts, even in the smallest, shaping and determining them all; and the second way, one that is adopted for works like *Faust,* for example, in which the general composition, more or less guided by mental concepts, does not entirely coincide with the poetic inspiration of the single parts, and in which one should distinguish the poetical parts from the unpoetical links; and the reader who is gifted with a poetic spirit passes over the latter in order to pause over and enjoy the former. In the *Furioso* there is not, or, there is only very slightly (that is, in the measure of imperfection that obtains in every most perfect human endeavor) the unevenness of this second type of work; there is, instead the evenness of the first; but it lacks the particular form of passionate seriousness that is in the whole of the first and in the individual parts of the second. We must therefore read in a third manner, which involves beyond the particularity of the tales and descriptions, a content that is always the same, that actualizes itself in ever new forms and attracts us with the magic of this: sameness which is, at the same time, an inexhaustible variety of appearances.

As we see, even with this we have come to accept, after correcting it, a common judgment on the *Furioso,* which we can say, began to accompany it from the time the poem first appeared in the world: the judgment that it is a work free of seriousness, light, gay, pleasant, frivolous. "Ludicro more," Cardinal Sadoleto, called it in the authorization written under the name of Leo X for the 1516 edition, although he added, perhaps translating the poet's own statement, "Longo tamen studio et cogitatione, multisque vigiliis confectum." Bernardo Tasso, Trissino, Speroni, and other grave pedantic personages, did not fail to reprove Ariosto for having directed his poem to the sole end of delight. Boileau judged it a simple collection of "fables comiques"; Sulzer defined it as "a poem directed to the simple end of delight, not guided by reason"; and Home called it "unrestrained and extravagant," full of interruptions, and annoying in its excessive variety. Even today in many school manuals we encounter, displayed as on a credit and debit balance sheet, its assets and deficits, and among the former, the perfection of the octaves, the vivacity of the narrations, the agility, and among the latter, the lack of profound sentiment, the light that shines and does not warm, the inertia it leaves in the heart: a judgment that may be accepted and corrected by simply observing that those who judge in this manner see and note well all that is on a level with their eyes, but they do not lift them to that which is higher than their heads and is the principal virtue wherein Ariosto's frivolity reveals itself as deep seriousness of a rare kind, a profound emotion of the heart, but of a gentle, exquisite heart somewhat aloof from the agitation of what is usually considered life and reality.

Aloof, but not detached, not alien, not indifferent: with this proposition, resuming and developing the analysis that we have already begun, it is useful to guard against a facile misunderstanding concerning the "destruction" of which we have spoken, which is brought about by Ariosto's tone and irony, almost a total destruction and annihilation, where we must understand "destruction" in the philosophical sense of the word, that is at the same time preservation. If it were otherwise, what would remain in the poem to make that varied material or emotional content which we have passed in review? Do perhaps the stars stand in the sky (as the sarcastic Don Ferrante would ask), like pins stuck in a pincushion? From total indifference of sentiment, from a lack of content is born the rhetoric of others, but not Ariosto's poetry: the rouge on the cadaver, and not the rosy blush that clings to and adorns the living. From indifference is born the soft, extrinsically musical versification of the *Adone;* and not the octaves of the *Furioso;* thus are born (to cite again the Ariostophile, Giraldi Cinzio, who warns us not to confuse the "facility" of the *Furioso* with the rhymes "of sweet sound and no feeling") the "eight hundred stanzas" of a contemporary composer that Giraldi once had to read "which when taken stanza by stanza, seemed to have been gathered from the flower gardens of poetry, they were so full of charm, but taken as a whole, they were so inane in regard to sense, that they seemed to have been born in the soil of childishness," because their author had been "exclusively intent upon the delight that derives from the splendor and choice of the sounds, and had entirely neglected the dignity and value that stems from judgment."

If Ariosto, in the act of composing, had not been enamored in the varied ways that we have been describing, of the various materials that entered his poem, he would have lacked the force, the liveliness, the thoughts, the accents to moderate and temper in the harmonious disposition of his soul. He would have poeticized coldly, and coldly one never succeeds to write poetry. Such was the case, as it seems to me, in the *Cinque canti,* which he excluded from the *Furioso* and for which he substituted others, where we perceive his touch above all in the skill of the clear descriptions and transitions, and there are also all the elements of his usual world, tales of wars, chivalric adventures, love stories (the love of Penticone for Ottone's wife, and Astolpho's love for Gismondo's wife), satirical tales (the foundation of the city of Medea with its law regulating sex, which she imposed there), astonishing fantasies (the knights imprisoned in a whale's body, replete with bedroom, kitchen and dining hall), and copious political and moral reflections (on jealousy, on ambition, against wicked masters, against mercenary troops). Despite all this, we feel that Ariosto wrote them during an unpropitious moment, Minerva being uncooperative or hostile, and when he did not take sufficient interest and lacked the necessary warmth. And in the *Furioso* itself, isn't there some part wherein the poet languishes? It would seem so, not indeed in the forty cantos of the first edition, which germinated during his twelve-year poetic springtime, but in the later additions, all (as could be demonstrated), some more, some less, somewhat intellectualistic in origin, and therefore (excepting the Olympia episode) are not among the most often read and the most popular; most intellectualistic of all is the long delay introduced at the end of the poem, the double engagement of Bradamant and the contest in courtesy between Leo and Rogero where in some passages the tone becomes positively pedestrian. True it is that the philologists given to the criticism of art have recognized an improving Ariosto who was becoming "serious" and—most amazing—was extending a hand to Torquato Tasso precisely in these listless passages and especially in the *Cinque canti,* in this disoriented and untuned Ariosto.

The process of "destruction" carried out on the material, could perhaps be made clear, to the person who does not like philosophic formulas or who finds them too difficult, through a comparison with what in the technique of painting is called "veiling a color," which does not mean to cancel it, but to tone it down. In such an even toning down, all the sentiments that form the scheme of the poem keep not only their own physiognomy but also their reciprocal relations and proportions; so that, though they indeed become dim to our sight "like pearls on a white brow" in the "smooth and transparent glass" and "clear and tranquil waters"[15] of the octaves, they remain as varied as they were before and more or less strong according to the greater or lesser force they possessed in the poet's soul. The comic, simultaneously muted and highlighted, still remains comic, the sublime sublime, the voluptuous voluptuous, the reflective reflective, and so forth. And sometimes it happens that Ariosto reaches a limit which, were he to pass beyond it, would cause him to depart from his tone, but he never does because, having reached this limit, he always respects it. Everyone knows by heart the most moving gestures and words that are in the *Furioso:* Medoro, surrounded by enemies who had unexpectedly come upon him, circles about like a capstan lathe, taking cover in the trees and never abandoning the body of his master, and Zerbino who, on the point of killing him, looking upon his beautiful face, feels compassion, and stops; Zerbino, who in dying despairs at leaving his Isabel alone, a prey to unknown men, while she dissolves into tears and utters sweet words of eternal fidelity; Flordelice, who receives the news or, rather guesses the death of her husband. . . .

Always, when repeating these and other such verses, the throat tightens and a something I know not what veils the eyes. Here is Flordelice, for instance, who has a shiver of foreboding:

> E questa novità d'aver timore
> le fa tremar di doppia téma il core.[16]

The deathly news arrives. Astolpho and Sansonet, the two friends who happen to come to the place where she is staying, keep it from her for a few hours, and then resolve to go to her in order to prepare her for the misfortune that has befallen her:

> Tosto ch'entraro, e ch'ella loro il viso
> vide di gaudio in tal vittoria privo,
> senz'altro annunzio sa, senz'altro avviso,
> che Brandimarte suo non è piú vivo . . . [17]

The trembling that seizes the dear unfortunate lady quivers in the images and rhythm; we feel the blow and quickly afterwards, the plunge into the black abyss of desolation. Another moment in the same tale, wherein grief seems to gain force and grow upon itself, occurs when Orlando, who was expected, enters the temple where the funeral rites of Brandimart are being celebrated: Orlando, friend, companion, witness to that death:

> Levossi, al ritornar del Paladino,
> maggiore il grido e raddoppiossi il pianto . . . [18]

Confronted by figures and words like these, De Sanctis used to say to his students, explicating the *Furioso* to them: "See how much heart Ariosto had!" But he also impressed upon them the truth: that "Ariosto never develops his situations to the point of torture," being forbidden to do so by the tone of the canto; and he demonstrated how, in order to contain the agony ready to break through, he alternatively employed interruptions, charming similes, pauses of reflections, and rhetorical devices. There are critics, overly exacting, or rather who demand what is unwarranted and too much, those who, for example, hesitate over the octaves on Isabel's name (designated by God thenceforth to adorn the most beautiful, kind, courteous, wise, and chaste women: an homage to the Marchioness of Mantua, Isabella d'Este). The tale of the sacrifice Isabel makes of her life in order to keep faith with Zerbino concludes with these octaves; and they do not understand that these octaves, along with the *Proficiscere* ("Depart in peace") preceding them ("Vattene in pace, alma beata. . . . "), and the very tale of Rodomont's drunken bestiality, and preceding it, the semi-comical scene of the holy hermit who, "like a skilled pilot," sits at the helm of Isabel's honesty and willingly prepares "a sumptuous, splendid repast of spiritual food," and whom Rodomont seizes by the neck and hurls three miles away into the sea—all these are words and representations intoned to produce the effect of allowing Isabel to die without overturning the *Furioso* and plunging it into tragedy and the correlative tragic catharsis— the *Furioso* that has a general, perpetual harmonic catharsis, now sufficiently clarified.

It is precisely the handling of the sentimental passional material, both in spite of and by means of the muting achieved—the varied coloring that this brings to the poem, the character of humanity that it confers on it— that counseled us to declare at the start of our analysis that in defining Ariosto as the poet of *Harmony,* we intended only to indicate where the *stress* on this work falls, because he is the poet of Harmony and, at the same time, something more, of Harmony that develops in a particular world of sentiments; and, in sum, that the harmony realized by him, is not Harmony in general, but an *entirely Ariostesque harmony.*

9

Shakespeare's Poetic Sentiment[1]

Everyone possesses in the depths of his soul an abbreviated image of a poet who, like William Shakespeare, belongs to the common cultural heritage, or discovers in his memory definitions which have been given of him and have become current formulas. It is useful to fix upon that image, to recall those formulas, and to extract their principal determinations, in order to obtain, at least in a preliminary and provisional way, the character of Shakespeare's spiritual attitude, that is of his poetic sentiment.

The first observation that strikes us and upon which there is general agreement, is that in him no one particular feeling or order of feelings prevails: he cannot be called a love poet, like a Petrarca, or a sad and despairing one like a Leopardi, or a heroic one as is said of Homer. Instead his name is adorned with epithets of *universal* poet, perfectly *objective*, supremely *impersonal*, extraordinarily *impartial*. Sometimes there has even been talk of his *coldness,* a coldness indeed sublime "of a sovereign spirit who has covered the entire curve of human existence and has survived sentiment" (Schlegel).

Nor is he a poet, as is usually said, of *ideals*—religious, ethical, political, or social, which explains the antipathy frequently felt for him by apostles of various kinds, the latest one being Tolstoy, and also explains the unsatisfied desires kindled in self-righteous folk, always eager to ask for extra, a supplement from any great man; such folk, even while admiring him, regretfully concluded that in truth he lacks something, that he is not to be counted among the fighters for more liberal political forms and for more equitable social conditions, that he does not have feelings of compassion for the humble, and for the common people. To the determined end of opposing such apparent accusations, or in fact in every case opposing them, a school of German critics (e.g., Ulrici, Gervinus, Kreyssig, Vischer, etc.)— of whom, to tell the truth for humanitarian considerations, I do not recommend to others the reading, which I out of duty was compelled to complete—began to represent Shakespeare as a deep teacher of morality, one of the shrewdest and most reliable of the casuists for whom no ethical problem existed that he did not justly resolve, as a prudent and austere political counselor and, above all, as an infallible judge of actions and a

dispenser of rewards and punishments, graded according to merits and de-
merits, who saw to it that not the slightest fault went unpunished.

Now setting aside the fact that the actions thus attributed to him, were
intolerable to his character as a poet and only attested to those critics' poor
taste; setting aside the fact that the imagined and praised intention attributed to him, of dispensing punishments and rewards according to a moral
scale was absolutely inexecutable by any man or even by a God, rewards
and punishments being concepts that are entirely extraneous to moral consciousness and purely practical and juridical; setting aside these matters
that, in general, in the most recent criticism are considered no longer worthy of discussion and are jeered at as ridiculous beliefs of an earlier time:
even if we choose to translate these affirmations into a less illogical form,
and in that way show nothing other than a concern in Shakespeare about the
above mentioned problems, they show themselves openly incompatible with
simple reality. Shakespeare did not cherish ideals of any sort, least of all
political ones; and however magnificently he represents even political struggles, he always goes beyond their specific character and aim, always arriving, through them, at the only thing that profoundly attracts him: life.

This *sense of life* is the source of the other high praise that is usually
given to his work which, for that reason, is held eminently *dramatic,* that
is, animated by the sense of life in itself, in its perpetual discord, in its
bitter-sweetness, in all its contradiction and complexity. To feel life powerfully outside of every determinate passion or ideal means to experience it
unilluminated by a faith, not disciplined by a law of goodness, not rectifi-
able by human will, not reducible to the serenity of idyllic enjoyment or to
the rapture of joy; and in fact, Shakespeare has from time to time been
judged not religious, not moral, not an affirmer of free will, and not an
optimist. But no one dares then to judge him for this reason irreligious,
immoral, a fatalist and pessimist—adjectives that, as soon as we try to
pronounce them, we notice that they do not suit him. Even on this matter,
Taine's strange, fantastic aberrations and his singular incapacity to experience clear impressions of reality were needed in order to portray the
Shakespearean sentiment about man and life as one based on fundamental
irrationality and blind deception, on a series of hasty impulses and teeming
fantasies, without an autonomous center, where truth and wisdom are accidental and transient effects or insubstantial appearances. These are descriptions of a manner repeated with variations by others and do not yield of
Shakespeare's art even a caricature, which after all requires a real connection with fact. Shakespeare has so strong a feeling of the limit that binds
human will and when the limit is overcome, he possesses in equal measure
a feeling of the power of human liberty; he who (as Hazlitt observed) in a
certain aspect is both ''the least moral of the poets,'' is in another aspect
''the greatest of the moralists.'' He who sees the irremovable presence of

evil and of pain, has his eyes no less open and intent on the resplendence of the good, on the smile of joy, and he is healthy and virile, as the pessimist never is; he, who nowhere in his works points to a God, holds constant the obscure consciousness of a divinity, of an unknown divinity. The spectacle of the world, taken in itself, seems to him without significance, and men and their passions appear a dream, that, as such, has for its intrinsic and correlative, albeit hidden, end a more solid and perhaps deeper reality.

But we must not overly emphasize even these positive characteristics and present his sentiment so as to suggest that the negative determinations have been subdued and conquered. Goodness or virtue is doubtless stronger than evil and vice in Shakespeare; but not because it transcends and assimilates the other term in itself, but because it is light in the midst of darkness, because it is goodness, is virtue—in short, because of its very quality, which the poet discerns and grasps in its original purity and truth, without adulterating and weakening it. In effect, positive determinations and negative ones maintain equal strength in his feeling, and they tangle and clash with one another without becoming truly reconciled in a better harmony. Rectitude, justice, sincerity affirm their logic; but their logic and their character of natural necessity likewise affirm ambition, greed, egoism, satanic wickedness. The will goes safe to its target, but at other times, it also goes awry, being mastered by a power it does not recognize and nevertheless serves, as if captured by sorcery. The sky clears after a devastating hurricane; just men occupy the thrones whence the wicked have fallen; conquerors feel compassion for the conquered and praise them; but the desolation of betrayed trust, of oppressed goodness, of innocent creatures destroyed, of noble hearts broken remains. The God who quiets hearts is longed for, perhaps anticipated, but he never appears.

The poet does not stand apart from these opposing emotions, from attraction and repugnance, from love and hate, from hope and despair, from joy and pain; but he stands apart from the unilaterality of each of these. He gathers them all unto himself, and not in order to endure them all and to shed tears of blood over them, but to form a single world out of them: the Shakespearean world, which is the world of these unresolved opposites.

What two poets appear, and even are, more clearly unlike one another than Shakespeare and Ariosto? Yet they do have this in common: they both look toward something that is beyond particular emotions; and therefore, of the one as of the other, it has more than once been said that they "speak little to the heart," and certainly they show themselves to be sentimental and passionately excited to only the slightest degree. With regard to both one and the other there has been talk of "humorism," a word we avoid here since it is of such uncertain meaning and of so little use in defining profound spiritual activities. Ariosto veils and tones down all the particular emotions that he represents, thanks to his divine irony; and Shakespeare, taking a different route, by giving all of them the same vigor and prominence manages, through their reciprocal tension, to create a sort of equilibrium everywhere else which, by reason of its genesis, is wholly different from the harmony in which the singer of the *Furioso* delights.

Ariosto surpasses good and evil, reserving interest only for the constant, yet varied rhythm, of the life that is born, expands, dies and is reborn in order to grow and die once more; Shakespeare surpasses all individual emotions, but he does not surpass, indeed he potentiates interest in good and evil, in pain and joy, in freedom and necessity, in appearance and reality; and the vision of this struggle is his poetry. Thus Ariosto has been metaphorically called "fanciful," and Shakespeare "realistic," and the one the opposite to the other; and they are opposites, but still they meet at one point, which is not the general one of both being poets, but a specific one, as cosmic poets: not indeed merely in the sense in which every poet is cosmic, but in the other, particular one, that has been drawn above. We hope that it will not be necessary to insist that this be understood with the required restrictions, that is, as the feature which in different ways dominates in the two poets, and which does not exclude the other individual features that characterize them, and above all which does not exclude what belongs to any poetry. The impassible limits of every characteristic criticism, that should by now be well known, are set by the impossibility of ever rendering the fullness of a poem or other artistic work into logical terms, because it is clear that if such a translation were possible, art would be impossible; that is, replaceable and superfluous. Nevertheless within those limits, criticism performs its proper task, which is to discern and to point out where the poetic motif is really located and to devise the schemata that may help to distinguish the characteristic of each work.

As for the rest, if Ariosto has very willingly been compared to painters who were his contemporaries, with the intent of drawing attention to his harmonious inspiration, so too for Shakespeare, Ludwig could not restrain himself from making the same comparisons; and he found the most suitable image of his plays in the figures and scenes produced by Titian, Giorgione, and Veronese, when contrasted to Correggio's charm, Carracci's insipidity, Guido's and Carlo Dolci's affectation, Caravaggio's and Ribera's harshness. In Shakespeare, as in those great Venetians, there is everywhere "existence," earthly life, transformed to be sure, but devoid of frenzies or halos and sentimentalism—serene even in the tragic.

Such sense of oppositions in their vital unity, such a profound sense of life, insures that the vision will not be simplified and made superficial in a dualism of good and bad beings, of the elect and the reprobate, and that the opposition will be introduced with varying gradation and measure for every being and that thus the conflict be fought out truly within the very bosom of things. Hence the aspect of mystery that surrounds the actions and events Shakespeare represents, which is not to be understood in the general sense in which every vision is mystery, but rather in the particular sense of a course of events for which the poet not only does not possess (and cannot possess) the philosophical explanation, but in which he can never find the terminal resting point; peace after war, the acceptance of war for a greater peace. For this reason there is a diffused fear of the Unknown that surrounds us on every side and that conceals a countenance that may perhaps be more dreadful than the dreadfulness of life itself, in the unfolding of which human beings are caught up—a countenance dreadful for what it will disclose, and perhaps, in this dreadfulness, may at one and the same time be ecstatic, tremulous, and rapturous.

The mystery is not solely in the images of ghosts, demons, and witches that sometimes appear in poetry, but in the entire atmosphere in which these images are nothing other than a part that defines itself in a more direct manner through personification; and this mystery, ruling generally, was well expressed by the first great critics of Shakespearean poetry, by Herder and by Goethe, to whom belongs the analogy between Shakespeare's plays and "open books of destiny, where the wind of stirred life blows, and here and there violently unleafs them." The throb of pleasure in the face of mystery beats in the musicality which is felt everywhere, and which, at times reflects upon itself and proclaims the nexus between music and love, between music and sadness, between music and the unknown Deities.

I must insist on the term I have adopted in describing this condition of spirit: "sentiment" ("sentimento"); lest it be mistaken for a concept, thought, or philosophic doctrine, as happens when the formula "mode of conceiving life" or "conception," adopted in reference to Shakespeare and to poets in general, is taken in a literal and material sense and when one, for example, seeks to discover by what marks Shakespeare's "conception of tragedy" differs from that of the Greeks or the French, and so forth, as though there were in such a case a question of concepts or systems. Shakespeare is not a philosopher, and his spiritual disposition is directly opposed to that of the philosopher who masters sentiment and the spectacle of life in the thought that understands and explains them and reconciles opposites dialectically with some one or other unitary principle; whereas Shakespeare gathers and restores them, unaware of criticism or theory, in their vital motion, and he resolves them in no other way but by the evidence of his representation. Therefore, when the epithets and praises for "objectivity," "impersonality," and "universality" conferred on him are not restricted to designating—even in inapt terms—the real psychological differences noted above, but proceed to attribute a philosophic character to his spiritual attitude, it is advisable to reject them all, setting his poetic subjectivity against objectivity, his personality against impersonality, and the individual form of his way of feeling against universality.

The cosmic opposites, in the images of which he represents reality and life, not only are not philosophic solutions for him, in his plays, they are not even problems of thought, and in some few of his works they only barely take on the form of bitter questions that remain unanswered. And the numerous systematic elaborations that have been made of Shakespeare's philosophy (from time to time presented as theistic, pantheistic, dualistic, deterministic, pessimistic, optimistic) must be termed fantastic and arbitrary, being extracted from his plays by the same method whereby one extracts the philosophy implicit in a political or historical treatise. In these last cases, there is most certainly a philosophy incorporated in the political and historical judgments, but in Shakespeare's case, which is that of poets in general, to extract a philosophy amounts to inventing it, that is, to thinking and to concluding on our account upon the stimulus of the poet's images, and by means of a psychological illusion, to put our own questions and our replies into his mouth. It would be possible to speak of Shakespeare's philosophy only if he, like Dante, had expounded one, in didactic form, in philosophical sections of his poems: this he did not do, because the very thoughts he enunciates do not fulfill any other task but that of poetic expressions, and, taken out of their contexts, where they sound so profound and powerful, they lose their strength and seem indeterminate, contradictory, or fallacious.

An entirely different question is then whether this his sentiment rests on what are called philosophical or mental *presuppositions,* and what these really might be; because, on the first point, we ought immediately to agree that a sentiment must emerge from certain mental presuppositions or concepts, that is upon certain convictions, affirmations, negations, doubts; and on the second point, we ought to admit the legitimacy of the inquiry, and note too that this is one of the many historical inquiries concerning Shakespeare in regard to his poetry whose rightful place has been wrongly usurped by trifling and extraneous remarks about his private affairs, his domestic relations, his business dealings, and his alleged love-relations with Mary Fitton and the hostess Mrs. Davenant.

It is true that even the inquiries about Shakespeare's mental presuppositions have often wandered into the extraneous and into the anecdotal, as into the still open questions about the religious persuasion he followed and about his political opinions, which, when proposed in this way, also degenerate, into problems of biography, indifferent to art. Whether Shakespeare adhered to Anglicanism or to Catholicism instead (as several still maintain; and in 1864, Rio wrote an entire volume on this thesis), and in one or the other condition, he opposed Puritanism; whether he favored the success of Essex's plot or took the side of Queen Elizabeth instead—these are matters that have nothing to do with mental presuppositions imminent in his poetry. In his active and practical life, he could have been as impious and profane as a Greene or a Marlowe, or a devout papist, worshipping superstitiously in secret like a disciple of Mary Stuart; yet nonetheless he could have poeticized upon diverse presuppositions, upon concepts that had introduced and shaped themselves and become dominant in his spirit without, for this reason, changing his chosen and practiced religious creed. The inquiry of which we speak does not concern the superficial character, but the deep one, not the frozen and solidified layer, but the flux that flows beneath it and that others would call "the unconscious" in respect to "the conscious," whereas, more precisely, the two qualifications should be reversed. Presuppositions are the philosophical tenets that each individual carries within him, gathering them from the times and from tradition or forming new ones for himself from his own observations and reflections, and that, for works of poetry, produce a condition far removed from that psychological attitude from which poetic fantasies are generated.

At this depth of consciousness, Shakespeare clearly reveals himself to stand not only outside of Catholicism and Protestantism, not only outside of Christianity, but outside of every religious conception or, rather, of every transcendent and theological one, being even in this—albeit even in this in dissimilar ways and with dissimilar consequences—like the other poet of the Renaissance, the Italian Ariosto. If a theological conception, if the Christian belief in eternal life, in God the judge, in other-worldly punishment and reward, in a consideration of earthly life as a test and a pilgrimage had been alive and active within him, his sentiment would have been composed in a fundamentally different way. He does not recognize any life other than the earthly one—vigorous, passionate, troubled, beaten about between joy and pain, with the shadow of mystery about and above it.

There is reason, therefore, to be amazed when (especially among German writers) we read of Shakespeare as of a spirit entirely dominated by the Christian ideas of the Reformation, whereas with regard to Christianity, he lacked the theology of Judaic-Hellenistic origin just as he lacked an inclination toward the mystical and ascetic. On the other hand, we cannot admit the opposite qualification of him as a pagan understood in the somewhat popular sense of satisfied hedonist, because it is no less evident that his moral discernment, his sense of the sinful, his delicate conscience, and his humanity bear the strong imprint of the Christian ethic. Indeed, precisely from his deep and exquisite ethical judgment, conjoined to his vision of a world that moves by its own force or in any case mysteriously, often opposing or overthrowing or perverting the forces directed toward the good, arises the tragic conflict.

To this double presupposition we must add a third, as an inference: a denial, a scepsis, or an ignoring of the concept of a rational course of events and of a Providence that governs it. He no longer accepts inexorable Fate as sole master of men and of Gods; he does not even accept (as is believed by some interpreters) the determinism of individual character, which is another kind of Fate, a naturalistic Fate; and he will have nothing to do with the hard Asiatic or African dualistic idea of predestination. On the contrary, he recognizes human spontaneity and liberty as forces that prove their true reality in the deed itself; nonetheless he permits liberty and necessity to clash and the one from time to time, to overcome the other, without establishing a relation between the two, without suspecting their identity-in-opposition, without discerning that the two warring elements form the only current of the real, and therefore without rising to the level of modern theodicy, which is History. From this we have new cause for marvel when we hear the historicism of Shakespeare's thought and of his tragedies insistently affirmed (by Ulrici, for example), whereas what is entirely, missing in them is precisely, the historical concept of life, which Dante yet possessed, though in the form of medieval philosophy of history. And since historicism is at the same time political and social idealism, Shakespeare ought to lack and as I have said, does lack a true faith and passion. This has been imagined and bestowed upon him as passion which they would even crown with doctrinal wisdom, by publicists and political polemicists (like Gervinus), who are eager to enlist so great a name among their own.

By what ways and means such propositions were formed in the depths of his spirit it is difficult to ascertain, because with a query of this nature we resume a biographical question concerning the education received, the company he kept, his reading, his experiences, all matters about which we are little or not at all informed. Did he, with vigilant eye and participating spirit, note the fervor of life in its diverse and contrasting aspects, which the England of his day had entered upon? Did he listen to theological and metaphysical disputes, carrying away an impression of vacuity? Did he keep company with the young university men who were just then contributing several "university wits" to literature and drama, his predecessors and colleagues in the theatrical arena? Did he read Erasmus, the *Praise of Folly,* the moral dialogues and treatises, the English humanists, the Platonists, and the ancient and modern historians, as he certainly later read Montaigne? Did he read Machiavelli and the other Italian political writers and authors like Huarte and Charron, who had begun to sketch the doctrines of the temperaments and passions? Did he know Giordano Bruno, or rather know of him and of his doctrines? Did the influence of these men and their books reach him by various and indirect ways, by second and third hand, through conversation, and as is imaginatively said, through the environment? And to what extent were his doubts, negations, and persuasions the result of his sure and lively intuition or of his continuous, tenacious self-querying rather than the fruit of his learning? In truth, even if we possessed abundant reports on this matter, we would still be little informed, because the processes of individual formation for the most part escape the observation of others and frequently even the memory of individual himself, and finally the ease with which they are forgotten proves that it is not important that they be saved, but rather their consequences.

What is important here lies in the relation of those mental presuppositions to the life of the time, with the general culture of the epoch, with the historical phase which the human spirit was then traversing; and in such a relationship Shakespeare was truly what he has appeared to be to his best interpreters, a man of the Renaissance: of that age which, with the wars between the great States, with the navigation, the commerce, the philosophies, the religious battles, the science of nature, the poems, paintings, statues, and the elegant architecture, had given full prominence to life on earth, and would not allow it to fade, grow pale, and dissolve before the rays of another and unfamiliar world, as had happened in the long medieval centuries. But he was not a part of that merry and joyous, paganistic Renaissance, which was only a minor aspect of that great movement; rather he belonged to that other one, animated by new needs, by new religious impulses, by searches for new philosophical orientations, troubled by scepsis, streaked with flashes of the future. These flashes, however, that sparkled only in its major thinkers, who were not yet sufficiently strong to gather them together to produce a steady, constant light, could not be reduced to a radiant fire in its major poet, for whom philosophizing served as a presupposition and did not constitute the regular, principal activity of his mind; and therefore, it is vain to seek in Shakespeare what neither Bruno nor Campanella, and later not even Descartes or Spinoza attained, that is, the aforementioned historical concept, and it is likewise vain to speak of his Spinozistic or Schellingian pantheism.

Yet Shakespeare did assume in the past, and sometimes assumes even to our eyes, the semblance of philosopher and teacher, or of harbinger of the highest truths that later came to light; and it is a fact that toward no other poet has modern philosophy, idealistic and historical, been so attracted as toward Shakespeare, recognizing him as a fraternal soul. How can this be? The answer lies in what we have been noting and confirming: through his mental presuppositions which rejected medieval views and represented the heights of the new era that wanted and had not found integration and harmony, and, above all through his strong sentiment of cosmic oppositions which burst forth from them and became elevated to poetry, Shakespeare seems to offer material already prepared and in some way shaped to the dialectic, and at times he almost suggests the word to the moralist, the politician, the philosopher of art. Because of his singular power to stimulate, he could almost be called a "pre-philosopher": a name that would also have the advantage of making it clear that it is useless to try to make him into a philosopher. From his pre-philosophy and poetry, precisely because we cannot extract a determinate and particular doctrine out of it, we can draw many and various ones according to the diversities of our minds and the developments of the times. Consequently, if someone has maintained that the logical complement of this poetic vision is speculative idealism, dialectic, anti-ascetic morality, romantic aesthetics, realistic politics, or the historical conception of the real and has sustained this rationally, moving from doctrines he holds to be true, and rightly thinking that the logical complement of beauty is truth; others by chance can arrive, and have arrived at pessimistic conclusions from that vision and affirmation of opposites; and still others have tried and try to proceed from that vision to a restoration of some of the presuppositions that are denied there or are absent, such as faith in another world and in a divine and transcendent justice. This last point is documented in the best possible way, by a great Italian genius, who was both a strict Catholic and fervent Shakespearean. Manzoni, in fact, discovered the most efficacious morality in Shakespearean pessimism, and he noted that "the representation of profound sorrows and indeterminate terrors," provided by Shakespeare "comes near to virtue," because "when a man imaginatively departs from the well-worn ground of familiar things and unforeseen events, with which he is accustomed to battle, and find himself in the infinite region of possible evils, he feels his weakness: his cheerful ideas of defense and strength abandon him, and he thinks that in that state of things only virtue, an upright conscience, and God's help can provide some comfort to his mind"; and therefore, he concluded with characteristic certainty: "Let everyone consult himself after reading one of Shakespeare's tragedies, whether he does not feel a similar effect in his heart."

10

Shakespeare's Art[1]

Having outlined the motifs of Shakespearean poetry,[2] there is no place for the further question about the way in which Shakespeare translated them into concrete poetry, or about the *form* that he gave to the affective content. In art, form and content cannot be disconnected and considered separately. Accordingly nothing that is said of Shakespearean form (provided that it point to something real and that has been well observed) escapes these two alternatives: either to repeat with application to Shakespeare the exposition of the characteristics, indeed of the unique characteristic of all poetry; or to provide under the name "formal characteristics" more or less completely, nothing other than the characteristics of Shakespearean sentiment or sentiments, and thus to repeat the review that has already been provided of his various poetic motifs. Nor is there a reason to investigate Shakespeare's "technique," since there is not in him or in any other poet a trade secret that can be communicated, "a part" that (as has been claimed) "can be taught and learned."

One can obtain easy confirmation of what we say by testing any one of the many books on Shakespeare's "form" or "technique;" for example, the most intelligent of all, written with great insight into art in general and into Shakespeare's art in particular, that of Otto Ludwig, from which I have taken the phrases cited above. And in it one will read that in Shakespeare,

everything is individualized, and at the same time idealized, through elevation and reinforcement: every speech according to the sentiment that produces it; every sentiment, every action according to character and situation; every character and every situation, the one thanks to the other; and both thanks to the individuality of the time; and every speech and every situation still more individualized by means of time and of place, even by means of natural phenomena; such that every one of his dramas, according to the occasion, has its own atmosphere, sometimes clearer, other times murkier.[3]

And of what poetry that is poetry, cannot one affirm, or from what cannot one demand, such individuated idealization? One reads in the same book that "Shakespeare is never speculative, but keeps to experience, as

Shylock keeps to his signed bond". And what poetry that is poetry, ever abandons the force of the sensible for concept or reasoning? His "supreme truth" is praised, that rests in every particular of his representations and that does not exclude the use of "symbolism," that is, of particulars that are not found in nature, but signify what they must signify, and "give the impression of a most persuasive reality, although—or rather precisely because—not a word of them can be called faithful to nature." With this observation we come at the most to another confutation of the superstition about art imitating nature. His "Shakespearean totality" is exalted, wherein "a passion is like the common denominator of a principal figure, and that principal figure, for its part, becomes the common denominator of the drama": "totality," that is clearly synonymous with the lyrical character proper to all poetry, even to what is called epic and dramatic, or rather, narrative and dialogue. It is noted that in a certain sense almost all the tragedies assume "the form of a sonata" that carries its theme, the idea of the hero, in the middle "in close exchange and opposition with its counter-theme" and "in the so-called passages, develops the motifs of the theme in an harmonious and contrapuntally characteristic manner," while "in the third part, it resumes the entire theme in a more tranquil manner." And this other imagined technical merit is what has been called the "musical character" intrinsic to every art, which, like the "lyrical character," should certainly be emphasized against the materially figurative and realistic interpretation of artistic representations.

Similar observations apply regarding the "ideality" of "time" and of "place" that Ludwig discovers in Shakespeare and that are also found in every poetry where rhythm and structure always conform to measures, not arithmetic or geometric but simply internal and poetic; and regarding all the other things that Ludwig and the other critics take note of, like typicality, impersonality, constancy, which is at the same time variability, of the characters, and the like. These are all synonyms or metaphors for all poetry. It is true that at times we perceive that some of these things are noted precisely for the sake of differentiating Shakespeare from other poets, and they therefore take on a particular significance, the "truth" being then understood as Shakespearean "truth," his very own vision of things; the "constant-variable treatment of the characters" being understood as his sense of the indivisible bond between good and evil in every man; the "impersonality" being understood as his attitude of unsolved, yet energetic dialectic, and so forth. But in other such cases, we are no longer dealing with the form of Shakespeare, and rather as has been pointed out, with his way of feeling, with the motifs of his inspiration.

Only in one case do we manage truly to separate form from content and to consider it in itself, that is when we apply to Shakespeare, as to any other poet and artist, the rhetorical method, whereby form is abstracted and treated as a garment that covers or adorns the living body. In romantic rhetoric (for there was also a romantic rhetoric) the so-called mixture of comic and tragic, of prose and verse, the so-called "humorous" or "grotesque," the so-called "fantastic," the apparitions of mysterious and supernatural beings, and further, the way in which Shakespeare proceeds in the "exposition" of the play and handles the conflict and determines the catastrophe, the manner in which he makes the characters speak, the quality and richness of his vocabulary, were enumerated as "characteristics of his art" and as rediscoveries that others could take for their own use. From this, for Shakespeare as for other poets, also comes these misleading praises of his "ability," of his "devices," of his knowing how "to convey necessary information without appearing to do so," as if he was a calculator and constructor of devices for certain practical ends, and not a divine creative imagination. But enough of these matters.

Certainly one could take one or another of Shakespeare's plays, or all, one after the other and, having expounded them in their fundamental motif, as we have done, illuminate the aesthetic coherence of their representation and point out their subtleties part by part, scene by scene, stroke by stroke, word by word. One could, for example, show the robust and potent unity of the movingly tragic representation in *Macbeth,* which breaks forth and flows like a single lyric outburst, with full agreement of all its various tones, wherein the single scenes seem strophes: this from its opening with the speedy announcements of Macbeth's new victories and the joy and gratitude of the aged king, immediately followed by the fateful meeting with the witches and by the voracious kindling of Macbeth's resisted desire; to the arrival of the king, unwary and trusting, at the castle of ambush and death; and then to the darkening of the scene, to the execution of the assassination in the dreadful night; and slowly slowly to the crescendo of crimes Macbeth is drawn into, down to the uncoiling of the terrible tension in the furious battle and slaying of the hero.

King Duncan, arriving at the gate of the castle, serene and happy as he is over the victories that have brought peace to his kingdom, pauses to enjoy the caresses of the sweet air and to admire the pleasantness of the site; and Banquo echoes him, his soul delighting in its surrender to trustfulness and innocent pleasure as he recites an exquisite variation on the swallow, "This guest of summer, the temple-haunting martlet" that, everywhere along the walls of the castle, has made his "bed and procreant cradle," a "sign" as he has always observed, that "the air is delicate."[4]

In the ensemble of this short, tranquil conversation, there is sympathy for the kind old man, a shudder for what is in preparation, a painful, piteous irony. When crossing swords with Macduff, Macbeth is still bound to the last scrap of the witches' prophesy, which he believes propitious, but at that moment of disclosure that Macduff is indeed the man destined to overthrow him, he shudders and the first words that burst forth are: "I'll not fight with thee."[5] It is a violent shock, an instinctive exertion of the will to live that tries to evade destiny.

And we could pause over any part of *Othello:* Desdemona, for example, who intercedes for Cassio, with the sweetness and coquettishness of a woman in love, who knows that she is loved, and speaks like a child who knows that she has the right to be a little spoiled; or Desdemona at the moment of being slain, who does not give vent to the lamentations about slandered innocence, or behave with the dignity of a victim unjustly sacrificed, but rather, like a poor creature of flesh, who loves life, loves love, who for love has with childish egoism abandoned her father, she breaks into childlike pleas seeking to put away, to delay death at least momentarily: "Oh, banish me, my lord, but kill me not! . . . Kill me to-morrow; let me live tonight. . . . But half an hour! . . . But while I say one prayer!"[6]

Likewise, we could make one feel, if he does not feel it immediately by himself, the human fable-like character of *King Lear,* by analyzing the great opening scene of Lear and his three daughters, where, at the stroke of the poet's pen, this tale and these characters from legend immediately acquire a reality through the very force of our abhorrence at the dry egoism which is cloaked in words of affection, through the very force of our tender admiration for a real goodness that conceals itself and does not speak ("What should Cordelia do? Love, and remain silent.")

But actually this insistence on analysis and praise will be useful to those who, either because of habitual inattention or obstructing preconceptions, or little experience in the art, or even weak penetration, do not immediately feel by themselves. It will be suitable in school for teaching to read well and, outside of school for softening hard heads, which are sometimes the heads of literati; but it does not belong to our purpose, nor does it seem to us the chief task of the criticism about Shakespeare: one of the clearest, plainest, most comprehensible poets even to men of scant and elementary culture. We scan the many, prolix so-called "aesthetic" commentaries we have on Shakespeare's plays with impatience, as we would listen to someone who has set out to make you realize that the sun shines in the sky, and gilds the countryside with its light, and makes the dew glisten, and plays its beams amid the foliage.

On the other hand, it is not inopportune to recall that for a long time Shakespeare's merit as an artist was denied or disputed and that this was the general judgment of his own contemporaries, for by now we know what we ought to think of the words in his praise that are found in books of his time which, diligently tracked down and collected by scholars, were more or less deliberately misunderstood, their clear sense reversed. This amounted to a kind indulgence and condescending praise for a poet of popular art, approximately what we would now say about a lively and pleasing writer of romanticized adventures. Expressed in a different style, in a different time, this judgment reappeared in Voltaire's famous sayings, variant intonations, according to the mood, on the *barbare aimable,* the *fou séduisant,* the *sauvage ivre,* and the like. These, as is thought, have not lost their power, especially in France, where even recently (1914) a Monsieur Pellissier has blown them up into a large volume, coming to the conclusion that Shakespeare's work, "malgré tant de beautés admirables, est, à tout prendre, un immense fouillis," and that it usually resembles the work "d'un écolier, d'un écolier génial, qui, n'ayant ni expérience, ni mesure, ni tact, gaspille prématurément son génie abortif." And (something that deserves greater prominence) even a learned historian of English literature, Jusserand, discussing Shakespeare with great erudition, presents him as "un fidèle serviteur" of his theater-going public and speaks of his "défauts énormes." In his essay of 1801, Chateaubriand, playing the Voltaire on his own, credited him with "le génie" and denied him "l'art," that is, observance of the "règles" and of the "genres" which are "nés de la nature même;" but later he clearly recognized that he had made the mistake of "mesurer Shakespeare avec la lunette classique;" and with this he put his finger on the fundamental error of that kind of criticism, judging a work of art not by means of intrinsic reasons, but by other and different works of art, taken up as models. This same error was renewed even when French tragedy was no longer taken as the model, but the realistic art of the novel and of modern dramas instead. Here the principal document is Tolstoy's book, where at every word and gesture of Shakespeare's characters, he cries out that men do not speak like that—men, that is, who are not man in the universal sense, but the characters of Tolstoy's novels, who are, however, more like Shakespearean characters than their great but scarcely reasonable and not at all critical author thought. Tolstoy went so far as to prefer the popular and unpoetic play of *King Lear* to Shakespeare's *King Lear,* because there he found greater logic in the development of the incidents; and so he preferred the little prose tale to the sublime poetry.

An attenuated version of these judgments on the lack of art in Shakespeare is the theory defended by Rümelin better than by any others, arguing that his characters have much greater value than the plots or the actions, which are disconnected, broken up, contradictory, having neither necessity nor verisimilitude; that he worked scene by scene, without heeding or not having the strength to keep his eye on what had come before and what followed; that the characters themselves do not respect dialogical and dramatic truth in their speaking-tone, which is always fiery, fantastic, splendid; and, in sum, it could be said that he composed beautiful music for more or less disjointed libretti.

Now, if this theory had aimed to assert (even if emphatically and with exaggeration) that in a work of poetry the materiality of the fable, the fabric of facts, does not count and that what alone is valuable is the soul that circulates within it, just as in a painting it is not the materiality of the things portrayed that counts (what painters and critics of painting call the "literary element," that taken in itself, is extraneous and without importance), but the rhythm of the lines and colors, it would be just, at least as a reaction. Coleridge had already noted that in Shakespeare's plays, dramatic interest is independent of the plot and of the quality of the fable, which was drawn from the most ordinary and best-known subjects. But the intention with which Rümelin devised his theory, and as it is usually supported, aims instead to establish a dualism, a contradiction in the art of Shakespeare, a poet who would be "strong" in one capacity of mind and "weak" in another, yet both being "necessary" to generate perfect work. We must, therefore, firmly reject the admission of this dualism and non-existent contradiction, because the distinction between characters and actions, between style of dialogue and style of work, is arbitrary, scholastic, rhetorical; and in Shakespeare there is a single poetic current, the waves of which can be neither differentiated nor counterposed like characters and actions, discourses and dialogues, and the like. So true is this that we take no notice of these supposed contradictions, leaps, and improbabilities, except with a cold mind, that is, when we step outside of the poetic condition of the spirit and begin to examine what we have just read as the report of a past event. No more admissible is the charge brought against the speech of the Shakespearean characters, which is perfectly consonant with the nature of these poems, whence from the lips of Macbeth, of Lady Macbeth, and of Othello and of Lear emerge true and fitting lyrics that are not interruptions and incongruities in the drama, but movements and heightenings of the drama itself, not superimpositions of one life upon another, but the outpouring of the life located within the central motif. The often criticized jests, conceits, and puns in *Romeo and Juliet* are explained quite naturally, for the most part at least, by the character of the play, by the comedy that precedes and colors the ensuing tragedy and that is embellished with the language of gallantry and fashion.

With this we do not wish to deny that in Shakespeare's plays we encounter (besides the historical, chronological, and geographical errors, unimportant to the poetry, yet unnecessary and therefore avoidable and to be avoided) sayings, and at times entire scenes that are justifiable only for theatrical needs. However, we do not know to what extent they had the author's consent and to what extent they may simply be the consequences of a very confused tradition through which the text of his works was formed and came down to us. And we should not even wish to deny that he fell into minor lapses and contradictions, and that he was perhaps negligent in general. But it is useful, in any case, to understand and keep present the psychological root of this negligence, which lies in the sort of indifference and casualness that develops toward the easy perfecting of certain details when one is carrying out broad and weighty endeavors. A great spirit who resembles Shakespeare both in the full and harsh way he had of feeling life, and in the vicissitudes that touched his work and fame, Giambattista Vico also slipped often into mistakes and errors of details. He firmly maintained: "Painstaking accuracy must disappear in arguments that partake of greatness, because it is a minor thing and, being minor, it is a delayed virtue"; and he openly vindicated the right of excitement and heroic fury, both intolerant of delays in the small and the secondary matters.

Just as Vico was nevertheless most accurate in regard to essentials and did not spare the most persistent meditations in order to investigate his concepts thoroughly, so it is impossible to think that Shakespeare did not give the greatest and best part of himself to his plays, that he was not continually alert in observation, reflection, comparison, in scrutinizing his own feelings and seeking out and weighing their expression, in gathering and sifting the impressions of the public and of his colleagues in art, in studying, in sum, his art. The precision, the delicacy, the gradations, the shadings of his representations are direct and irrefutable proof of this study of his art.

Even those who admire him, usually deny him the sense of the classical, according to a partial and antiquated idea of the classical, made to consist in certain external regularities; but classical he was, because he has a force that is sure of itself, that does not force itself, that does not proceed by fits and starts, that carries its own moderation and serenity with it; besides, he had taste, taste that belongs to genius, that is commensurate with genius, because genius without taste is the abstraction of treatise writers. The rare places in which he happens, incidentally, to theorize on poetry prove that he had also meditated deeply on the activity that he exercized. In some famous verses of the *Dream,* he makes Theseus say that:

> The poet's eye, in a fine frenzy rolling,
> Doth glance from heaven to earth, from earth to heaven;
> And as imagination bodies forth
> The forms of things unknown, the poet's pen
> Turns them to shapes, and gives to airy nothing
> A local habitation and a name.

And

> . . . strong imagination,
> That, if it would but apprehend some joy,
> It comprehends some bringer of that joy,

> Or in the night, imagining some fear,
> How easy is a bush supposed a bear![7]

Namely, he demonstrates awareness of the creative power of poetry, poetry
that originates in the emotions and transforms them into figures that enclose the airy sentiment. But in another not less celebrated passage in *Hamlet,* he insists on the other aspect of artistic creation, on its universality, and
hence on calm and harmony; because what Hamlet above all recommends
in his speech to the players, is "moderation" and to acquire "in the very
torrent, tempest, and as I may say, whirlwind of your passion . . . a tem-
perance that may give it smoothness."[8] To take Shakespeare as representative of the art of disordered and raging outbursts, as has been done many
times, is to say precisely the opposite of truth; and in this regard, it is
useful to read the dramatic art of his contemporaries in order to measure
the difference, indeed the abyss that sets him apart. In Kyd's famous *Spanish Tragedy,* there is a scene (perhaps written by another hand) in which
Hieronimo asks a painter to paint the portrait of his son's assassin, and he
cries out: "There you may show a passion, there you may show a passion . . . make me rave, make me cry, make me mad, make me well again,
make me curse hell, invocate heaven, and in the end leave me in a trance;
and so forth." Then seized with doubt, he asks breathlessly: "May it be
done?" And the painter responds: "Yes, sir."[9] This was not the mode of
Shakespeare's art, which would not have been able to respond with "yes,"
but with a "yes and no" together.

His art was not, therefore, defective or faulty at any point of its constitutive character, although assuredly in the vast production that goes under
his name, as is obvious, we encounter works that are weak and parts that
are weak in his works. The works of his youth, *Love's Labour's Lost, The
Two Gentlemen, The Comedy of Errors,* are not notable except for a certain
ease and grace and bear traces of his profound spirit only in a few places.
The "history plays," for the reason already ascribed, remain fragmentary
and are not rounded off in poems animated by a single breath of passion;
and some, especially the first part of *Henry VI,* are dry and anecdotally
disconnected; others, like *Henry IV* and *Henry V,* permit purposes of patriotic edification to shine through and are weighted down by purely informative scenes; *Coriolanus,* composed later, it appears, and drawn from a
different kind of sources, also lacks full internal justification, being reduced
above all to a study of characters; *Timon* (assuming that it is his) is developed mechanically, even though social and ethical observations abound in it
and it does not lack oratorical warmth. *Cymbeline* and *Winter's Tale* have
very charming scenes but, taken in their entirety, are not works of the first
order, and the Shakespeare of tales and the idyllic appears somewhat deca-

dent in them in comparison to the author of the earlier plays of the same sort, which are animated by a different liveliness.

Measure for Measure displays profoundly Shakespearean sentiments and characters, in the protagonist Angelo, inexorable justician, sure of his own incorruptible virtue, who rushes into sin and crime at the first sensual temptation; in Claudio, who wishes to die and does not wish to die; and in the already mentioned Barnardine. But instead of being composed as a sarcastic-sorrowful-horrifying play, it oscillates between the tragic and the comic, with a happy ending, and it does not persuade us that it should unfold and conclude thus. There is something of the composite in the structure of the admirable *Merchant of Venice;* some scenes of *Troilus and Cressida,* like Ulysses's speeches and the contrasting one of Hector and Troilus, seem echoes or actual pieces of historical plays, transferred into a comedy of ironic intonation. Even in the major tragedies we can point to some things: in *King Lear* the adventures of Gloucester and his sons inserted among those between Lear and his daughters are not completely satisfying, either because they introduce an overly realistic element into the fable of the play, or because they form a multilateral parallelism (greatly admired by an Italian critic, who tried to reduce *King Lear* to a schema with a geometric configuration), a parallelism that perhaps owes its origins to the need for theatrical variation, complication, and suspension, rather than to the moral intention of giving emphasis to the horror of ingratitude. The fool, who accompanies the king, sometimes goes too far with expressions that are not all opportune and significant. But if the cutting up of the beauties of the Shakespearean plays has seemed superfluous and annoying to us, so in another way—pedantic and irreverent besides—does the investigation of the defects which are noted in them, and which are opaque points that the eye does not heed in the radiance of so much light.

Another judgment, also very widespread, seems to refer to a constitutive and general defect of his poetry and points out a limit or barrier in it, a narrowness, albeit an ample and rich one. About this judgment it is useful to distinguish two forms, the first of which could be represented by the epigrams of Platen[10] who, after recognizing Shakespeare's power to stir the hearts and energies of his characters, said that "so great a truth is a fatal gift," and that Shakespeare describes with such incisiveness only because he does not know how to elevate human miseries to the sphere of grace, so that in the end, he yielded to admiration for the comic figures, for Falstaff and for Shylock, an "incomparable pair," but he denied Shakespeare the true tragic dimension which "ought to open up the deepest wounds and then heal them anew." The second form of this judgment is the more common one and Mazzini can be taken as its representative, for he regarded Shakespeare as the poet of the real and not of the ideal, of the isolated individual and not of society, as not dominated by the concept of duty and responsibility to others and to politics and history, as a voice still out of the medieval period and not yet of modern times, of which, in drama, Schiller ought to be considered the initiator instead, the poet of humanity and Providence.

Even Harris's[11] book ends with a series of reservations: that Shakespeare was neither a philosopher nor a sage; that he never conceived a character who opposed and battled against his own times; that he had only a vague sense of those spirits by whom, in every epoch of history, humanity is transported to new and more lofty ideals; that he could not understand a Christ or a Mohammed; that, instead of studying it, he mocked Puritanism, with the result that he remained closed in the Renaissance; and that consequently, *Hamlet* notwithstanding, he does not belong to the modern world; that the best of someone like Wordsworth or Turgenev is beyond him, and so on. All things which can largely be admitted and may perhaps even serve to restrain hyperbolic and superlative expressions, like Coleridge's where he calls Shakespeare *anér myriònous [sic]*, a myriad-minded [ἀνήρ μυριόνους] man (although even myriad-mindedness can seem a most ample narrowness, if myriad is a finite number!)

Shakespeare could admire neither the ideal of Beauty that frequented the soul of the peevish, rough Platen, nor the humanitarian and social ideals of a Schiller and a Turgenev. But he had no need of that to attain the infinite, which every poet attains, arriving from any point of the periphery to the center of the circle; and for this reason no poet, whatever the historical context in which he is born and by which he is limited, is ever poet solely of one historical epoch; and Shakespeare, having been formed in the Renaissance, transcends it, not merely with his practical personality, but, precisely, with his poetry. Nothing remains, therefore, for those who would set limits on him but to manifest their dissatisfaction with the poetry itself, always limitless-limited. This, it seems to me, is what happened with Emerson, when he complained that Shakespeare (though in good company with Homer and Dante) "had settled for the beauty of things, and never took the step that seemed inevitable to such a genius of investigating the virtue that resides in symbols," and had converted "the elements that awaited his command" into an entertainment, supplying "half truths to half men"; where the whole truth for whole men can be given by a personage, whom the world still awaits, and who seemed very attractive to Emerson, but to others may seem perhaps as little lovable as some possible Antichrist: a personage, he denominated the "poet-priest."

11

Corneille's Ideal[1]

And yet, when we have demonstrated and concluded in this way,[2] the impression of the whole of Corneille's work remains that it has something of the grandiose, and it brings to our lips the homage that subsequent generations paid to the author, calling him "the great Corneille." No one, let us hope, will be deceived about the aim of our commentary up to this point, which is directed not against Corneille, but against the critics—indeed, not actually against those who have written many other beautiful and just things (and among the most recent ones we remember the shrewd Lemaître, the diligent and loving Dorchain, and, the most solid of all, Lanson), from whom we shall draw profit subsequently—but against their particular theories and presuppositions that are disfigurements of the very subject of judgment. The negative criticism that we have explained, does not inspire faith but makes us suspect its fallaciousness, or at least its incompleteness and one-sidedness, only for this reason: it does not explain that impression of grandiosity. From the way this criticism is presented, it would seem well suited to a writer who is splendidly luminous and fervent in rhetorical warmth, an able craftsman of the theatre, inwardly unmoved, light, and frivolous. But Corneille looks at us and those critics with so serious and severe a face that it deprives us of the courage to treat him in so unceremonious and so very hasty a manner.

Whence this serious and severe air, that is not only in his portraits but precisely in every page of his tragedies, even in those and in those parts of them where he does not strike his proposed target, or he appears tired, lost, and constrained? It comes simply from this: Corneille had an ideal, an ideal in which he believed, and to which he was bound with all the forces of his soul, and he never lost sight of it and strove to actualize it in situations, rhythms, and words, seeking and finding in the boldness and solemnity of those scenes and those sounds his own deepest satisfaction, the incarnation of that ideal.

This his contemporaries felt, and for this reason Racine wrote that, above all, "what was special to Corneille consisted in a certain force, in a certain elevation that astonishes and fascinates and makes even his defects, if there are some to reproach him for, more praiseworthy than the virtues of others'' and La Bruyère likewise pronounced that ''his most eminent possession was his mind, and that was sublime.''

The Corneillian ideal has been located by the most recent interpreters in will for its own sake, in ''pure will,'' superior or anterior to good or to evil, in the energy of will as such, apart from its particular ends. With this the false concept that described it, instead, as the ideal of moral duty and of the triumphant struggle between duty and the passions is completely eliminated; and agreement is attained not only with the reality of those tragedies, but also with what the author himself, theorizing, said in his *Discours* about the dramatic character, who in fact, like Cleopatre (in the *Rodogune*), can immerse herself in crimes, but (the author noted), ''all her crimes are accompanied by a greatness of mind so lofty that at the same time her actions are detested the source from which they flow is admired.''

Moreover, the concept of the pure will runs the risk of being perverted by certain interpreters who, proceeding to determine it further, identify it with the other will, the ''will to power,'' and they associate Corneille's notion with that of Nietzsche, who liked thus to understand and admire the French tragedian. The ideal of the will to power has entirely modern origins in the protoromantic and romantic superman, in excessive and abstract individualism, and it existed neither in Corneille's time nor in his heart which was very healthy and simple. In order to see the figures of his tragedies with such colors and gestures, we must look at them not through clear eyes, but through many-colored, distorting lenses, supplied by fashionable literature.

A further specification that, rendering the first conception more exact and authentic, at the same time closing the door on these new fantasies, is that this ideal does not grasp the pure will in the surge of its violent rise and actualization, but in its moment of deliberation and resolution instead, that is, insofar as it is a deliberating will. This Corneille truly loved: the spirit that deliberates calm and serene and, having reached a resolution, sticks to it firm and unshakable, as upon a ground laboriously conquered and fortified step by step. Here for him lay the highest force, man's greatest dignity. ''Laissez-moi mieux consulter mon âme,'' says one, and all Corneillean characters say and think and do this. ''Voyons,'' proposes the king of the Gepidi to the king of the Goths, in the *Attila,* ''voyons qui se doit vaincre, et s'il faut que mon âme / À votre ambition immole cette flamme, / Ou s'il n'est point plus beau que votre ambition / Elle-même s'immole à cette passion.''

Augustus long hesitates, after discovering that Cinna is plotting against his life; and he gives vent to anguished groans, as if to relieve his mind and to open it and dispose it to deliberation, which now begins, passionately, with anguish in the midst of his anguish. Has he the right to lament and be angry? Has he too not caused rivers of blood to flow? Therefore, let him resign himself in turn; let him yield himself up as a sacrifice to his own past. But no: he has a throne and must defend it, and therefore will punish the assassin. Yes: but when he will have shed more blood, he will be surrounded by new and greater hatreds and new and greater dangers. Better to die then. But why, die? Why not once more enjoy both vengeance and triumph? This is the tumult of indecision which, although felt as sharp and desperate torment, although seeming to hold the will suspended, in reality makes it move, insensibly guiding it toward its goal: "O rigoureux combat d'un cœur irrésolu!" The more truly deliberative process enters his breast with the entrance of Livia on the scene, whose counsel he resists, contesting and fighting it, and yet listening to it and pondering it. In the end, he still seems undecided, and yet he has already reached a resolution: he has already set his heart upon an act of political clemency— one so dazzling and thunderous as to stun and hurl his enemy, conquered, at his feet.

In the *Rodogune*, the two fraternal princes deliberate while they wait to have revealed to them, which of the two is the legitimate heir to the throne and at the same time, as a result of that revelation, which of the two will become the happy spouse of Rodogune, whom both love with equal ardor. How will they face, how will they bear the decision of fate? One of the two, uncertain and worried about the future, proposes to renounce the throne to the other, provided that he give up Rodogune; but the other counters with the same proposal. Consequently, their mutual satisfaction, through a reciprocal renunciation, is precluded. But the other way is also precluded, that of conflict and combat, because their brotherly love remains firm, firm too is their feeling of moral duty. This also prevents one sacrificing himself for the other, because neither of the two would accept such a sacrifice. What can be saved from a collision course out of which nothing, it seems, can be saved? After these various, vain attempts to escape the dilemma, one of the brothers, in self-reflection, descends into the depths of his soul and draws out the best course to follow and is the first to formulate the only solution: "Malgré l'éclat du trône et l'amour d'une femme, / Faisons si bien régner l'amitié sur notre âme, / Qu'étouffant dans leur perte un regret suborneur, / Dans le bonheur d'un frère on trouve son bonheur." And the other, not the first to perceive and take this course, "Le pourrez-vous, mon frère?" The first replies: "Ah! / que vous me pressez! / Je le voudrais du moins, mon frère, et c'est assez; / Et ma raison sur moi gardera tant d'empire, / Que je désavôuerai mon coeur, s'il en soupire." And the other, resolute in his turn: "J'embrasse comme vous ces nobles sentiments."

Loving the work of the deliberative will in this way (I have recalled only two situations in his tragedies, and could cite hundreds of them) Corneille did not love love, which is a thing that subverts deliberation, an illness that a man discovers in his body like a fire in his house, without having willed it and without knowing how it came. The deliberating ideal is sometimes surprised by it and is at least momentarily thrown into confusion. It then cries out like Attila: "Quel nouveau coup de foudre! / O raison confondue, orgueil presque étouffé!''; and he struggles against the enchantment of this "cruel poison de l'âme et doux charme des yeux.'' But usually he drives it out forthwith disdainfully and coldly, subduing it and employing it, availing himself of it as a means and aid in far weightier matters, ambition, politics, the State; or he accepts it to the extent that he is able to transmute it into a political and moral choice for whatever utility and worth it contains and as such, it becomes the object and fruit of deliberation. "Ce ne sont pas les sens que mon amour consulte: / Il hait des passions l'impétueux tumulte.'' Certainly this is an intransigent, ascetic, hard attitude: but so what? "Un peu de dureté sied bien aux grandes âmes.'' Certainly, love comes out of it diminished and humiliated: "L'amour n'est point le maître alors qu'on délibère''; but it deserves such a fate, and almost deserves the taunt: "La seule politique est ce qui nous émeut; / On la suit, et l'amour s'y mêle comme il peut: / S'il vient, on l'applaudit; s'il manque, on s'en console.'' Love manages as best it can and, under this pressure to which it is subjected, it becomes thin and marvelously pliable, ready to bend in whatever direction reason commands. Sometimes it remains suspended between two persons, like a scale that awaits an additional weight to tip it:

> . . . ce cœur, des deux parts engagé,
> Se donnant à vous deux ne s'est point partagé,
> Toujours prêt d'embrasser son service et le vôtre,
> Toujours prêt à mourir et pour l'un et pour l'autre.
> Pour n'en adorer qu'une, il eût fallu choisir;
> Et ce choix eût été au moins quelque désir,
> Quelque espoir outrageux d'être mieux reçu d'elle . . .

On another occasion it might have some desire, some inclination toward the one more than toward the other side; but it keeps this very secret, resolved to stifle it if reason should pronounce that it ought to love contrary to that inclination. One dares to tell Corneille's characters to their face not only "Il ne faut plus l'aimer,'' the sort of renunciation to ask of a saint, but also "Il faut aimer ailleurs,'' which is work to impose on a martyr.

He does not love love, but not, in sum, because it is love, but because it is passion, which carries one away and, if it were allowed, it would not agree to set the right terms of the debate, and to deliberate, which is confirmed by his objection to intoxication, both of hatred and rage that blind or confuse the sight, and that insofar as they are passions, are also foreign to his ideal, "Qui hait brutalement permet tout à sa haine, / Il s'emporte, il se jette où sa fureur l'entraîne /. . ./ Mais qui hait par devoir ne s'aveugle jamais: / C'est sa raison qui hait. . . . " The characters of his ideal, facing a hostile man, sometimes declare: "Je te dois estimer, mais je te dois haïr."

Conversely, we clearly perceive why Corneille admired and loved the will even when devoid of moral light, indeed, when it worked outside of morality and against it—the will that however has the merit of not yielding to the passions and of dominating them; of not being a violent weakness, but a force, or, as it was called in the Renaissance, a *virtú*. In this sphere of deliberation, there was a common ground between the honest and the dishonest man, between the hero of good and the hero of bad, both obeying, each in his way, one duty, both in agreement on opposing the follies of passion and in despising them.

And we can also see why the domain toward which Corneille turned his glance and fixed upon as his predilection had to be politics, where *virtú*, in the meaning that it took in the Renaissance, had the means to unfold freely and to be enjoyed for its own sake. In politics one finds oneself continually in difficult and contradictory situations; here shrewdness and farseeing skills have their value; here the calculations of interests and of the passions of men; here one needs to weigh things precisely, and energetically put what is decided upon into action; to be prudent and firm at the same time. It was noted jokingly by William Schlegel that Corneille, a most just and honest man, was, in his political cogitations and representations, more Machiavellian than any Machiavelli, and he paraded the art of deceiving; but with all that he had no feeling for practical politics, which is much less complicated and more pliable and skilled; and even Lemaître admitted that in this regard, he was "fort candide." But who does not go to excess in the things that he loves? Who is not in these things, at times, too candid—with that candor or simplicity that grows hand in hand with enthusiasm and faith? His very inexperience in real politics, the oversimplification and exaggeration with which he imagined it, serve to confirm the vigor of his affection for the ideal of the political in which for him that of the deliberating and pondering man was condensed and heightened. How he always returns in his thought and on his lips to *raison d'état* and *le maximes d'état*! Words and formulas that (we feel it clearly) arouse him, edify him, and transport him into an ecstasy of admiration.

Free determination and full submission to reason, duty, objective utility, and advantage—and not at all the spirit of courtly adulation—led him to regard high-placed personages and those at the peak of the pyramid, the monarchs, with the same ecstasy of admiration. He did not admire them at all because they can do all, and much less because they can enjoy all, but, on the contrary, because through position, discipline, and tradition, they are accustomed to sacrifice their private desires and to act upon higher motives than personal ones. Even kings have a heart, even they are open to the sweet snares of love; but they, better than every one else, know how they should conduct themselves. " . . . Je suis reine et dois régner sur moi: / Le rang que nous tenons, jaloux de notre gloire, / Souvent dans un tel choix nous défend de nous croire, / Jette sur nos désirs un joug impérieux, / Et dédaigne l'avis et du cœur et des yeux." And elsewhere: "Les princes ont cela de leur haute naissance, / Leur âme dans leur rang prend des impressions / Qui dessous leur vertu rangent leurs passions; / Leur générosité soumet tout à leur gloire." They love, yes, as happens to all, but not for this, like the vulgar, do they yield to the allurement of the senses. "Je ne le cèle point, j'aime, Carlos, oui, j'aime; / Mais l'amour de l'État, plus fort que de moi-même, / Cherche, au lieu de l'objet le plus doux à mes yeux, / Le plus digne héros de régner en ces lieux." His predilection for history had the same root (especially Roman history which, through a long process of idealizing elaboration—already evident in the imperial period, but still more in the Renaissance and post-Renaissance, and even in the schools of the Jesuits—had been transformed into an exemplary history of civic virtues, of sacrifices and heroic deeds, of self-willed grandiosity). That this predilection was entirely different from—indeed, opposed to—historical knowledge and to the so-called "historical sense" we shall avoid demonstrating, because this question, along with the eulogies to Corneille as an "historiographer," are now to be considered out of date.

With these outlines and clarifications we have sufficiently indicated or at least sketched out, the historical connections of the Corneillean ideal, its background and genesis, which is to be sought, as we have said, on the one hand in the theory and practice of the Renaissance bearing upon politics and upon the office of the sovereign or prince; and on the other, in the ethics of stoicism, that had wide use in the second half of the sixteenth century, in France no less than elsewhere. In our fancy, Corneille's image is surrounded, almost as a natural complement to it, by all those volumes with Baroque historiated frontispieces, which then saw the light in every part of Europe, from the moralists, the Machiavellians, the Taciteans, the counselors in the art of courtly conduct, and by the Jesuit casuists: Botero and Ribadeneyra, Sánchez and Mariana, Valeriano Castiglione and Matteo Pellegrini, Gracián and Amelot de la Houssaye, Jean Louis de Balzac and Naudé, Scioppio and Justus Lipsius—in short, we would say, by an entire conspicuous section among those that compose the library of Manzoni's Don Ferrante, the "intellectual" of the seventeenth century.

Such literature and the very history of the times (from the religious wars to the Fronde upheaval) have been opportunely and often remembered with reference to the poetic inspiration that is Corneille's own, and, in truth, they spontaneously come to mind to anyone who is informed about the particular thought and the particular customs that were dominant in the various ages of modern society. It is regretable, therefore, that through annoyance with the obvious and only, in this case, true explanation, some people have fished to find different and remote origins for it in an obscure racial or regional determinism, pointing out "an energy" in Corneille "that comes from the North," that is, from the Germanicity that produced Luther and Kant, or even from the country once occupied by his Norman forebears, the Scandinavian pirates who landed under the leadership of Rollo; or more prosaically (if this fancy is personal to Lemaître, all repeat it), finding the character of his poetry in the subtlety and litigious spirit of the Norman, and of the lawyer or magistrate that he was.

Nor is there much truth to the usual association between his ideal and Descartes' theory (of whom, moreover, chronological incongruence would in any case preclude derivation or repercussion), it being possible at the most to concede that there were common elements in the one and in the other, both deriving from one same source of culture, from the already mentioned moral stoicism, and in general from the cult of wisdom. In Descartes, as later in Spinoza, the tendency was toward the overcoming of the passions by means of the intellect or pure mind, which by knowing them and thinking them, dissolved and dispersed them, whereas in Corneille, the overcoming was to be completed entirely through the force of will. Corneille's *raison* has an emphasis quite different from Descartes', which was not pondering and deliberating reason, but illuminating reason, so that he, and not the tragedian of *Cinna* and *Rodogune,* was the spiritual master and the symbol of the new century.

The historicity of the Corneillean ideal does not signify that its value is restricted to the author's time and must be considered to have set with the passing of its customs and doctrines, because every period expresses human and eternal truth in historically determined forms, and strongly highlights particular aspects or moments of the spirit. The idea of the deliberative will has been able, in different times or in this age in which we live, to withdrawn to a place of secondary import, almost losing itself in the background, superseded by other forces, and other more urgent aspects of reality; nonetheless it preserves a perpetual vigor, and returns perpetually to the mind and heart, thanks to the philosophers and poets and thanks to the very interlacing of life, that makes us feel again its importance and beauty. The efficacy with which it is endowed is attested by the history of customs, of patriotism, of the moral and military spirit in France, which found and still finds one of its supports and one of its propelling forces in the Corneillian tragedies. By means of these, like the tyrannicides of the Renaissance by means of Plutarch's *Lives,* the heroic, tragic Charlotte Corday trained her own feelings, actualizing in her own person one of those willful figures, ready to take every risk, one of those "aimables furies," whom her great

predecessor had with so much satisfaction described on paper—pages that
Napoleon contemplated with admiration for that ideal world, that world of
his own thoughts, his own deliberations and resolutions, with the result that
he considered Pierre Corneille as his own poet, and the poet of the age
which he believed he had opened, in which classical "fate" was replaced
by "politics." It seems inconceivable that one would compare and confuse
creatures like these, with their sublime, yet pondered volitional force, and
men like Bonaparte, with impulsive and weak beings, admired by the philosophers and artists of the "will to power," from Stendahl to Nietszche,
who readily took the wretched inmates of prisons as their model.

   The entire life of Corneille, all his long work was dominated and
governed by the ideal here described, with a constancy and coherence that
is luminously clear to anyone who examines it in its particulars. As a young
man he struck various chords—the Senecan tragedy of horrors (*Médée*),
bizarre comedy (*L'illusion comique*), romantic drama of adventure and
spectacle (*Clitandre*), comedies of love and intrigues; but even in these
works, and especially in the comedies, we discern numerous signs of the
tendency to portray the will in its particular modification as well of purpose and choice. After his novitiate (in that period that partly includes
Le Cid, which is more an attempt than a realization, more a beginning
than an end), he proceeded straightforward with ever greater resolution and
awareness.

   And it is a prejudice, born from an extrinsic or certainly not very
acute consideration, to put a separation between the *Cid* and the later
works, as Schlegel, Sainte-Beuve, and many others, foreigners and French-
men have done and to complain that Corneille thereafter abandoned the
Spanish medieval and chivalrous genre, so suitable to his generous, grand,
and imaginative inclinations, and so promising for future Romanticism, and
that he locked himself up in the Greco-Roman world and in political tragedy. About *Le Cid* (as we have already demonstrated in passing), it is impossible to establish its originality and beauty so long as it is placed in
comparison with the Spanish drama, and with the model that Guillén de
Castro directly provided for Corneille; and if not precisely beauty, a sort of
originality is certainly discoverable in the Corneillean element that corrodes
the popular epic-like quality of the model and replaces it with a study of
deliberating situations. These, harmoniously versified, explain in great part
the luck that the drama met in a society that was accustomed to debating
the "questions of love" (as they were called from the period of the trouba-
dours to the Renaissance), along with those about honor and chivalry, about
challenges and duels; but on the other hand, the reason for its luck indubi-
tably derived from what persisted in it, here and there or vaguely, of the
ardor and tenderness of the original play, which moved the spectators and
made them fall in love with Chimène: "Tout Paris pour Chimène a les yeux

de Rodrigue." And yet those tender words and those powerful expressions, beautiful taken in themselves, are felt as somewhat foreign in the play's new form; and there is some truth in Klein's bizarre remark: that "in that atmosphere filled with exhalations from the *antichambre,* there is not enough Cidian electricity, not enough material of electric-dramatic insults to produce a slap of such pathetic force and consequence" as the *bofetade,* that, in the Spanish drama, the Count Lozano impressed upon the face of the decrepit Diego Laynez. And there is even some truth in the judgment of the Academy that the subject of *Le Cid* is "defective in its essential part" and "improbable"; to be sure, not because this was so in Guillén de Castro's version or that a subject or raw material can in itself be good or evil, probable or improbable, poetic or unpoetic, but because it had become defective and discordant in Corneille's elaboration and refinement. Rodrigue, Jimena, the lady Urraca are simple souls, spontaneous, almost childish, characteristically popular-heroic types; and Chimène, Rodrigue, and the Infanta are reflective and dialectical spirits, and, since their new psychological attitude does not well accord with the former behavior, at times Rodrigue and the father seem conceited charletans, Chimène at times even a hypocrite, and the Infanta insipid and superfluous. Even when in the *Don Sanche d'Aragon,* Corneille returned to the "Spanish genre," he loaded it with reflections, ponderings, and deliberated resolutions, and he did not aim at the picturesque, as later the romantics did, but at dialectic and subtlety. That all this regarded from another angle, also represents an improvement must be recognized: not in the artistic effect obtained, but in mentality and culture, in a more advanced and more complex humanity.

Thus the *Cid* should be considered truly a work of transition, transition to the *Horace* that to one German scholar, seemed substantially nothing other than *Le Cid* itself, revised after the criticisms of his adversaries and of the Academy, which Corneille, in the depths of his being, felt to be just, at least to a certain extent. But it is also prejudice to place a disjunction between the four so-called principal tragedies, the *Cid,* the *Horace,* the *Cinna,* and the *Polyeucte*—"the great Corneillean quadrilateral," eulogized in Péguy's rambling prose—and the later works, as if in the succeeding plays Corneille had changed his manner and had taken to pursue a new ideal, "political tragedy." Setting aside for now the question of greater or lesser artistic value, it is certain that substantially he never changed his manner; that in the *Horace* there is not at all a sense of the fierce patriotic sanctity of a primitive society; in the *Cinna,* there is not the dreamed up tragedy of satiety or lassitude, with which the blood-thirsty Augustus had been seized; in the *Polyeucte* there is no shadow of the fervor, of the rapture and fanaticism of a nascent religion, but, as Schlegel well said "a firm and constant faith rather than a true religious enthusiasm"; that in these four *le cœur* does not reign, whereas in the later plays only *l'esprit* reigns, but in

all these—in some more, in some less—there is already "political tragedy," in its essential sense of a representation of calculations, deliberations,
resolutions, and often too in the more visible sense of affairs of state. And
not withstanding the disfavor of the public and the critics who wanted other
things, such forms of representation continue, unheeding, firm, and obstinate, going ever more deeply into themselves, divesting themselves of extraneous elements, arriving at the perfection that had been aimed at from
the beginning; as can be seen in one of the very last, in the *Pulchérie,*
about which the author congratulated himself for its partial success or the
shadow of success that it had achieved, declaring that "it is not always
necessary to follow the infatuations of the time to get listened to on the
stage"; and a little earlier, he was pleased with Saint-Évremond's approval
of the secondary place assigned in the tragedies to love, "a passion too
burdened with weakness to be the dominating one in a heroic drama." Voltaire was struck by such constancy of development, and in the conclusion of
his commentary he felt constrained to note, not without amazement and
against current opinion:

> He wrote very unevenly, but I do not know if he possessed an uneven
> genius, as it is said; because I see him always, in his best works and
> in his worst, intent on the solidity of the reasoning, on the strength
> and profundity of the ideas, almost always more given to argue than
> to excite, rich in expedients even in his most unrewarding arguments,
> but in expedients often scarcely tragic, selecting his subjects badly
> from the *Oedipe* on and inventing intrigues, but little ones without
> warmth and without life, and in his last works seeking to delude
> himself.

But he did not delude himself; on the contrary he knew himself, and he, the
author himself, was a personage who had deliberated, and, once and for all,
had resolved himself.

The vigor of this resolution and the conciseness of the work that came
out of it are not diminished but, on the contrary, gain prominence from
noting that Corneille possessed other aptitudes and sources of inspiration,
of which he made no use, or very little, and neglected. Certainly, the poet
who, collaborating with Molière, versified the delightful *Psyché,* would
have been able, if he had wished, to engage in the graces of those
"doucereux" and "enjoués" that he despised. And among his scattered
poems there are witty, tender, and melancholy ones. In some parts of the
paraphrase of the *Imitatio,* as well as in some other moral and sacred composition, there is a religious afflatus that is lacking in the *Polyeucte;* in the
comedies of his youth, there is an observation of life that is filled with

emotional participation, and they foreshadow what will later be bourgeois drama. We refer in particular to some characters and scenes of the *Galerie du Palais,* the *Veuve,* and the *Suivante*; to certain figures of marriageable girls, amenable to the decisions of their parents, and of mothers who still carry in their hearts how much that submission had once cost them and do not want to abuse the power they now have over their daughters; and to certain tremulous meetings of lovers who have been separated and who, in the bliss of their effusions, are annoyingly interrupted by the arrival of their parents and friends, that is, by prosaic reality ("Ah! / mère, sœur, ami, que vous m'importunez!"); to certain psychological dispositions, odious and painful, like that of Amaranthe, the poor girl of good family, who, having been given as a companion to a girl who is rich, but not superior to her either in attractiveness, or in spirit and grace, or in blood, burns with envy and works against her covertly to separate her from her betrothed, and, finally defeated, hurls bitter words against society and pours out venomous maledictions.

"Curieux," "étonnant," "étrange," "paradoxal," "déconcertant," say the critics from time to time about the character of Alidor, in the *Place Royale*; and Corneille himself, in the critique he later wrote of his work, called him "extravagant." And "very Corneillean," "pure Corneillean" everyone has judged that radical lover of his own liberty who, being in love, fears love because it threatens to take away his inner freedom; and therefore he deceitfully seeks to throw his lady-love, who adores him, into the arms of another, but he does not succeed, and, left at last by the lady herself who becomes a nun, instead of being grief-stricken, or at least mortified, he rejoices at his good fortune. In fact, not withstanding this late epithet "extravagant" that he plants on him, he does not jeer at him in the comedy; he does not condemn him; he does not criticize him. And, indeed, in the dedication—addressed to an anonymous gentleman, who could even be himself—he approves of the theory that is represented in Alidor. "From you I have learned," he writes, "that the love of an honest man must always be voluntary; that one must never love to the point where one cannot not love; that if one reaches such an extreme it is tyranny, and one must shake off its yoke; and that, finally, our beloved must be more obligated by our love when it is the result of our choice and of her merit, than when it comes from blind inclination, forced by some ascendent at birth which we cannot resist." But the confused performance and perplexity that this play gives rise to, have their origin in this, that Corneille had not yet succeeded in repressing and suppressing spontaneous affections, and for this reason he casts the creature of his ideal among characters who have softer limbs, warmer and more tumultuous blood, and who love, suffer, and despair, like Angélique. These would have nullified that ideal or rendered it extravagant, if the poet for his part had not thought it through and felt it as entirely serious and positive. In its every part the play is run through by a fine fault line and it lacks fusion and unity in its fundamental motif. This, without doubt, is a grave defect, but a defect that increases the evidence for the psychological proof it offers, of the absolute power that the ideal of the deliberating will was gaining over Corneille.

12

In Goethe's *Faust*

Wagner, The Pedant[1]

I confess that I harbor a certain fondness for Wagner, the *famulus*, the assistant to Doctor Faust. I like his candid and boundless faith in science, the honorable ideal of a serious scholar, the simple rectitude and unaffected modesty, the reverence he shows and the unfailing gratitude he preserves unaltered for his eminent master. His taste for tranquilly unrolling parchments, his aversion to crowds, to shrill noises and street organs, to promenades and excursions, his preferring above these things, to withdraw in the evening to his little room amid books and ink-stand, to read, meditate, and take notes touch my heart. And I feel disarmed by his little weaknesses, which all combine in his desire of one day meriting the admiration of society, praised as a scholar, consulted as a wise man. And I do not have the heart to reproach him for his way of judging and arguing everything with phrases and maxims drawn from common opinion, because how could I reprove him for what is the very reason for his living and working?

Certainly, Wagner is irritating (though he is not to blame) to anyone whose disposition is the contrary of his, just as the sight of calm and satisfied sanity is unbearable to one who suffers from nerves, or the sight of prosaic happiness is to one who is being tossed about by the hurricanes and tempests of the passions. And he becomes unbearable to Faust who, at certain moments, almost even fears him; fears that face, that voice. And he never speaks to him except with impatience, annoyance, and sarcasm. These are not really dialogues that Faust carries on with him, for Wagner never understands, nor does Faust hope at all to be understood by such a listener. But the one wishes only to vent his ill-témper against the universal lie and against himself; and the other is all intent on increasing the treasure of judgments and counsels that he has already gathered from his master, and he drinks in Faust's words with devotion, with mouth gaping, without any one of the concepts that these express passing effectively into his brain, where it runs up against the barrier of those sensible maxims. The one pursues his feverish inner monologue in which the other takes part only by casting into its midst unwitting, discordant phrases, that are so many pricks and goads to his agitated, struggling, fuming master, whose haughty and deprecating replies again seem to the disciple, nothing other than a "so gelehrt" discourse, so erudite, and, as such he is not confounded, but admires them!

However open Faust's disdain, sarcasm, and contempt may be, Wagner does not notice, and cannot notice; so far is he from suspecting that his own virtuous ideal of science and of intellectual absorption should present any ridiculous side, and so much is his reverence for the great man, whom fortune has placed at his side, that it submerges and drowns in him the self-love which ought to render him sensitive to these pricks. And you do well, poor Wagner, with your ingenuous dignity and your affectionate dedication, to listen deferentially and not to feel wounded! Faust is really always a philosopher and a man, and his ferocity toward you is entirely intellectual. Pay attention to what you do, if you decide to take a wife; for if you do not make certain to choose one of those timid, silent creatures, whom Jean Paul[2] frequently couples with his learned maniacs, if instead a Faust in skirts should turn out to be your companion, a titaness, a Valkyrie, you will no longer get simple, albeit stinging, philosophic lashes across your face, but you will feel (and you do not deserve such a thing) that you are entirely enveloped in aversion, hatred, nausea: as in fact will happen to one of your colleagues, the diligent researcher, the historian Tesman, who will get the bright idea of marrying Hedda Gabler![3]

Many times critics have had the idea of comparing the Faust-Wagner pair with Don Quixote and Sancho Panza; but really there is nothing of Don Quixote in Faust, and in Wagner there is very little of Sancho Panza. If anything it is really Wagner himself who has something of Don Quixote and, in a certain sense, he *is* the Don Quixote of the old science. For Wagner's ideal is neither more nor less than the humanistic one conjoined with the Baconian: the devoted study of ancient histories in order to draw from them maxims and prudential rules, both political and moral, and the investigation of the laws of nature for purposes of social utility. An ideal that precisely at the time of Goethe was dissolving, being worn away by skepticism about naturalistic and abstract methods; by scorn for arid erudition and pragmatic reflections, replaced or being replaced by a revived Augustinian zeal to *redire in se ipsum*, to search the heart and intellect of man; by a new feeling of the religious mystery of history; and by a new heroic and rebellious ethic. Wagner has no inkling of this movement of thought, which seethes about him and upsets his master's heart. He is chivalrously loyal to the science that is by now antiquated, and he dreams as the highest good, a library rich in codices and parchments, a cabinet with many natural curiosities and instruments for observation and experiments, a medical art that kills patients by all the rules inscribed in books, and, for his own appearance in the world, upon a professorial chair, an acquired dexterity in the use of persuasion and the rhetorical *actio*. The insatiable desires, the vertiginous dreams of the superman are disturbances that, thank heaven, he has never experienced; even if (as he amiably says) "he too, at times, had his hours of fancy," precisely as Don Quixote had around him a little of the real world in his maid-servant and his niece.

I would say that the pleasure that is always renewed when we reach the pages in *Faust* where Wagner enters upon the scene must be equalled only by the rage that grips his master at that point.[4] An amusing character enters upon the scene, and with what an entrance, so entirely worthy of him! Faust is still hot and trembling from his brief, excited conversation with the Spirit of the earth, quickly conjured and vanished; and Wagner, who had heard the sound of voices and, simple as he is, believes that the master himself was declaiming a Greek tragedy, and declares his desire to make some progress in the art of declamation. And, like this entrance, every slightest stroke of the two conversations he holds with Faust is a marvel of brilliant naturalness, of a perfect fusion of the serious with the comic. The figure of the pedant was not new in literature, and all remember the satirical rough sketches of rusty scholastic disputants that Erasmus sketched, the Ciceronian humanists in our sixteenth-century comedy, the old, fanatical Aristotelians in the philosophic polemics of Bruno and Galileo. But those representations were satire, or rather criticism in its negative aspect, developed with witty eloquence or, at the most, caricatures and not poetry. Poetry is at times barely grazed, but not felt or taken up, as in Bruno's Polihimnio, who is "a Jupiter who from the heavenly observatory looks down at and reflects upon the life of other men, subject to so many errors, calamities, miseries, useless labors," and "he alone is happy, he alone lives the celestial life when he contemplates his divinity in the mirror of a miscellany, a dictionary, a Calepino,[5] a lexicon, a Cornucopia, a Nizzolio[6]. . . . " But Goethe, like every true poet, does not want to hear about satires or encomiums, nor about deep black or raw white, and he loves only the play of lights and shadows, knows only humanity, humble or grand as it may be; and the pedant, ridiculed by the polemicists of the sixteenth century, the pedant whom writers of comedies, in their rage to heap every sort of abuse upon his patient back, frequently end up by attributing to him the qualities of a pederast and thief, becomes in Goethe's fantasy, an idyllic creature, rich in virtues, at times even interesting and moving. What does it signify to call a character good or bad, virtuous or vicious, wise or foolish? These are abstractions, because the terms thus separately taken are abstract; and, though the aestheticians are in the habit of affirming that the perfectly good and virtuous characters are not poetic, we must explain and add that the perfectly vicious and wicked ones also are not, surely not at all because of an artistic demerit of virtue or vice, but because such perfection as one would wish to represent in one or other opposing one-sidedness ia a dead thing, an abstraction. And in truth, who can ever say which of the two, Faust or Wagner, is right? Who can assign complete wrong to the two-fold intellectual limitation of the one—the cult of the science that desiccates the origins of life and of science itself—and complete approval to the opposite two-fold limitlessness of the other, and his desperate, mad drive to conjoin and exhaust both criticism and life, both science and sensual delight in a single act?

In his particular form, Goethe's Wagner, the humane pedant, admirably suits the modern sentiment of the unity of opposites, of undivided humanity that has had a long, varied, and honorable progeny, to which belong among the latest representatives, some of the small figures Anatole France used to lightly sketch, as Silvester Bonnard, a member of the Institute, who, before committing himself to protecting and marrying off the good girls, also unrolls parchment, with "magnanimous ardor," expecting from those modest labors the arrival of "I know not what, mysterious, charming, and sublime" thing.

So sentimental is the good Wagner, and so sweet an affectionate vein travels through his breast that, when conversing with his master, his accents become lyrical—not with the sublime lyricism that soars from the lips of the other, but precisely, with an idyllic lyricism, now content, now plaintive:

> Wie anders tragen uns die Geistesfreuden
> Von Buch zu Buch, von Blatt zu Blatt!
> Da werden Winternächte hold und schön,
> Ein selig Leben wärmet alle Glieder,
> Und, ach! entrollst du gar ein würdig Pergamen,
> So steigt der ganze Himmel zu dir nieder.[7]

Or else:

> Wie schwer sind nicht die Mittel zu erwerben,
> Durch die man zu den Quellen steigt!
> Und eh'man nur den halben Weg erreicht,
> Muss wohl ein armer Teufel sterben.[8]

And he is pleased above all in admiring and savoring images of glory, the glory of the scholar:

> Welch ein Gefühl musst du, o grosser Mann,
> Bei der Verehrung dieser Menge haben!
> O glücklich, wer von seinen Gaben
> Solch einen Vorteil ziehen kann!

Der Vater zeigt dich seinem Knaben,
Ein jeder fragt und drängt und eilt,
Die Fiedel stockt, der Tänzer weilt.
Du gehst, in Reihen stehen sie,
Die Mützen fliegen in die Höh',
Und wenig fehlt, so beugten sich die Knie,
Als käm' das Venerabile.[9]

On reading these cadenced verses, we seem to catch the manner, between enraptured and sorrowful, of someone savoring a mystic joy and feeling full of noble envy, the ecstatic aspect Wagner must have worn in pronouncing them, keeping the high and low notes of a voice well practiced in rhetorical delivery through the apostrophes, the exclamations, and the pompous descriptions.

Even a dog enters this idyll, the poodle that has placed itself behind Faust and in which the *famulus* notices nothing extraordinary; but, since his master appears to take some interest in it, Wagner is unable to deny the dog a little benevolent consideration, and so he offers it the homage of an aphorism and the caress of a compliment and, in a manner of speaking, elevates it, placing it in their very family, in the academic world:

Dem Hunde, wenn er gut gezogen,
Wird selbst ein weiser Mann gewogen.
Ja, deine Gunst verdient er ganz und gar,
Er, der Studenten trefflicher Skolar.[10]

A personage, so individualized and alive in the two scenes of Part One, Wagner does not lose his artistic vitality, not even among the allegories, the caprices, and oddities of Part Two, in the scenes with the Homunculus. On these, commentators have written many subtle things that turn out to be of very slight importance, precisely because, if one must resort to hermeneutic subtleties, it is a sign that these representations do not speak for themselves, and their idea (assuming that they have an idea) does not coincide with form. Nevertheless Wagner, now "Doctor Wagner," having become a celebrated, resplendent singular light occupying a professorial chair, surrounded by a dense throng of scholars, provided in his turn with a *famulus* called Nicodemus, has not allowed his head to be turned by his acquired fame; and he still venerates the memory of his old teacher and master, who vanished unexpectedly in some manner that is incomprehensible to him, and he has preserved his study intact with his hood still hanging upon its nail, and he hopes for and still awaits his return. He (says Nicodemus) will not admit, not even in fun, that his name can obscure that of Faust, of the sublime man. "Modesty is his allotted part." And then after

having distilled the Homunculus and heard it prettily call him "papa," he
sees his little creation turn wholly to Mephistopheles, quickly come to a
complete understanding with him, and announce its immediate departure
for the Pharsalian fields, in the company of his two associates: "And I?"
the poor man, who feels himself abandoned, cries out in anguish. "You,"
the offspring of science answers mockingly, "you shall remain here to ac-
complish great things, and you will reach a glorious destination. Farewell."
To which Wagner, resigned but moved:

> Leb' wohl! Das drückt das Herz mir nieder.
> Ich fürchte schon, ich seh' dich niemals wieder.[11]

Even in the midst of the chilling allegories, his eyes glisten with humane
tears.

13

Marcel Proust

A Case of Decadent Historicism[1]

The historical conception of reality is a profoundly religious and moral conception, the only one that is equal to the idea of religion and morality.
Determinism and fatalism do not affect or threaten it, because in it necessity turns out to be nothing other than an aspect of liberty itself. We can
never leap outside the course of history to reach a reality above or beyond
ourselves; hence history which, having happened, takes on the character of
logical necessity, is, in the actuality of its becoming, a continuous creation
of liberty. Nor is omnipotent time, lord of men and gods—mathematical
time that divides and mechanizes the single course of history—the frame
within which history moves, enclosing and dominating it, as popular
thought believes; but, on the contrary, history is time's frame and contains
it as the instrument that history shapes to its own use. The life of reality
engages all the work of the spirit in its complexity and in its unity as
thought and as action, as truth and as goodness; it is perpetual increase and
it is gain in perpetuity that remains after death, because nothing of what we
truly love, will, and value dies, and what dies of ourselves is solely our
transient suffering and enjoying, the pulse that is resolved and dissolved in
the eternal. Knowledge, which is always essentially historical knowledge,
unfolds itself in terms of moral life because out of history—so immense
within us—we make ourselves from time to time aware of those series of
facts which, as the objects of a particular need to know, are bound to our
new and particular need to act. Without moral stimulus we do not have a
reality historically thought out, an historical knowledge.

Now with these and similar propositions in mind, which after long
elaboration have become familiar to me, it may be imagined with what
mixed and curious feelings I read, now more than twenty years ago, the
volumes of Marcel Proust's *À la recherche du temps perdu,* about which at
that time there had arisen a great deal of debate and discussion including
astonishment for the writer's originality, endeavors to interpret and to define the new philosophy that he seemed to offer, investigations into the relations that bound it to Bergson's philosophy and to Einstein's physics, and
a bold affirmation that, the idea of time now having been re-formed by

Proust, the modern novel should assume an entirely different perspective in its narratives. Without allowing myself to be stunned by this admiring out- cry, nor seduced by these announcements or hopes for a philosophic and aesthetic revolution, it seemed to me that the true sense of Proust's work had not been grasped, because to grasp it required firm possession of the aforementioned concepts, without which one could not perceive that Proust's theory altogether was a flashing glimpse into, and at the same time an impoverishment and debasement of, the vision of reality as history.

The taste of a little biscuit dipped in a cup of tea or the unexpected sound of a doorbell are enough to stir, to rouse the mind, and to start the re-evocation of past events, the *recherche du temps perdu*. Seeking to hear that inner sound more near at hand, that bell that tinkled within, Proust writes,

> c'est en moi même que j'étais obligé de redescendre. C'est donc que ce tintement y était toujours, et aussi, entre lui et l'instant présent, tout ce passé indéfinement déroulé que je ne savais pas que je portais. Quand il avait tinté, j'existais déjà, et depuis, pour que j'entendisse encore ce tintement, il fallait qu'il n'y eût pas eu discontinuité, que je n'eusse pas un instant pris de repos, cessé d'exister, de penser, d'av- oir conscience de moi, puisque cet instant ancien tenait encore à moi, que je pouvais encore le retrouver, retourner, jusqu'à lui, rien qu'en descendant plus profondément en moi. C'était cette notion du temps incorporé, des années passées, non séparées de nous, que j'avais l'in- tention de mettre si fort en relief dans mon œuvre.[2]

Thus he describes the process that moves from the impression of a present to the reconstruction of a past; but with this difference in respect to the genuinely historical process just mentioned and briefly outlined: whereas in history, the point of departure is a moral need that seeks to shed light on the past in order to designate the action it has to carry out, and the satisfaction of that need is an act of thought, resulting in a judgment or series of judgments; in Proust, the point of departure is a sentiment of com- mingled pleasure and pain that awakens a sequence of like images, which were already bound to it when it first arose in his mind. We could represent the difference with the figure of the man who, preparing for action, works with his thought and, in contrast, that of the man when he gives himself to rest, to relaxation, to indolence, and to the amusements of indolence. In the second case what takes place is the simple hedonistic satisfaction of a phys- iological need, which is not a mental process, precisely because it is not at the same time a moral process. Confirmation of this is the ignoble material, the so-called good society—that "good society" which Goethe abhorred and considered unsuitable for inspiring poetry—of which Proust's reconstructions are composed, his *temps retrouvé,* and which is held together with no other unifying principle than the very obvious one of a prevailing sexual restlessness. The truly human drama—the drama of the man who strives in the creation of the spiritual world—is not in Proust's mind and not in his pages. For if he happens to mention it, he denies the causes that generate it, or, finding himself somehow in their presence, he is led to explain them as remnants of habits of a former life, which means denying them as effective forces and components of the only life that is lived and known.

> Tout se passe dans notre vie comme si nous y entrions avec le faix d'obligations contractées dans une vie antérieure; il n'y a aucune raison dans nos conditions de vie sur cette terre pour que nous nous croyons obligés à faire le bien, à être délicats, même à être polis, ni par l'artiste cultivé à ce qu'il se croie obligé à recommencer vingt fois un morceau dont l'admiration qu'il excitera importera peu à son corps mangé par les vers.... Toute ces obligations qui n'ont pas leur sanction dans la vie présente semblent appartenir à un monde différent fondé sur la bonté, le scrupule, le sacrifice, un monde entièrement différent de celui-ci, et dont nous sortons pour naître à cette terre, avant peut-être d'y retourner revivre sous l'empire de ces lois inconnues.[3]

His imaginary "anterior life" would be the world of the spiritual category, empty, because lacking the material of the terrestial world, and this, a blind world because it would move without spiritual afflatus—a separation of the world of the idea from the world of facts. This is a philosophic absurdity that the author does not formulate in these precise terms, precisely because he does not notice that what he says is absurd.

The sentiment that this decadentist vision gives rise to in him is of servitude, oppression and despondency, quite the contrary of that which the genuine vision of history excites in men sound of mind and heart, who from their historical visions draw counsel and comfort, the spirit of emulation, the courage to act:

> J'éprouvais un sentiment de fatigue profonde à sentir que tout ce temps si long non seulement avait sans une interruption été vécu, pensé, secrété par moi, qu'il était ma vie, qu'il était moi-même, mais encore que j'avais à toute minute à le maintenir attaché à moi, que j'étais juché à son sommet vertigineux, que je ne pouvais me mouvoir, sans le déplacer avec moi.[4]

Instead of a stronger inner unity, of an increased energy of the self, he feels dispersion and downright disintegration.

Mon amour pour elle n'avait pas été simple: à la curiosité de l'inconnu s'était ajouté un désir sensuel et à un sentiment d'une douceur presque familiale tantôt l'indifférence, tantôt une fureur jalouse. Je n'étais pas un seul homme, mais le défilé, heure par heure, d'une armée compacte, où il y avait selon le moment, des passionnés, des indifférents, des jaloux, —des jaloux dont pas un n'était jaloux de la même femme.[5]

Nothing remains but the torment of recollection, to which death alone can put an end.

Et c'est parce qu'ils contiennent ainsi les heures du passé que les corps humains peuvent faire tant de mal à ceux qui les aiment, parce qu'ils contiennent tant de souvenirs, de joies et de désirs déjà effacés pour eux, mais si cruels pour celui qui contemple et prolonge dans l'ordre du temps le corps chéri dont il est jaloux, jaloux jusqu'a en souhaiter la destruction. Car après la mort le Temps se retire du corps et les souvenirs—si indifférents, si pâlis,—sont effacés de celle qui n'est plus et le seront bientôt de celui qu'ils torturent encore, eux qui finiront par périr quand le désir d'un corps vivant ne les entretienne plus.[6]

It has been said that the catharsis of this tragedy, the solution to the problem that Proust proposes, is art, wherein alone life grows calm and becomes bright again. In effect, Proust persuaded himself that his search for time lost was art and poetry: "Or la récréation par la mémoire d'impressions qu'il fallait ensuite approfondir, éclairer, transformer en équivalents d'intelligence, n'était-elle pas une des conditions, presque l'essence même de l'œuvre d'art telle que je l'avais conçue tout à l'heure?[7] But, in its theoretical regard, this is not a definition of art, precisely because, as has already been observed, it is a definition of a process that is not contemplative but practical, of a true unburdening of the nerves by means of the imagination; and, with regard to Proust's own work, whatever the fine and subtle observations in it, the well analyzed and well described nuances and complications of sentiment, I find it difficult to feel poetic afflatus in it. A fact little noted, but of great importance, is the very slight and almost nonexistent development that the concept of historicity and the theory of historiography have had in French thought and literature. In this connection it is worth referring to the beginning of an article by Anatole France, "Les torts de l'histoire," written sixty or more years ago, in which the antihistorical French and Cartesian tradition is ingenuously commemorated:[8]

Les philosophes ont, en général, peu de goût pour l'histoire. Ils lui reprochent volontiers de procéder sans méthode et sans but. Descartes la tenait en mépris. Malebranche disait n'en pas faire plus de cas que des nouvelles de son quartier. Dans sa vieillesse, il distinguait le jeune D'Aguesseau et le favorisait même de quelques entretiens sur la métaphysique; mais un jour l'ayant surpris un Thucydide à la main, il lui retira son estime: la frivolité de cette lecture le scandalisait. Avant-hier encore, étant assez heureux pour causer avec un philosophe dont l'entretien m'est toujours profitable, M. Darlu, j'eus grand' peine à défendre contre lui l'histoire, qu'il tient la moins honorable des œuvres d'imagination.

And he goes on in the article to praise a book "tout à fait solide et puissant," the unfortunate *L'histoire et les historiens* by Bourdeau where, while denying truth-value to all histories, the author points out a safe exit from that world of fable and frivolities by substituting "statistical facts taken from ordinary life" in its place, a positivistic corollary to Cartesian antihistoricism. To this France raised no objection other than a plea of grace for the books of the narrative historians, because they speak to the imagination and are exciting or entertaining. When I think of those, and there are many, who once reasoned and still reason with ideas of this solidity (Valéry among our contemporaries, who has also had his say about history), I feel no rush to react, because truly, in regard to their mental outlook, to me they seem men *penitus toto divisi orbe*; and, in their far-off unattainable dwelling place, they seem content with themselves and happy, and rid of the assaults of doubt, persuaded that they move in the clearest light of truth, so that it is not possible to establish relations with them and engage in exchanges of ideas.

The only moment favorable to the formation of a more serious and profound concept of history occurred in France in the age of the Restoration, a golden age for this widening and reinvigoration of the French spirit under the influence of the German thinkers and of the Italian Vico. But that good beginning came to naught after a few decades, and was never renewed. And when some necessary premise of historical thought was proposed, as in Bergson's critique of the ordinary idea of a falsified and spatial time, it was not developed in the theory and logic of history, because Bergson stopped at his so-called "intuition" and never went up to the speculative concept and to its dialectic, and because his very culture was, and has remained, naturalistic in origin and foundation, and antihistorical or ahistorical. Bergson's philosophy of intuition, not treated as *fermentum cognitionis* but accepted dogmatically as conclusive *per se,* pleased the decadent literati, among them Proust who, without realizing it, made of the noble matron that is history, of the educator with stern thought for stern action, a sort of wanton hussy, a procuress of rare and exquisite excitations for jaded nerves.

14

Poe's Essays on Poetry[1]

Edgar Allan Poe's *Three Essays* on poetry, well printed, well translated into Italian, and well introduced and presented by the translator Elio Chinol (*Le Tre Venezie,* Padova: 1946) have brought me the joy that comes from beautiful things. But an unpleasant encounter befell me a little later in Yvor Winters' book, *Aspetti della letteratura americana* (French translation, ed. du Chêne, Paris: 1947),[2] where I read a violent and contemptuous diatribe against Poe as critic, short story writer, and poet.[3] I have always esteemed Poe among the rare spirits who profoundly penetrated the nature of poetry, even if the logical formulation of his doctrine may now appear insufficient to us. Chinol on his part confirms this reservation. For him as for me this does not signify censure, but is a means of opening the way to his thought in the minds of those who, too rigidly observing or rather believing to observe logic and system, reject or discard truths that are truths, both original and profound.

"But how," one may say "are the affirmations that a thought is true and at the same time logically not correct or indeterminate ever reconciled? Does not truth perhaps coincide with logic itself, and can it ever stand without it?" No, it cannot stand without it; nor in the case enunciated above, is this in question. We are dealing instead with a more simple, but fundamental consideration, which usually is not taken up or is forgotten: that is, that every truth must begin through the stimulus of doubt and as a response to a problem, and all truths, being born this way, are connected among themselves, and are continually increased and are forced to reforge their connection by the intervention of new truths; and this process that continues to infinity and weaves together the history of truth (or of philosophy, so to say), gives way to the appearance that there are incomplete or confused truths, whereas our every truth is perfectible, that is, our every truth is to be completed and clarified with other truths that are possessed, or will arise in other spirits, or in our own. Pedantic brains, and in reality impoverished and lazy ones that regard their concepts definitive and conclusive, reject or are reluctant to accommodate new truths or those of others, and to introduce them among their own and previous ones; but critical minds are always prepared for this, and indeed have highly developed in themselves a sort of sentiment or intuition that makes them quick to notice in the prop-

ositions that come before them whether they are the velleities of the ignorant and unreflective, and thus to be discarded immediately, or the real
thought of a spirit who has embraced the truth and from this embrace, obtained the enthusiasm and the warmth to affirm it to himself and to others.
Following common terminology, this will be called the thought of a non-
philosopher or of an unconscious philosopher; but these are modes of
speaking, if not professionalistic self-conceits, and this thinking is indeed
of a philosopher; and the non-philosopher Poe must be read no differently
than a Vico or a Kant, accepting and continuing the work he initiated in
conformity with new reflections.

For example, Poe denies that poetry should inculcate a moral and expound philosophical and historical truths, and he says that poetry's end is
poetry itself.[4] It is a denial that could and should have been formulated in
these terms in his time and that even today has not wholly lost its reality,
even if we are not overly keen to argue against the enslavement of poetry
and of all art, as desired by the old or by the new "totalitarianisms" and
disdain taking such absurdities seriously that by now are all too evident and
gross. But we can develop Poe's statement with another that could seem to
contradict it, but actually integrates and validates it: that is, that poetry
does not need to accept philosophy and morality into itself as ends proper to
it, because they are things that it already has in itself, in its contemplation
of the drama or the tragedy of the world, where thought and morality, cosmic powers, operate; hence the truth and purity of beauty, and the catharsis
it induces in particular and contending passions.[5]

Another example: seeking to determine in a direct and positive way
the true character of poetry, Poe distinguishes it from philosophy, which is
and must be simple, precise, lucid in its expression, without flourishes,
severe and hard, whereas he locates poetry in the elevation of the mind
seeking to attain supreme beauty, in a struggle toward the infinite that it
never reaches; hence the veil of melancholy which surrounds it.[6] But in
this, notwithstanding that he seems only to speak of a sentiment of longing
and that he is ignorant of or ignores the character of the truth—non-
philosophical truth, but truth—of poetry, still he does not fail to have a
presentiment of it in this same interior elevation that he describes with
lively images. Certainly, he did not notice that the striving toward the unattainable Infinite, as in poetry, also belongs to philosophy and to the practical and moral life, and that in every one of its spheres the human spirit
obtains only "a part of that Grace" (as he says) whose true elements belong, perhaps, only to eternity, and that from this the question about the
proper and distinctive character of this elevation in the sphere of poetry
logically arises.

The translation from one truth to, not indeed its negation, but its integration, is seen even better in observing another of Poe's theories, where

for the first time, or for one of the first times, a great and fruitful truth about aesthetics and about art criticism is enunciated, but he does not succeed in disengaging it from peculiar determinations of a quantitative nature; that is, that a poem must be short, to be read or sung within a short span of time, its intensity unable to endure for a "long" period of time. The simplism of the introduction in this part, on the criterion of time, where he is unable to determine the measurement of the short and of the long, becomes almost childishness when he adds the admonition that, moreover, the time must not be overly brief and that in every case it must not exceed a half hour at the most.[7] But why did Poe ever involve himself in these wild fancies if not because his heart was set on that great truth, we are alluding to, hidden away and in fact resisted by traditional aesthetics and criticism, which were superstitiously tied to the idea of the poem and the long poem, whether narrative or theatrical, as the highest form of poetry, whence the inferiority in which they held what was called the genre of the lyric (which, only with difficulty and through the work of some sixteenth-century Italian writers of poetry, was finally placed beside the other two, the epic and the dramatic): the truth, that is, that not everything in epic poems is poetry, and that the unity which in these is often praised and sought-after is not organic, but mechanical and allows the real and living unity of the poetry to escape? Accordingly, in a clear and vigorous manner Poe said that the great poems, beginning with the Homeric and passing through the classical and those of the Renaissance, up to *Paradise Lost*—all of which adopted the Homeric design—either carry in their bosom many extraneous things or are lyric sequences unified under one title.[8] A truth that, not without much resistance and scandal, has triumphed, lastly in the aesthetics and criticism of our day, thanks to the differentiation and distinction between "structure" and "poetry." And so little does this distinction have to do with material length or brevity that it may be found in a *canzone,* a sonnet, or madrigal as readily as in a so-called epic, or romance, tragedy, or comedy.

Conscious as I was of these great merits of the theorist and critical Poe (who had his predecessors in Coleridge, and in other sensitive spirits and acute minds, and, besides, was well acquainted with the earlier critics, including Italians, and cited pages of Boccalini and Gravina), one can imagine with what feelings I took up the diatribe of Winters, who, being truly ignorant of the problematic nature of these studies, with great assurance raises objections that appear so superficially dazzling and powerful as to blind and prostrate his adversary and abolish his stupidity. He says that Poe excludes human experience, or, rather, experience of the "moral life" from poetry, and gives it a "subject matter of an essentially supre-human order that the poet cannot in any way confirm"; that for Poe, poetry is "nervous excitation"; that (in the essay on Bryant) he even dares to affirm, as something self-evident, that "a satire cannot be a poem"; that in proposing beauty as the principle of poetry, he has ignored or has not understood that the "matter" of poetry is the "truth" and that, though there is "beauty" in poetry, it is only the "vehicle" of the "personal conception that the poet makes of a moral truth," and that the conception is what is essential, "whether it be embodied in the form of description, or of narration, or of exposition"; that in qualifying the severity and harshness suitable for philosophical exposition, Poe conceives of it as that of a lawyer or even of the disputant Thomas Aquinas, but not at all like that of the contemplator Dante; and in his essay on Horne, he does not even grant him the merit of having excluded passionality from poetry;[9] and with all this, he concludes that Edgar Allan Poe is "explicitly an obscurantist."[10]

As one sees from this definition, the author is an antiromantic, and of the antiromantics, quite a number recently have surfaced in America (I recall Irving Babbitt), to join the French antiromantics, the Maurrases, Lasserres, and Seillières—a polemic in which I would rather not enter, conducted as it is without any exactness of method or distinguishing of concepts; and therefore adhering to the theory of art, I restrict myself to noting that Winters does not even have a distant suspicion of the principle of art as truth of the intuition, the foundation of aesthetics and modern criticism. If one wishes to call this principle "romantic," let him say it, but it goes back beyond the romantic age; it was already outlined in Italy in the seventeenth century; it was vigorously validated by Vico; it gained prominence with Leibniz and his school; with Baumgarten, it gave a name to Aesthetics, and in the romantic period it is found wandering everywhere yet without being clearly conceived with conciseness and deepened philosophically. A great step forward was carried out only in Italy with De Sanctis, who explained art as "form," form not at all the dress of content, but rather content itself transfigured; however only after long and persevering work (this too mostly Italian) did this principle come to constitute a *doctrinal corpus* as part of a philosophy of the spirit. Winters instead—lucky him—still regards the "content" of art as moral concept and "beauty" as "manner" or "form" that adorns this content;[11] that is, he stands by the theory of rhetoric and literature, which is not the theory of poetry; and with this old or extraneous conception he claims to defeat the brilliant Poe, who, from profound inspiration, worked toward the new direction. When I published my aesthetic, there was more than one English and American writer who recalled Poe's similar thoughts (among others, see A. Ransome, *Edgar Allan Poe*. New York, pp. 120, 122), and I was happy because that similarity spoke to my mind and to my heart.

Of the three essays on poetry, only the first, "The Poetic Principle," is truly important, and I have referred almost exclusively to it; whereas the second, "The Philosophy of Composition,"[12] sets forth the process by which, through reflecting and searching, a poem may be constructed part by part and is not, it seems to me, exempt from a certain psychological illusion. In effect, the reflection can precede and can follow the discovery of the single forms; but these forms are created solely by the poetic power, or rather by the intuitive-expressive act to which, in regard to both talent and taste, the first and final word belong. The third essay, "The Rationale of Verse,"[13] is by nature not aesthetic but practical and prosodic, concerning the method of scanning verses, and therefore avails itself of such empirical concepts as quantity, accent, tonic syllables, atonic syllables, and the like—concepts so extraneous to poetry that, as is known, a verse can be entirely impeccable metrically, but equally ugly.

Poe, the short story writer and poet, is dispatched by Winters with the statement that premises his diatribe: that for a long time, "in the eyes of his friends and contemporaries, Poe was considered a bad writer, who owed his popularity to a fleeting accident"; and with the hasty demonstration of this thesis which he gives in his concluding pages.[14] Here, however, I have preferred to limit myself to his judgment regarding Poe's aesthetic theories, judgment that is mistaken even if Poe the short story writer was a "bad writer;" art and criticism, poetry and philosophy, being things independent of one another. But since, on the other hand, sound theory and sound criticism are strictly related to one another, it seems to me that Winters' judgment may not be very promising for the reader who expects to be guided by him in the interpretation of Poe's art.

15

Ibsen[1]

All of Ibsen's heroes and heroines are strained with expectation, consumed by the yearning for the extraordinary, the sublime, the unattainable, scornful of idyllic happiness in any form and degree and of virtue modest and resigned to its own imperfections. Hedda Gabler despises and scorns her hard-working, good-natured, and mediocre husband, and his old aunts, saintly women. She won't stand to hear even the slightest allusion to domestic life, children, and to obligations of any kind. She shrinks from unhappiness and adultery, as from matters equally common and vulgar; and yet she feels that she is drowning in the commonplace and the vulgar, and, looking about her, she is bored to death, because although she has no scruples about what means to use, she in vain seeks in the world for "something free and courageous, something illuminated by a ray of absolute beauty." Ellida's soul, undulating like the sea, is ever turned seaward, yearning for her native land and for the man from the sea, unknown, possibly criminal who one day approached her, spoke to her, and bound her to him, casting their engagement rings upon the waves. Nora, during the eight years of her married life, has patiently awaited the "miraculous," which alone would have given sense and flavor to the monotonous course of ordinary events, marriages, children, mundane relations; and since she had secretly committed a tiny falsehood in order to cure her husband's weakness, her heart beats at the thought that if the falsehood were discovered, her husband learning of it, will rush quickly forward to protect her, will take the blame upon himself, and will happily sacrifice all that he holds dear—well-being, social position, reputation, honor—for her who erred out of love for him. Rebecca West gets into the Rosmers' austerely religious and conservative ancestral home, desiring to conquer the last family survivor by the spell of her looks and her arts, and to make him the instrument of her own ambition and fortune in the struggle against old ideas, in which she engages for the sake of liberty and progress. Rita marries Allmers in order to possess him, all of him, jealous of his sister, of the studies he engages in, even jealous of their little son, with such fury of rapacious passion that at times she is afraid of herself.

And the men? Solness wants to be the only builder of churches, houses, towers, putting all others down or subjugating them to himself as assistants and workers, suspicious of the young men who can advance and steal the chief place from him, and he attempts the "impossible": suffering from vertigo, but mastering himself, he tries to climb to the pinnacle of the tallest tower he has built, in order to raise the inaugural wreath there. Rubek has renounced life to create art and now is consumed in a disconsolate drive to attain the rapture he had allowed to slip away. Borkman dreamed of getting into his hands all the sources of power and, under his yoke, all the treasures of the ground, the mountains, the forests, and the seas through his banking operations, in order to satisfy and gladden many thousands of men and, having slipped in his rush to power, having fallen under the penal code, been imprisoned and rejected, in solitude, he stands firm in his faith and waits daily for people to come to beg him and to plead with him to place himself at their head once again. Gregers Werle's dream is made of other stuff: to destroy the lies, the hypocrisies, the illusions, on which men ignobly rest their heads, as upon a soft cushion, to found upon the truth, the truth bravely unveiled and settled, a new life of forgiveness, of reciprocal help, and redemption.

And though these examples are drawn from the plays of his last period, that is, of Ibsen's maturity, we are not to believe that the same inspiration does not rule in his earlier plays, because between both the earlier and the later there is great variety in forms and in artistic merit, but no diversity of substance. Except in artistry, Ibsen underwent no true and distinct development—neither intellectual nor emotional—no profound changes or conversions; and anyone who has tried to create the history of his spirit, has been constrained to move continually over the same ground, because he finds before him, whether youth, adult, or old man, always the same soul, with its ever-present and unchanging desire for the extraordinary and the sublime. We go back to Peer Gynt, who goes about, he says, to actualize his "Gyntian self," that is "the army of wishes, appetites, desires, the sea of whims, pretensions and demands," all of what appropriately "swells here within my breast and by which I, myself, exist."[2] We go back further to Brand, obsessed by the idea of duty, duty for duty's sake, of this ultra-Kantian duty so pitiless and cruel to the very man who exercises it; Brand, whose motto is: "all or nothing," and who, with the overbearing energy of his character, tears Agnes from the side of the man who loves her, endows her with his hard faith, and allows her son to die for this faith, allows Agnes herself to die, tramples upon every one of his personal emotions, but never his own higher self, his inexorable will, which sees no alternative beyond all or nothing. And from Brand, we go back still further to the history play, *The Pretenders,* where, if the central figure, King Haakon is a *pius Aeneas* refashioned according to the ideas of German philosophy of history (having reached Ibsen in a direct or indirect way), among those surrounding him are characters of blazing passion, of mad desire, the

Duke Skule and, markedly, the terrible figure of the Bishop Nicholas. Or consider the poet Falk in *Love's Comedy*, with his ideal of love that overturns every barrier and that *omnia vincit*, and his declared war against lies and hypocrisies. And in a play of an entirely different kind, in *The Vikings in Hegeland*, we note the pathos of almost all the characters, but above all of Hjördis, who is Hedda Gabler in barbaric form and barbaric society, or rather in her true form and in the society appropriate for her.

This drive toward the extraordinary and the sublime is never realized or satisfied except as self-destruction, that is, as tragedy. It is obstructed by the surrounding reality, or rather, by mean and base men, by the laws, by society; and what is worse, by the very failings in the hero, his past sins, his present weaknesses, the impediment that rises from the depths of his being; and perhaps these two orders of obstacles reduce to only one, to the second, because, as Ibsen obscurely feels, the hero, who is not able to work upon society cannot be its superior, not even being its equal. In Peer Gynt, the fault is evident, but we may discover it even in Brand who, with horror, rejects ordinary prudence, and, after drawing the crowds for a while, he is abandoned and finds himself alone on the mountain, and a phantom appears to him and cries out: "Die then! The world can find no use for you!"[3] He feels that Jesus has slipped from his hand like a word he cannot recall; and when, at last, he questions heaven to learn whether a firm unshakeable will is enough to save him, he hears the answer that God is the "God of love!"[4]

Thus all are guilty: Solness who has created his own glory, sowing pain and unhappiness about him, sinning, if not by actual deeds, then by the force of a culpable desire that forces events; Borkman, who, in order to win power, renounces the woman who loved him and whom he loved, and fans the flame kindled in a kindred soul; Rubek, who likewise sees in a woman nothing more than lines for his sculpture, not realizing that those lines enclose a being of flesh and blood, a creature who loves the man in him, who, rejected or uncared for, is consumed with passion and survives as a spectre; Gregers Werle, who, with the arrogance of a reformer and ideologue manhandling the delicate fabric of life, pulls away some little pieces in order to be rid of lies, and disfigures the entire fabric, and, instead of redemption and purification, brings death upon whatever he touches; Hedda Gabler, who passes from mischief to mischief, from crime to crime, and, when she believes that she has caused a ray of absolute beauty to shine in the world, a "beautiful death," she realizes that she has not succeeded in preparing and inspiring anything other than the most trivial and unaesthetic of deaths in the house of a prostitute, by a wound in the belly; Ellida, who breaks her promise to the mysterious man, in order to marry another who has rescued her from misery and abandonment and thus prefers prosaic comfort to her poetic idol; Nora who allows herself to be dressed, cherished, and caressed like a doll and dreams about the "marvelous" that must lie ahead, neglecting to develop herself as a human being having duties and rights and never seeks to carry out the necessary effort to know herself and others; Rita who, in order to give herself over to the power of her unbridled love out of her egoistic desires to possess Allmers exclusively, has twice neglected and hurt her little boy in thought and deed, and has lost him, and, with him, has lost Allmers' affection and exhausted in his heart the bloom and pride of first love; Rebecca who, with her calculating ambition, has allowed herself to stray from her love for Rosmer, though she has driven his wife to her death for this love and, when left alone with this man, has little by little, in accord with his spirit, allowed herself to be won by honesty, by the pure moral force that radiates from him, so that now she can no longer love, neither impurely, because she has purified herself, nor purely, because of her past sin; and thus she has shut herself off from two possible types of happiness—the turbid, acrid happiness of the senses, and the sweet happiness of the heart.

Some of these and other Ibsen characters are saved by renouncing their senseless longing, like Ellida, the woman from the sea, who, by an act of free choice, refuses to follow the mysterious man who has returned to take her with him, and by so doing she attains peace and enters the circle of ordinary life. The Allmerses, parents of the little drowned Eyolf, about whom they feel guilty, propose a new life, dedicated to the well-being of abandoned waifs. Nora abandons husband and children and withdraws in order to meditate alone about herself and about reality, which until now she has neither understood nor sought to understand. Consul Bernick (in the *Pillars of Society*) publicly confesses his offense and attains the sublimity of expiation by condemning himself to a civil death. Gregers Werle, the calamitous moralist, and Mrs. Alving who, out of respect for the law and for human respectability, put up with her dissolute husband and endeavored to feign a respectable memory of him, remain desolate—the one with a broken, disunited family, deprived of trust and affection, before his eyes, and the dead body of a poor girl who, unable to endure estrangement of the one who she believed to be her father, has committed suicide; and the other with her son, heir to his father's disease, beside her, who must swear to administer a poison to him so that he will not outlive his approaching insanity. Desolations, these forerunners of death; but the majority of Ibsen's characters do not delay in awaiting death and meet it resolutely. Brand once again ascends the mountain, and there, as he asks the Lord for light on the work he has undertaken, an avalanche sweeps him away. Peer Gynt, at the conclusion of his wanderings and adventures, the realization of his Gyntian Ego having failed, must rest his head upon Solveig's breast—Solveig, the eternal feminine, a sort of Gretchen, who has always awaited him—and die. Solness climbs his tower in order to set the garland there, and, no sooner having done so, he is seized by vertigo, falls, and is smashed upon the ground. Hedda Gabler, having driven Løvborg to suicide, in order to destroy the only one who, to that day, had given her a feeling of the extraordinary and from whom she hopes for the excitement of the "beautiful death," becomes aware that her secret doings have become known by another man, who keeps watch on her, lusts after her, and now holds her fate in his hands, kills herself. Borkman and Rubek allow themselves to be guided gently to their deaths by the women whom they had abandoned; and, hand in hand, Rebecca West and Rosmer throw themselves into the torrent—she purified and no longer having the right to love, he who now loves her, but can join her only in death, marrying her before dying. Thus the expectation of the sublime is always disappointed in both its forms, as satanic sublime and as divine sublime, as sensual passion and as ethical passion: in the first form, because it conflicts with moral conscience; and in the second, because this conscience sins or has sinned against itself.

Poetry of despair, if there ever was such, and not of pessimism about the pleasure that whithers and the life that passes, but the pessimism that is the conscious impossibility that man can ever achieve the end that his own nature impels him to propose for himself or makes him to desire to propose. And, as we have said, Ibsen is fixed in this state of mind; the incidents and depictions change, but his life closes with the nostalgia and the delusion with which it had opened. His own moral character never becomes near and familiar to us like those of other great poets, because he never descends to our level, loving the simple things that we love, loving imperfectly as we do, suffering and enjoying like us. He sees all through his own lenses of a single color, and never with the colorless or variously colored panes through which we, the rest of humanity, look. But if his psychological attitude is constant, his art, as we have also said, develops, grows, and perfects itself. In his first period, Ibsen adopted forms of existing models, the historical drama of the Romantics, the philosophical, humorous, and ironic drama of the same school, the forms of Schiller, Goethe, Byron, and their Scandinavian imitators, who looked to the Germans for literary examples. *Peer Gynt* is influenced by the second part of *Faust* and is caught up in the difficulties and illegitimacies of that style; *Brand* is an incessant flow of powerful eloquence, but also redundant and verbose; the structure of other plays, like the *Love's Comedy* and *The League of Youth*, does not depart very far from that of the French comedy *à thèse*. This is not to say that we do not discern the lion's claw everywhere, especially in *The Pretenders*, but also in *Peer Gynt*, of which the scenes of the trolls and of the mother's death are justly admired, and very beautiful is the oration the priest pronounces over the grave of the man "whose hand had only four fingers"; and in *Brand*, where there is such austere emotion in the figure and speech of the hero and such anguish in the figure of his companion, Agnes, who has lost her son and does not dare to accuse the man who has let him die in order to remain faithful to an appointed duty. In *The League of Youth* there are profound moments, and the secondary figure Selma is clearly a precursor of Nora in *A Doll's House*. Anyone who studies Ibsen in detail is able to see these signs and allusions multipled and to better recognize the unity of his inspiration. But it is certain that only after 1875 did he fashion his own original form, particularly with *A Doll's House* and *Ghosts*; and this form is further perfected and is made pure after 1883, beginning with *The Wild Duck* and with *Rosmersholm,* which is already, in my opinion, his masterpiece. One might say that then his mind became completely disillusioned and despairing, and this is not so, because it was always so; but without doubt it did take fuller possession of his disillusionment and despair, which was not so much a moral change as a deepening of his art, or rather, a clearer perception of his own sentiment. He did not see clearly enough and did not take it sufficiently into account in *Peer Gynt,* where the representation unfolds in the outlandish, satirical, and playful form of the second part of *Faust*; nor did he in *Brand,* where the protagonist, on the contrary, is seriously, positively conceived as a hero and the action of which, even before reaching the catastrophe, unconsciously poses a critique of his conception and his character and reveals the chink in his armor, an error into which Ibsen rarely fell afterwards; and perhaps only in the character of Dr. Stockmann, the "enemy of the people," about whom, as about Brand, there remains some doubt as to whether the poet wishes to depict a hero or a fanatic, a profound spirit or an obtuse one, a character who tends toward the sublime or toward the grotesque. The true Ibsen is the Ibsen who is able to represent altogether, fused, the desire for the extraordinary, the sin that corrupts it, the renunciation, the desolation, and the death that awaits it; and to represent them in a form of his own.

This form is generated by a sort of monologue, by an impassioned monologue that is inconclusive and, insofar as it is inconclusive and split up and argumentative, it is dramatic: with the exception of a few lyrics, Ibsen wrote nothing but plays, so much was dramatization for him spontaneous, natural, and necessary. And his dramatic creations are moments and features of his very own spirit, that is, of such a spirit as we have described, wholly absorbed in the desire for that happiness that is attainable by attaining the sublime and the extraordinary, and at the same time most scrupulous and intransigent in its consciousness of responsibility and of guilt. Therefore, it should not be expected that they overcome obstacles and realize their ideal of life, shaping around them a life conforming to their desires, disposing themselves in pictures of harmonious perspective, bathed in an even light, and appearing out of the background with the determination and roundness of characters committed to action, and who only in action reveal themselves or that much of themselves as they can or wish to reveal.

His creations are souls who make confessions, and suffer until they do confess, and, even before confessing, they see through, divine, and understand one another, discovering themselves as in the light of the divine, which they do not yet feel worthy of, but which already falls upon them like souls in purgatory. Hence their dialoguing, as if by dialoguing, to arrive at an understanding of themselves, and the frequent tearing away at one stroke of the veil still standing between them. "Let us talk frankly, let us lie no more," says Rita to her husband. Allmers explains to his wife how he is determined to abandon his scientific work in order to devote himself entirely to his little crippled son. Rita, understanding him better than he had supposed or wished, answers: "Not out of any love for him." "Then why, in your opinion?" "Because of the self-doubt eating away at you. You'd begun to question whether you really had any great mission to live for in this world."[5] And Allmers, without trying to defend himself, as if himself had already known it: "That was something you saw in me?"[6] Both had inveighed against the people who had been around the lake, because they had not risked their lives to save their little Eyolf from drowning; but when their spirits calm and their judgment of themselves and of the others gains strength, though he nevertheless repeats his assertion: "If you consider, Alfred" (Rita says, speaking slowly) "Are you so sure that—that we would have risked our own?" And the guilty man, trying to divert the conversation: "You mustn't ever doubt *that*, Rita!" "We *are* so earthbound, you know."[7] Ibsen's creations say out loud—things we scarcely or rarely say to ourselves and that more often whisper within us without our bending to hear; and they are priests to one another, not just for the sake of the confession, but for comfort and encouragement, the one helping the other.

Rita
(slowly nodding)

There *is* something changing in me now.
It's such a painful feeling.

Allmers

Painful?

Rita

Yes, like something giving birth.

Allmers

That's it. Or a resurrection. A
passage into a higher life.

Rita

(gazing blankly straight ahead)

Yes—with the loss of all, all of
life's happiness.

Allmers

The loss—that's the heart of the
victory.

Rita

(explosively)

Oh, fine phrases! Great God, we're
still human beings born of earth.

Allmers

We've some part of the sea and the
stars in us too, Rita.[8]

The final scenes of *Rosmersholm* reach the summit of this reciprocal
fathoming and fusion of souls who have renounced happiness, purifying
themselves, and renounce life.

When Ibsen's art, as is said, overcame the long indifference of the
public, and there gathered around him fervent admirers, fanatical zealots,
interpreters and imitators, in sum a "school," which insofar as it was such,
endeavored to differentiate itself from other preceding and contemporary
ones, that art was defined and celebrated as the "problem art," and its
special characteristic consisted in posing moral and social problems, instead
of setting forth ready-made solutions as in the French comedies à thèse,
static ideals, or in realistically representing emotions, passions, and actions. This difference was well received, but the same cannot be said for the
positive definition it was given as "problem art." Problems relate to a
thinker, and no one is less a thinker than Ibsen, notwithstanding his rich
observation and keen perception of the agitations of the mind; and woe to
him if he had been one, for all his ardent, passionate world would suddenly
have been extinguished by the critical breath of wisdom, more swiftly and
completely than the youthful sentimental world of Goethe had been extinguished before the gently smiling Goethe turned sage. And, on the other
hand, how can things that are so perpetually stormy and disordered be
termed problems, mental problems? It is true, however, that Ibsen tends
here and there to propose problems, but they are precisely those sorts of
problems that have never been resolved, as the history of Ethics teaches,

and which Logic clarifies as being unsolvable—problems of moral casu-
istry. Who is in the right in *A Doll's House*? The husband? But he is an
egoist. The wife? But she has no moral sense. Who is in the wrong? The
husband? But he is respectful of law and honor. The wife? But she wished
to save her husband from illness and death. Who is right in *John Gabriel
Borkman*? Is it Borkman who, in order to carry out the mission he believed
assigned to him, has rejected the woman who loved him? But he has killed
a soul. Is it the woman? But she could not justly claim that for the sake of
her happiness thousands and thousands of men should not obtain happiness,
and should not rise to a higher societal level. Who is in the wrong? Borkman? But he first of all sacrificed himself, his own heart, because he too
loved. The woman? But she could not stifle her immediate and urgent need
for happiness and spiritual salvation, both hers and that of the man she
loved, for the sake of the remote and problematic happiness of future name-
less mobs. No wonder that these unsolvable problems won popularity for
these plays, and that they particularly interested the not very critical feminine brains, the least critical among them, those of the feminists, and that
they, with their psychological, moralizing or amoralizing disputations,
quickly made them tiresome and hateful to the point that some Scandinavian families (the anecdote is well-known) in sending their dinner invita-
tions, took pains to add this recommendation at the bottom of the card:
"Please do not discuss *A Doll's House*."

Ibsen himself touched upon casuistic problems, but never became
profoundly engaged with them, being restrained by his artistic feeling; and
it seems to me perfectly just that when an English critic (while visiting
him) suggested the idea that in his works the concept must have preceded
the dramatization, he responded by denying it, and what the critic further
reported all the more just, namely, that "from his statements, there
emerged at least this, that in the history of his labors there was a phase
when they could have become critical treatises in the same way as they
became plays." Indeed, but they never did become critical treatises, and
Ibsen never wrote a page of doctrinal prose: instead all always became
plays, because they were plays from the beginning, in their primordial cell;
and the soul of the poet was profoundly, uniquely dramatic.

For this reason his creatures are not cold-blooded animals; they are
not "fish" (precisely as one of them says), as personified abstractions always are, but they desire, suffer, and emit savage cries in words trembling
with emotion, in solemn expressions. Hedda Gabler destroys the manuscript
written by a man whom she herself does not know whether she loves or
detests, but by whom she is solely attracted and preoccupied—a manuscript
he had written supported by the loving care of another woman—and while
throwing those pages into the fire, she exclaims with a fierce smile: "Now
I'm burning your child, Thea! You with your curly hair! Your child and

Eilert Løvborg's."[9] After many years, Irene encounters the sculptor Rubek for whose masterpiece she had posed, and, while the two talk together of that time, sadly and gently she reproaches him for the really great gift she had given him: "I gave you my young, living soul. And that left me empty inside. Soulless. That's why I died, Arnold."[10]

When Ella Rentheim hears Borkman, now aged and almost senile, confess how, loving her, he had resolved to abandon her, she judges and condemns him, setting herself above Borkman and herself, above her passion, and in that act she is instead the most passionate incarnation of femininity, of that femininity that is elevated to a religion of itself: "You've killed the capacity to love in me. Can you understand what that means? In the Bible it speaks of a mysterious sin for which there *is* no forgiveness. I've never known what that could be. Now I know. The great unforgivable sin is—to murder the love in a human being."[11]

The poet gave them faces, gestures, and garments, actualizing them completely, because for him they belonged to reality and not to schemata of thought. Borkman, of somber appearance and refined profile, penetrating eyes, with curly gray hair and beard, dressed in black, out of fashion clothes, alone, withdrawn from his friends, confined to the upper floor of the house, paces up and down all day, ruminating about the past and awaiting the future, to which he is more tenaciously attached than ever. Hedda Gabler has a "noble carriage, pale skin, calm and cool appearance, medium brown hair," and she presents herself at home dressed "in tasteful morning gown, rather loose-fitting."[12] Beside her and in contrast to her, her husband George Tesman shows a "youthful appearance, medium sized, blond hair and beard, wearing spectacles and somewhat shabby."[13] So we see them all; nevertheless, Ibsen's plays that have such plastic poetic force, are developed with a simplicity which, at times, is almost simplistic. This, coming from so expert an artist, is not an indication of impoverishment and impotence, but of willed inattention to externals; just as the symbols that at times he introduces, serving as lyrical images and similes, are not signs of impoverishment and weakness: the tower from which Solness will fall; the Alving asylum that will burn; the wild duck forgetful of sea and sky, that wallows and fattens in the loft of the Ekdal house. It happens that the style and ingenuous procedures of the primitives are well suited to this art of courageous and chaste confession, to this almost religious art; and Ibsen has recourse to them, confident of his own strength and, with this determined simplicity, gives proof of strength.

16

An English Jesuit Poet

Gerard Manley Hopkins[1]

Hopkins (1844–1889) was a Jesuit-poet, and certainly not a poet-Jesuit—defining formulae that are not only different, but opposite, because the first affirms and the second denies the poet's condition. It is a common observation that the Jesuits, though they have cultivated literature and poetry a good deal, have never produced a talent who, in this matter, rose to true originality. Another poet, the Anglican canon Dixon repeated this observation in his *History of the Church of England, from the Abolition of the Roman Jurisdiction*;[2] and, replying to his friend and admirer, Hopkins himself supported it with many historical references and argued it on the reasonable principle that in Jesuit thought, literature, science, and philosophy are solely "means to an end." "We have had for three centuries often the flower of the youth of a country in numbers enter our body; among these how many poets, how many artists of all sorts, there must have been! But there have been very few Jesuit-poets and, where they have been, I believe that it would be found on examination that there was something exceptional in their circumstance or, so to say, counterbalancing in their career."[3] In effect, anyone with the soul of a poet did not become a Jesuit (the many potential poets in the troop of youths received by the Jesuits do not count, as it is clear, since they belong to the world of the imagination); and in any case a soul endowed with the poetic spirit could certainly not have divested himself of it by donning the habit of the Society, and he would unconsciously have rejected or bent the rule of the Society to his own purpose and would have treated poetry as end and not as means. Such a one was Hopkins who spoke from his own experience, of the way poetry flashes upon the mind and of the labor that follows it, with the awareness and insight of a Shelley. His last verses, addressed to his friend, the poet Robert Bridges, declare:

> THE fine delight that fathers thought; the strong
> Spur, live and lancing like the blowpipe flame,
> Breathes once and, quenchèd faster than it came,
> Leaves yet the mind a mother of immortal song.

Nine months she then, nay years, nine years she long
Within her wears, bears, cares and combs the same:
The widow of an insight lost she lives, with aim
Now known and hand at work now never wrong.

Sweet fire the sire of muse, my soul needs this;
I want the one rapture of an inspiration.
O then if in my lagging lines you miss

The roll, the rise, the carol, the creation,
My winter world, that scarcely breathes that bliss
Now, yields you, with some sighs, our explanation.[4]

The theory of inspiration and of the long slow work whence the embryo develops toward image and word, and a new poem comes to inhabit
the earth, is here itself a poem, effective in images, as in that "leaves yet
the mind a mother of immortal song" and "the widow of an insight lost."

Hopkins, at twenty-two, left the Anglican for the Catholic church and
at twenty-four entered the Society of Jesus. The conversion, during which
he sought counsel and aid from Cardinal Newman, did not occur as the
result of an intellectual process, or, if this preceded it, he did not feel the
need to give any account of it or to talk about it. It occurred through that
self-surrender of the soul, which is the decisive moment, designated
"grace" in theological terms. But it was a serious matter and affected his
life profoundly. However, Hopkins did not become a Jesuit in the current
sense of the word, that is a representative of the πρῶτον ψεῦδος (original
fallacy) of the Society, of that political treatment of religion, thought, morality, and of every other human virtue, all reduced from ends to means.
The great anti-Jesuit polemicist Pascal had already distinguished Jesuitism
from the good, holy, and pious people who were found among the Jesuits,
of whom the leaders of the Society indirectly, and without being aware of
it, availed themselves for their goal to maintain the reputation of the Society; and Jean-Jacques with words of affection recalled his confessor who,
"quoique jésuite, avait la simplicité de l'enfant,"and taught a morality
"moins relâchée que douce."[5] For his part, Hopkins was a Jesuit of austere
and ascetic mind; nor does it seem that he rendered many practical services
to the Society,[6] which ended with using him perhaps in the best way, when
it sent him to Dublin to teach Greek literature in which he was most expert.
He was always on guard concerning his poetic disposition, resisting and
repressing it. While in training for the novitiate, he burned all the verses he
had composed until then and, having become a Jesuit, for seven years he
wrote no more.[7] But not to write verses does not mean not creating them
inwardly, and in those seven years his poetic spirit did not, for it could not,

cease to feel and to conceive poetically, and to increase and refine his experience of art, so that one day when one of his superiors spoke to him of the opportunity for someone to commemorate the death-in-shipwreck of some nuns who had been expelled from Germany, he quickly seized upon that invitation or pretext and, with exquisite skill, composed a little poem on the subject, which was like the introduction to his new and mature poetic activity. Nevertheless, he continued to torment himself as to whether he not merited God's severe judgment for his having wavered in renouncing that disposition of his; for the reservations he may have made in his heart, for time lost to the detriment of more sacred and pressing obligations, for his uneasiness and the thoughts of vainglory that he had allowed to slide; for his not certainly having wavered in his religious vocation, but for his not having lived exclusively for it.[8] It seemed to him that just as being a gentleman is something more fundamental than being an artist, so is the duty assumed toward God.[9] While redoing his probationary year or second novitiate, his *schola affectus,* he felt more at peace than ever before, purified of all interests and ambitions, ever more distanced from things and occupied exclusively with God, approaching the ideal of "the man who in the world is as dead to the world as if he were buried in the cloister."[10]

Therefore, though still opening out to poetry from time to time, and never neglecting to inquire into problems of art and the works of poets, and to treat and discuss them in his letters to Bridges, Dixon, and Patmore, he always resisted publishing his verses, of which some few fragments were known outside the circle of his friends, and the entire collection, which constitutes a small volume, did not see the light until about thirty years after his death in 1918, with Bridges as its editor.[11] Even after this publication, Hopkins's poetry was very slow to win the attention and admiration of the critics and only now can it be said that it has become known and has received general recognition.[12]

Certainly, this struggle between the man of the church and the poet revealed itself here and there in his compositions, but not in the sense that he worked from a practical aim and, without any poetic inspiration, arranged images and versified, as the Jesuits did, chiefly in the great age of their pseudo-poetry, the seventeenth century. He is almost always guided by a poetic motive; although he sometimes adds reflections and exhortations of a religious character, or other times even provides a religious frame for his poetic motives. For example, the sonnet "In the Valley of the Elwy," is the touching memory of a friendly family:

> I REMEMBER a house where all were good
>   To me, God knows, deserving no such thing:
>   Comforting smell breathed at very entering,
> Fetched fresh, as I suppose, off some sweet wood.

> That cordial air made those kind people a hood
> All over, as a bevy of eggs the mothering wing
> Will, or mild nights the new morsels of Spring:
> Why, it seemed of course; seemed of right it should.[13]

The lyric finishes at this point, or it could not continue to expand without going more deeply into itself and drawing from itself the impetus for further development. Instead, the two quatrains followed by these tercets, which, although held together with much stylistic art, contain a somewhat intellectual and contrived transition:

> Lovely the woods, waters, meadows, combes, vales,
> All the air things wear that build this world of Wales;
> Only the inmate does not correspond:
>
> God, lover of souls, swaying considerate scales,
> Complete thy creature dear O where it fails,
> Being mighty a master, being a father and fond.[14]

Perhaps a linkage of the same sort may be found in the other sonnet, "Duns Scotus's Oxford," the Duns whom Hopkins favored among the medieval philosophers for his strong sense of individuality, though as Jesuit he should have felt rather more inclined toward Aquinas. Poetic inspiration comes to him from his vision of that ancient university city:

> TOWERY city and branchy between towers;
> Cuckoo-echoing, bell-swarmèd, lark-charmèd,
>   rook-racked, river-rounded;
> The dapple-eared lily below thee; that country and town did
> Once encounter in, here coped and poisèd powers;
>
> Thou hast a base and brickish skirt there, sours
> That neighbour-nature thy grey beauty is grounded
> Best in; graceless growth, thou hast confounded
> Rural rural keeping—folk, flocks, and flowers.[15]

The two tercets are linked to the quatrains with a "Yet ah!", a patent discontinuity, and they differ from them in tone and feeling, if in this case one can speak of feeling and not rather of an intentional celebration, of a tiny eulogy which the author wished to execute, setting it in a poetic frame:

> Yet ah! this air I gather and I release
> He lived on; these weeds and waters, these walls are what
> He haunted who of all men most sways my spirits to peace;

Of realty the rarest-veinèd unraveller; a not
Rivalled insight, be rival Italy or Greece;
Who fired France for Mary without spot.[16]

There are, at any rate, insertions and linkages, always executed with refined taste and art. Thus the warm pleasure that he feels at the sight of the variety and contrasts among earthly things, is turned into a psalm on the glory of God. "Pied Beauty":

GLORY be to God for dappled things—
  For skies of couple-colour as a brinded cow;
    For rose-moles all in stipple upon trout that swim;
Fresh-firecoal chestnut-falls; finches' wings;
  Landscape plotted and pieced—fold, fallow, and plough;
    And áll trádes, their gear and tackle and trim.

All things counter, original, spare, strange;
  Whatever is fickle, freckled (who knows how?)
    With swift, slow; sweet, sour; adazzle, dim;
He fathers-forth whose beauty is past change:
    Praise him.[17]

One of his short poems that is among the best known by virtue of its singularity of theme and treatment—"The Bugler's First Communion" (or the first communion of the regiment's boy bugler) is also perhaps the one that most clearly retains the aspect of a devotional work. After recounting how, in a hillside encampment, the young soldier asked him for the gift of first communion and how Hopkins himself took his first communion in his own church, he writes:

Here he knelt then ín regimental red.
Forth Christ from cupboard fetched, how fain I of feet
  To his youngster take his treat!
Low-latched in leaf-light housel his too huge godhead.

There! and your sweetest sendings, ah divine,
By it, heavens, befall him! as a heart Christ's darling, dauntless;
  Tongue true, vaunt- and tauntless;
Breathing bloom of a chastity in mansex fine.

Frowning and forefending angel-warder
Squander the hell-rook ranks sally to molest him;
  March, kind comrade, abreast him;
Dress his days to a dexterous and starlight order.

How it dóes my heart good, visiting at that bleak hill,
When limber liquid youth, that to all I teach
  Yields tender as a pushed peach,
Hies headstrong to its wellbeing of a self-wise self-will!

Then though I should tread tufts of consolation
Dáys áfter, só I in a sort deserve to
  And do serve God to serve to
Just such slips of soldiery Christ's royal ration.

Nothing élse is like it, no, not all so strains
Us: fresh youth fretted in a bloomfall all portending
  That sweet's sweeter ending;
Realm both Christ is heir to and thére réigns.

O now well work that sealing sacred ointment!
O for now charms, arms, what bans off bad
  And locks love ever in a lad!
Let mé though see no more of him, and not disappointment.

Those sweet hopes quell whose least me quickenings lift,
In scarlet or somewhere of some day seeing
  That brow and bead of being,
An our day's God's own Galahad. . . . [18]

What remains live in the creative fancy is that figure of the young soldier, in his red uniform, that youth who is open to life, neither stained nor spoiled by the passions, who has come with dutiful fervor to fulfill a religious rite, while priestly unction emphasizes the representation, and is forced to resort to somewhat clipped forms and images, like those about the consecrated host, about the "ration of Christ" that is administered to soldiers, and suchlike.

At such times one admires how Hopkins, thanks to his poetic feeling, succeeds in conquering the unrewarding theme that he has set for himself or has been set before him. He must celebrate saint Alphonsus Rodriguez, a Jesuit saint who had no apparent merit other than to have held, for forty years, as a lay brother, the office of porter of the College of Palma in Majorca, and of whom it was related that he had with divine aid resisted the malignant spirits that tormented him. What should he say about him? But Hopkins is poetically inspired by the idea of battles that the eye does not see, so much more lofty and harsh and fierce than those that unfold in thunderous events, celebrated by fame and the poets:

HONOUR is flashed off exploit, so we say;
And those strokes once that gashed flesh or galled shield
Should tongue that time now, trumpet now that field,
And, on the fighter, forge his glorious day.
On Christ they do and on the martyr may;
But be the war within, the brand we wield
Unseen, the heroic breast not outward-steeled,
Earth hears no hurtle then from fiercest fray.[19]

And from this point he descends toward the soul of the poor Spanish
brother in order to raise him, as a hero of the inner life, to this lofty sphere
of thought:

Yet God (that hews mountain and continent,
Earth, all, out; who, with trickling increment,
Veins violets and tall trees makes more and more)
Could crowd career with conquest while there went
Those years and years by of world without event
That in Majorca Alfonso watched the door.[20]

The religious intention, as happens with poets, gives way to purely
human inspiration, which at times overwhelms the other to such a point
that one no longer knows whether to be moved or to smile while yet being
moved, as in these two little stanzas in "A Nun Takes the Veil":

I HAVE desired to go
Where springs not fail,
To fields where flies no sharp and sided hail
And a few lilies blow.

And I have asked to be
Where no storms come,
Where the green swell is in the havens dumb,
And out of the swing of the sea.[21]

The poet has relived and shared enough of the little nun's feelings—
that flight from human hardships, from travails and sorrows, that fought-for
sweetness of peace—to paint a little picture of purest, childish egoism, of
an egoism that is unaware of itself and somewhat innocent. Therefore re-
specting and admiring Hopkins's serious religious and devout mind, and in
addition tolerating its intervention when it occurs in the composition of his
poems, it is at the same time necessary to assign it its place and circum-
scribe it, in order to avoid confusing it with his true poetic force. This

originates principally from a most profound feeling for the vital forces or, as is usually said, for nature which he, at the same time, elevates to longing, anguish, and moral aspiration; such that, extremely sensitive as he shows himself to be to the spectacle of nature, there is nothing in him of the sensuality and impressionistic disintegration customary today. But it seems that he ultimately detaches himself and withdraws even from the contemplation of the things of nature, in order to pass beyond to a more retiring and exclusive inwardness, notably in a series of lyrics that has been considered as his later manner with respect to his earlier and, as a whole, comes afterwards chronologically. I leave aside the observations of the English critics on the relation that he shows to Milton in his poetic style, particularly to the Milton of the sonnets and Samson, or to Donne, and, in another way, to Wordsworth, all predecessors who certainly influenced him, but did not make an imitator, an eclectic, or a virtuoso out of him, because Hopkins always manifests his own, original personality. Rather, in order to understand what is said of his poetic style and of his two manners, I find it useful to remind Italian readers of the Leopardi of the short idylls, and of the relationship that runs between these and "Il pensiero dominante" or "L'amore e morte."

Let it not displease that samples of Hopkins's poems are offered here in some abundance, since he is little known in Italy, and a further, more specialized discussion of him would not be fruitful unless this knowledge preceded it, and some familiarity with the author were acquired. We present them translated into prose, not only thus subjecting them to the usual diminishment that results from translation, and especially from translation into prose, but also to the much greater one that an artist like Hopkins, exquisite in rhythm, in verse, and in the blending of language,[22] must necessarily suffer.

"Inversnaid" a place not far from Glasgow, rendered famous by Wordsworth and by Matthew Arnold[23] provided the title of a sonnet in which the representation of a gloomy landscape, entirely bathed with water, is filled with the sensation of life that flees from dryness, and is fed and grows in the wild wet:

> THIS darksome burn, horseback brown,
> His rollrock highroad roaring down,
> In coop and in comb the fleece of his foam
> Flutes and low to the lake falls home.
>
> A windpuff-bonnet of fáwn-fróth
> Turns and twindles over the broth
> Of a pool so pitchblack, féll-frówning,
> It rounds and rounds Despair to drowning.

Degged with dew, dappled with dew
Are the groins of the braes that the brook treads through,
Wiry heathpacks, flitches of fern,
And the beadbonny ash that sits over the burn.

What would the world be, once bereft
Of wet and of wildness? Let them be left,
O let them be left, wildness and wet;
Long live the weeds and the wilderness yet.[24]

How much "of wet and wildness" there is, not only in physical sensation, but in the higher spiritual life that also flees from dryness as from death and continually re-emerses and renews itself in the eternal virginity of lively impressions and surging natural passions.

The eternal youthfulness of nature and the dryness from which human work and civilization suffer from time to time also shape another lyric, "The Sea and the Skylark":

ON ear and ear two noises too old to end
    Trench—right, the tide that ramps against the shore;
    With a flood or a fall, low lull-off or all roar,
Frequenting there while moon shall wear and wend.

Left hand, off land, I hear the lark ascend,
    His rash-fresh re-winded new-skeinèd score
    In crisps of curl off wild winch whirl, and pour
And pelt music, till none's to spill nor spend.

How these two shame this shallow and frail town!
    How ring right out our sordid turbid time,
Being pure! We, life's pride and cared-for crown,

    Have lost that cheer and charm of earth's past prime:
Our make and making break, are breaking, down
    To man's last dust, drain fast towards man's first slime.[25]

Here, as in the preceding lyric, one does not notice the intervention of religious faith standing out as a separate element. In "God's Grandeur," the divinity intervenes in mythological-naturalistic form, full of poetic and philosophic significance, presented as a cosmic force, that perpetually summons the springs of life from the deep bosom of the earth, perpetually rejuvenating the world:

THE world is charged with the grandeur of God.
    It will flame out, like shining from shook foil;
    It gathers to a greatness, like the ooze of oil
Crushed. Why do men then now not reck his rod?
Generations have trod, have trod, have trod;
    And all is seared with trade; bleared, smeared with toil;
    And wears man's smudge and shares man's smell: the soil
Is bare now, nor can foot feel, being shod.

And for all this, nature is never spent;
    There lives the dearest freshness deep down things;
And though the last lights off the black West went
    Oh, morning, at the brown brink eastward, springs—
Because the Holy Ghost over the bent
    World broods with warm breast and with ah! bright wings.[26]

In the poem "The Starlight Night," the vision is commingled with a pious allegorizing interpretation:

LOOK at the stars! look, look up at the skies!
    O look at all the fire-folk sitting in the air!
    The bright boroughs, the circle-citadels there!
Down in dim woods the diamond delves! the elves'-eyes!
The grey lawns cold where gold, where quickgold lies!
    Wind-beat whitebeam! airy abeles set on a flare!
    Flake-doves sent floating forth at a farmyard scare!—
Ah well! it is all a purchase, all is a prize.

Buy then! bid then!—What?—Prayer, patience, alms, vows.
Look, look: a May-mess, like on orchard boughs!
    Look! March-bloom, like on mealed-with-yellow sallows!
These are indeed the barn; withindoors house
The shocks. This piece-bright paling shuts the spouse
    Christ home, Christ and his mother and all his hallows.[27]

Or as in "The Lantern out of Doors," the religious pronouncement stands like a final gloss on a representation infused with sadness and loss:

SOMETIMES a lantern moves along the night,
    That interests our eyes. And who goes there?
    I think; where from and bound, I wonder, where,
With, all down darkness wide, his wading light?

Men go by me whom either beauty bright
    In mould or mind or what not else makes rare:
    They rain against our much-thick and marsh air
Rich beams, till death or distance buys them quite.

Death or distance soon consumes them: wind
    What most I may eye after, be in at the end
I cannot, and out of sight is out of mind.

Christ minds: Christ's interest, what to avow or amend
    There, éyes them, heart wánts, care haúnts, foot fóllows kínd,
Their ránsom, théir rescue, ánd first, fást, last friénd.[28]

    In the sonnet "Windhover," the magnificent celebration of a bird, in the movement of its flight, which is expanded in the two quatrains, is followed by two tercets that have yielded numerous moral and religious interpretations, all uncertain, indicating that their manifold "suggestiveness"[29] has been recognized:

I CAUGHT this morning morning's minion, king-
    dom of daylight's dauphin, dapple dawn drawn Falcon, in his
        riding
    Of the rolling level underneath him steady air, and striding
High there, how he rung upon the rein of a wimpling wing
In his ecstasy! then off, off forth on swing,
    As a skate's heel sweeps smooth on a bow-bend: the hurl and
        gliding
    Rebuffed the big wind. My heart in hiding
Stirred for a bird,—the achieve of, the mastery of the thing!

Brute beauty and valour and act, oh, air, pride, plume, here
    Buckle! AND the fire that breaks from thee then, a billion
Times told lovelier, more dangerous, O my chevalier!

    No wonder of it: shéer plód makes plough down sillion
Shine, and blue-bleak embers, ah my dear,
    Fall, gall themselves, and gash gold-vermilion.[30]

    But Hopkins did not want the obscurity of these last verses to produce an ensemble lacking determinate meaning which, with its mysteriousness, was capable of yielding infinite interpretations, as with the followers of Stéphane Mallarmé, and other tormented-tormentor artificers of France and other countries, whose presumed and vaunted richness is poverty. It is an obscurity resulting from excessive condensation and the absence of transitions, and in which his thought remains entangled. His general tendency is toward expressive clarity.

　　Human anguish in the presence of death and the fulfillment of ecclesiastical duties of assistance and of administering the sacraments are set down in the sonnet "Felix Randal," with a slight clash between two differing attitudes that control different tones of expression:

> FELIX RANDAL the farrier, O is he dead then? my duty all ended,
> Who have watched his mould of man, big-boned and
> 　　hardy-handsome
> Pining, pining, till time when reason rambled in it and some
> Fatal four disorders, fleshed there, all contended?
>
> Sickness broke him. Impatient, he cursed at first, but mended
> Being anointed and all; though a heavenlier heart began some
> Months earlier, since I had our sweet reprieve and ransom
> Tendered to him. Ah well, God rest him all road ever he offended!
>
> This seeing the sick endears them to us, us too it endears.
> My tongue had taught thee comfort, touch had quenched thy tears,
> Thy tears that touched my heart, child, Felix, poor Felix Randal;
>
> How far from then forethought of, all thy more boisterous years,
> When thou at the random grim forge, powerful amidst peers,
> Didst fettle for the great grey drayhorse his bright and battering
> 　　sandal![31]

The sonnet "Andromeda" is noteworthy for its essential departure from those skillfully objective or wholly sensual representations that we find in the art of Hérédia and other such, who are much more refined and exquisite and yet substantially akin to authors, both Baroque and Arcadian, of sonnets describing Moses, Hannibal, or Caesar. Here instead we have the representation of the soul that is tormented by horror of the danger threatening it, and nonetheless hopes and awaits help:

> Now Time's Andromeda on this rock rude,
> With not her either beauty's equal or
> Her injury's, looks off by both horns of shore,
> Her flower, her piece of being, doomed dragon food.
>
> Time past she has been attempted and pursued
> By many blows and banes; but now hears roar

A wilder beast from West than all were, more
Rife in her wrongs, more lawless, and more lewd.

Her Perseus linger and leave her tó her extremes?—
Pillowy air he treads a time and hangs
His thoughts on her, forsaken that she seems,

All while her patience, morselled into pangs,
Mounts; then to alight disarming, no one dreams,
With Gorgon's gear and barebill / thongs and fangs.[32]

Most charming in its melancholy wisdom is the short exhortation mentally directed at a girl, as if to explain what she feels and does not understand. "Spring and Fall":

MÁRGARÉT, áre you gríeving
Over Goldengrove unleaving?
Leáves, líke the things of man, you
With your fresh thoughts care for, can you?
Áh! ás the heart grows older
It will come to such sights colder
By and by, nor spare a sigh
Though worlds of wanwood leafmeal lie;
And yet you *will* weep and know why.
Now no matter, child, the name:
Sórrow's spríngs áre the same.
Nor mouth had, no nor mind, expressed
What heart heard of, ghost guessed:
It ís the blight man was born for,
It is Margaret you mourn for.[33]

With concentration and renewal of moral energy, the poet combines an impression of evening and the ending of life, the thought of death, in "Spelt from Sibyl's Leaves":

EARNEST, earthless, equal, attuneable, / vaulty, voluminous, . . .
    stupendous
Evening strains to be tíme's vást, / womb-of-all, home-of-all,
    hearse-of-all night.
Her fond yellow hornlight wound to the west, / her wild hollow
    hoarlight hung to the height
Waste; her earliest stars, earlstars, / stárs principal, overbend us,

Fíre-féaturing heaven. For earth / her being has unbound; her dapple
    is at an end, as-
tray or aswarm, all throughther, in throngs; / self ín self steepèd and
    páshed—qúite
Disremembering, dísmémbering / áll now. Heart, you round me right
With: Óur évening is over us; óur night / whélms, whélms, ánd will
    end us.
Only the beakleaved boughs dragonish / damask the tool-smooth
    bleak light; black,
Ever so black on it. Óur tale, O óur oracle! / Lét life, wáned, ah lét
    life wind
Off hér once skéined stained véined varíety / upon áll on twó spools;
    párt, pen, páck
Now her áll in twó flocks, twó folds—black, white; / right, wrong;
    reckon but, reck but, mind
But thése two; wáre of a wórld where bút these / twó tell, each off
    the óther; of a rack
Where, selfwrung, selfstrung, sheathe- and shelterless, / thóughts
    agaínst thoughts ín groans grínd.[34]

A philosophical meditation, and yet not a metered, versified gnomic work,
but something more intimate and moving are the strophes didactically entitled: ''To What Serves Moral Beauty?''

To what serves moral beauty / —dangerous; does set danc-
ing blood—the O-seal-that-so / feature, flung prouder form
Than Purcell tune lets tread to? / See: it does this: keeps warm
Men's wits to the things that are; / what good means—where a
    glance
Master more may than gaze, / gaze out of countenance.
Those lovely lads once, wet-fresh / windfalls of war's storm,
How then should Gregory, a father, / have gleanèd else from swarm-
èd Rome? But God to a nation / dealt that day's dear chance.
To man, that needs would worship / block or barren stone,
Our law says: Love what are / love's worthiest, were all known;
World's loveliest—men's selves. Self / flashes off frame and face.
What do then? how meet beauty? / Merely meet it; own,
Home at heart, heaven's sweet gift; / then leave, let that alone.
Yea, wish that though, wish all, / God's better beauty, grace.[35]

Lyrics follow that express the interior struggle of the unhappy soul
with its lamentations, its cries, its accents of despair:

No WORST, there is none. Pitched past pitch of grief,
More pangs will, schooled at forepangs, wilder wring.
Comforter, where, where is your comforting?
Mary, mother of us, where is your relief?
My cries heave, herds-long; huddle in a main, a chief-
woe, world-sorrow; on an age-old anvil wince and sing—
Then lull, then leave off. Fury had shrieked 'No ling-
ering! Let me be fell: force I must be brief'.
O the mind, mind has mountains; cliffs of fall
Frightful, sheer, no-man-fathomed. Hold them cheap
May who ne'er hung there. Nor does long our small
Durance deal with that steep or deep. Here! creep,
Wretch, under a comfort serves in a whirlwind: all
Life death does end and each day dies with sleep.[36]

The desperation of the damned is felt and likened to the unsur-
mounted individuality that is realized in the rebellious body:

I WAKE and feel the fell of dark, not day.
What hours, O what black hoürs we have spent
This night! what sights you, heart, saw; ways you went!
And more must, in yet longer light's delay.

With witness I speak this. But where I say
Hours I mean years, mean life. And my lament
Is cries countless, cries like dead letters sent
To dearest him that lives alas! away.

I am gall, I am heartburn. God's most deep decree
Bitter would have me taste: my taste was me;
Bones built in me, flesh filled, blood brimmed the curse.

Selfyeast of spirit a dull dough sours. I see
The lost are like this, and their scourge to be
As I am mine, their sweating selves; but worse.[37]

"Carrion Comfort"[38] has to do with moments frightfully endured and
yet overcome, overcome by the strong mind that repulses the raging, men-
acing, seductive desperation:

NOT, I'll not, carrion comfort, Despair, not feast on thee;
Not untwist—slack they may be—these last strands of man

In me ór, most weary, cry I CAN NO MORE. I can;
Can something, hope, wish day come, not choose not to be.

But ah, but O thou terrible, why wouldst thou rude on me
Thy wring-world right foot rock? lay a lionlimb against me? scan
With darksome devouring eyes my bruisèd bones? and fan,
O in turns of tempest, me heaped there; me frantic to avoid thee and
    flee?

Why? That my chaff might fly; my grain lie, sheer and clear.
Nay in all that toil, that coil, since (seems) I kissed the rod,
Hand rather, my heart lo! lapped strength, stole joy, would laugh,
    chéer.
Cheer whom though? The hero whose heaven-handling flung me,
    fóot tród
Me? or me that fought him? O which one? is it each one? That
    night, that year
Of now done darkness I wretch lay wrestling with (my God!) my
    God.[39]

Moments of self-indulgence in the suffering self alternate with this
heroic impulse:

    MY own heart let me more have pity on; let
    Me live to my sad self hereafter kind,
    Charitable; not live this tormented mind
    With this tormented mind tormenting yet.

    I cast for comfort I can no more get
    By groping round my comfortless, than blind
    Eyes in their dark can day or thirst can find
    Thirst's all-in-all in a world of wet.

    Soul, self; come, poor Jackself, I do advise
    You, jaded, let be; call off thoughts awhile
    Elsewhere; leave comfort root-room; let joy size

    At God knows when to God knows what; whose smile
    's not wrung, see you; unforeseen times rather—as skies
    Betweenpie mountains—lights a lovely mile.[40]

Charges against the Lord that turn into supplications, form upon his
lips as they once had upon Job's:

THOU art indeed just, Lord, if I contend
With thee; but, sir, so what I plead is just.
Why do sinners' ways prosper? and why must
Disappointment all I endeavour end?

Wert thou my enemy, O thou my friend,
How wouldst thou worse, I wonder, than thou dost
Defeat, thwart me? Oh, the sots and thralls of lust
Do in spare hours more thrive than I that spend,

Sir, life upon thy cause. See, banks and brakes
Now, leavèd how thick! lacèd they are again
With fretty chervil, look, and fresh wind shakes

Them; birds build—but not I build; no but strain,
Time's eunuch, and not breed one work that wakes.
Mine, O thou lord of life, send my roots rain.[41]

The yearning of his entire being is for peace, full and steady peace. "Peace":

WHEN will you ever, Peace, wild wooddove, shy wings shut,
Your round me roaming end, and under be my boughs?
When, when, Peace, will you, Peace? I'll not play hypocrite

To own my heart: I yield you do come sometimes; but
That piecemeal peace is poor peace. What pure peace allows
Alarms of wars, the daunting wars, the death of it?

O surely, reaving Peace, my Lord should leave in lieu
Some good! And so he does leave Patience exquisite,
That plumes to Peace thereafter. And when Peace here does house
He comes with work to do, he does not come to coo,
      He comes to brood and sit.[42]

"Patience" is the final word:

PATIENCE, hard thing! the hard thing but to pray,
But bid for, Patience is! Patience who asks
Wants war, wants wounds; weary his times, his tasks;
To do without, take tosses, and obey.

> Rare patience roots in these, and, these away,
> Nowhere. Natural heart's ivy, Patience masks
> Our ruins of wrecked past purpose. There she basks
> Purple eyes and seas of liquid leaves all day.
>
> We hear our hearts grate on themselves: it kills
> To bruise them dearer. Yet the rebellious wills
> Of us we do bid God bend to him even so.
>
> And where is he who more and more distills
> Delicious kindness?—He is patient. Patience fills
> His crisp combs, and that comes those ways we know.[43]

From the lyrics we have related we can form a conception of Hopkins's poetry which could better be determined by reading and translating the others that we have omitted (though there are some very notable ones among them) to avoid over-crowding.

But Hopkins, as we have already said, studied matters of poetry and art a good deal, and his published letters contain always notable judgments, especially on the English poets Milton and Campbell, as well as Keats, Wordsworth, and Tennyson, at times severe ones, as on Walter Scott, Carlyle, and Swinburne. Among his "poetic fragments" there is one, "On a Piece of Music," where he illuminates the objectivity of the work of art (what Flaubert used to call "l'air bête" of beauty), its interior necessity, where every intention is surmounted and can no longer be recovered.

> How all's to one thing wrought!
> The members, how they sit!
> O what a tune the thought
> Must be that fancied it.
>
> Nor angel insight can
> Learn how the heart is hence:
> Since all the make of man
> Is law's indifference.
>
>
> [. . . . .]
>
> Not free in this because
> His powers seemed free to play:
> He swept what scope he was
> To sweep and must obey.

Though down his being's bent
Like air he changed in choice,
That was an instrument
Which overvaulted voice.

. . . .

Therefore this masterhood,
This piece of perfect song,
This fault-not-found-with good
Is neither right nor wrong,

No more than red and blue,
No more than Re and Mi,
Or sweet the golden glue
That's built for by the bee.[44]

Great and studious artificer of forms in themselves, as he was, it did
not occur to him, moreover, as it did to the aestheticizers and virtuousi of
art for art's sake, to locate beauty and poetry anywhere but in the soul. "A
true humanity of spirit, neither mawkish on the one hand, nor blustering on
the other, is the most precious of all the qualities in style. . . . After all it is
the breath of his human nature that we admire in Shakespeare."[45]

Hopkins's concepts and theories on English metrics (he announced
but did not publish them, as also on Greek metrics); his insistence on the
"sprung rhythm" in order to distinguish it from counterpoint; his views on
the use of the "blank verse" or that of the sonnet; his oft expressed judgment that, except for Milton's verse, all those of the other English poets
offended him as being "licentious," and that "the vision and strictly poetic
inspiration of English poetry is indeed one of the most beautiful and perhaps more beautiful than the Greek, but that rhetoric, or the teachable element of literature, equivalent to grammar for language, to the ground bass
[*basso continuo*] for music, to theatrical experience for the playwright,
turns out to be inadequate;"[46] and the other curious judgment, which is
paired with this, that in painting and sculpture, nothing as yet has been
produced of what there is to produce, and they remain greatly inferior—
what value, whether scientific or critical, do all these statements have?
They have the usual value of artists' statements of this kind, expressions of
their innermost personal tendencies, not philosophic statements or judgments that are entirely defensible and demonstrable. Dixon rightly doubted
that Hopkins's "new prosody" could be fitted into a system of rules; and
having argued with him, he wisely concluded that even if "sprung
rhythm," insofar as it was distinct from common rhythm and also from

counterpoint, was not such a thing as to be used generally (which besides was not desirable nor desired by Hopkins), yet "it may do great good in poetry, in making writers careful."[47] All taken up in his studies of rhythm and meter, Hopkins sometimes called his lyrical poems "rhythmical experiments" or "metrical experiments,"[48] which were much more than that. But that there remain traces here and there in them of the forced and of the bizarre deriving from pseudotheoretical preconceptions was a matter noted by his friend and editor Bridges and about which critics have made observations, whose importance is useful for a detailed study of his poetic form.[49]

NOTES

Introduction

1. For anyone who does not read Italian, Cecil Sprigge's *Benedetto Croce: Man and Thinker* (Cambridge, England: Bowes & Bowes, 1952; reprinted in Benedetto Croce, *Philosophy, Poetry, History,* trans. C. Sprigge [London: Oxford University Press, 1966]), provides the most detailed biography of Croce's life. Also see H. S. Harris, "Croce, Benedetto," *Encyclopedia of Philosophy* (New York: Macmillan, 1972); E. Caserta, "Croce, Benedetto," *Dictionary of Italian Literature* (Westport: Greenwood Press, 1979); G. Gullace, "Benedetto Croce," *Critical Survey of Literary Theory* (Pasadena: Salem Press, 1988); Gian N. G. Orsini, *Benedetto Croce: Philosopher of Art and Literary Critic* (Carbondale: Southern Illinois University Press, 1961), ch. 1; Angelo A. De Gennaro, *The Philosophy of Benedetto Croce* (New York: Harcourt, Brace & Co., 1922); Giovanni Gullace's introduction to Benedetto Croce, *Poetry and Literature,* trans. G. Gullace (Carbondale: Southern Illinois University Press, 1981); Edmund E. Jacobitti, *Revolutionary Humanism and Historicism in Modern Italy* (New Haven: Yale University Press, 1981). Croce's autobiographical statements that have been translated into English may be found in *Benedetto Croce: An Autobiography,* trans. R.G. Collingwood (Oxford: Clarendon Press, 1927); and Benedetto Croce, *My Philosophy and Other Essays on the Moral and Political Problems of Our Time,* selected by R. Klibansky, trans. E. F. Carritt (London: George Allen & Unwin, 1949), ch. 1. For several recent books in English on aspects of Croce's life and thought see Ernesto Caserta, *Croce and Marxism* (Naples: Morano, 1987); M. E. Moss, *Benedetto Croce Reconsidered: Truth and Error in Theories of Art, Literature and History* (Hanover: University Press of New England, 1987); and David D. Roberts, *Benedetto Croce and the Uses of Historicism* (Berkeley: University of California Press, 1987).

2. See Moss, *Benedetto Croce Reconsidered,* chs. 1 and 2.

3. Benedetto Croce, *Contributo alla critica di me stesso* (Naples: 1918), translated into English as *Benedetto Croce: An Autobiography,* tr. R. G. Collingwood, with a preface by J. A. Smith (Oxford: Clarendon Press, 1927).

4. Croce, *Autobiography,* p. 37.

5. *Ibid.,* pp. 86–87.

6. For a discussion of Croce and Vico, see Angelo De Gennaro, "Croce and Vico," *Journal of Aesthetics and Art Criticism.,* 22 (1963–65): 43–46; and Angelo De Gennaro, "Vico and Croce: The Genesis of Croce's Aesthetics," *The Personalist,* 50 (1969): 508–525.

7. Benedetto Croce, *"Intorno ai saggi del Poe sulla poesia,"* in *Letture di poeti* (Bari: Laterza, 1966), pp. 197–203. See pp. 151–155 below.

8. See p. 154 below. For a discussion of Croce and Francesco De Sanctis, see Angelo De Gennaro, "Croce and De Sanctis," *Journal of Aesthetics and Art Criticism*, 23 (1964–65): 227–231.

9. Benedetto Croce, *Estetica come scienza dell'espressione e linguistica generale* (Milan-Palermo-Naples: Sandron, 1902). For an English translation see *Aesthetic as Science of Expression and General Linguistic*, trans. D. Ainslie (London: Macmillan, 1909). This translation was revised by Ainslie and published in 1922 by Macmillan, but without the Heidelberg lecture that had been included in the 1909 edition. The 1922 version also presented all of Part 2 ("History of Aesthetics") of the *Estetica*, which had been summarized in the 1909 work. In the pages that follow, unless otherwise indicated, I shall quote from the paperback edition of the 1922 *Aesthetic* (New York: Noonday Press, 1958).

10. See p. 30 below.

11. Croce, *Aesthetic* (1958), p. 11.

12. *Ibid.*, p. 221.

13. Benedetto Croce, "Tesi fondamentali di un'Estetica come scienza dell'espressione e linguistica generale,"*Atti dell'accademia pontaniana*, 30 (1900): pp. 88.

14. See p. 117 below. For a review of Douglas Ainslie's translation of Croce's *Ariosto, Shakespeare and Corneille*, see "Briefer Mention," *The Dial*, 71 (1921): 244; and for a review of Robertson, *Croce as Shakespearean Critic*, see Samuel C. Chew, "The Shakespeare Canon," *The New Republic*, 32 (August 30, 1922): 24–25.

15. Benedetto Croce, "Il sentimento shakespeariano," in *Ariosto, Shakespeare e Corneille* (Bari: Gius. Laterza & Figli, 1968), pp. 83–96. See pp. 107–116 below.

16. Benedetto Croce, *"Carattere e unità della poesia di Dante,"* in *La poesia di Dante* (Bari: Gius. Laterza & Figli, 1966), pp. 163–172.

17. See pp. 69–74 below.

18. Benedetto Croce, *"Dante: l'ultimo canto della 'Commedia',"* *Poesia antica e moderna* (Bari: Guis. Laterza & Figli, 1966), pp. 153–163. See pp. 75–82 below.

19. Benedetto Croce, *Logica come scienza del concetto puro*. 2d ed. rev. (Bari: Laterza, 1909). (The 1st edition of this work was entitled *"Lineamenti di una Logica come scienza del concetto puro,"* *Atti dell'accademia pontaniana*, 35 [1905]: 140). The 2d edition was translated into English by D. Ainslie as *Logic as the Science of the Pure Concept* (London: Macmillan & Co., 1917).

20. Croce's *Breviario di estetica: Quattro lezioni* (Bari: Laterza, 1913) was translated by D. Ainslie and published first in English under the title "The Breviary of Aesthetic," *The Book of the Opening of the Rice Institute* (Houston: The Rice Institute, 1912) 2: 450–517. This translation was subsequently revised and republished under the title *The Essence of Aesthetic* (London: Heinemann, 1921). More recently the *Breviario* was retranslated by Patrick Romanell under the title *Guide to Aesthetics* (Indianapolis: Bobbs-Merrill, 1965).

21. Benedetto Croce, *Poesia e non poesia: Note sulla letteratura europea del secolo decimonono*, 7th ed. (Bari: Laterza, 1964); translated by D. Ainslie under the title *European Literature in the Nineteenth Century* (London: Chapman & Hall, 1925). For a review of Ainslie's translation of this work, see "Briefer Mention," *The Dial*, 78 (1925): 523.

22. Croce, *Aesthetic*, p. 13.

23. Benedetto Croce, *"Omero: interpretazione moderna di taluni giudizî antichi,"* in *Poesia antica e moderna*, pp. 31–38. Also see pp. 27–31 below.

24. See p. 28 below.

25. See p. 119 below.

26. Benedetto Croce, *"Terenzio," Poesia antica e moderna*, 1–30. Also see pp. 33–48 below.

27. See p. 72 below.

28. See p. 125 below.

29. See p. 80 below.

30. See p. 66 below.

31. See p. 124 below.

32. Benedetto Croce, *"Lucrezio e Virgilio. Il 'De rerum natura' e i 'Georgica',"* *Poesia antica e moderna*, pp. 39–54. See pp. 49–59 below.

33. For a discussion of the evolution of Croce's theory of intuition as art see Moss, *Benedetto Croce Reconsidered*, ch. 3.

34. Croce, *An Autobiography*, p. 104. Also see Benedetto Croce, "Intuizione, sentimento, liricità," *La critica*, 5 (1907): 248.

35. Benedetto Croce, *Problemi di estetica* (Bari: Gius. Laterza, 1954), p. 17; also see p. 22.

36. See pp. 50–51 below.

37. Even the addition of lyricality to Croce's concept of art would prove difficult for some U.S. critics to understand, See W. K. Wimsatt Jr. and C. Brooks, *Literary Criticism: A Short History* (New York: Knopf, 1957), p. 504. Also see

Norman Foerster, "The Esthetic Judgment and the Ethical Judgment" in Edmond Wilson, Norman Foerster, John Crowe Ransom, W. H. Auden, *The Intent of the Critic*, ed. D. A. Stauffer (Massachusetts: Peter Smith, 1963), pp. 63–88.

38. In a scathing dismissal of Croce's philosophy of art, the English aesthetician and critic I. A. Richards quoted from Giovanni Papini's *Four and Twenty Minds:* "If you disregard critical trivialities and didactic accessories, the entire aesthetic system of Croce amounts merely to a hunt for pseudonyms of the word 'art.' " See I. A. Richards, *Principles of Literary Criticism* (London: Kegan Paul, 1934), pp. 255–256.

39. Benedetto Croce, "Il carattere di totalità dell'espressione artistica," *Nuovi saggi* (Bari: Laterza & Figli, 1958), pp. 119–146. This essay was translated into English by C. Sprigge and appears in *Philosophy, Poetry, History*, pp. 261–273. "Il carattere di totalità" was published first as an article in *La critica*, 16 (1918): 129–140.

40. Croce, *Guide to Aesthetics*, p. 32.

41. Croce, *Nuovi saggi*, p. 119. My translation. Cf. Croce, *Philosophy, Poetry, History*, p. 263.

42. Croce, *Philosophy, Poetry, History*, p. 269. Unfortunately, some U.S. critics, such as Irving Babbitt, having identified Joel Spingarn as Croce's American spokesman, falsely accused Croce of belonging to the Romantic tradition, which he so severely criticized. See Irving Babbitt, *On Being Creative and other Essays* (New York: Biblo and Tanner, 1968), pp. 8, 18, 19, 174.

43. See *The Nation*, 75, no. 1943 (Sept. 25, 1902): 252.

44. See Guido Calogero, *Estetica, semantica, Istorica* (Turin: Einaudi, 1947), chs. 4 and 5.

45. Croce, *Philosophy, Poetry, History*, p. 262.

46. Benedetto Croce, *The Defence of Poetry*, trans. E. F. Carritt (London: Oxford, 1933), p. 28. This work consisting of the Philip Maurice Deneke Lecture, delivered at Lady Margaret Hall, Oxford, 1933, was published first in English and subsequently in Italian under the title *"Difesa della poesia," La critica*, 32 (1934): 1–15.

47. Croce, *Defence of Poetry*, p. 28.

48. John Paul Pritchard, in his *Criticism in America* (Norman: University of Oklahoma Press, 1956), cited Paul Elmer More as an illustration of this point, p. 210. Also see Irving Babbitt, "Genius and Taste" (1918) in Irving Babbitt, Van Wyck Brooks, W. C. Brownell, Ernest Boyd, T. S. Eliot, H. L. Mencken, Stuart P. Sherman, J. E. Spingarn, and George E. Woodberry, *Criticism in America: Its Function and Status* (New York: Harcourt, Brace, 1924), pp. 162, 165. Babbitt believed that Joel Spingarn was Croce's American spokesman. So when Babbitt mis-

interpreted Spingarn's views, he misunderstood Croce's aesthetic as well. Also see Norman Foerster, "The Esthetic Judgment and the Ethical Judgment," in *The Intent of the Critic*, pp. 63–88.

49. Croce, *Nuovi saggi*, p. 122.

50. See p. 110 below.

51. See p. 118 below.

52. Benedetto Croce, *Poesia popolare e poesia d'arte* (Bari: Gius. Laterza, 1967), pp. 76–77.

53. Benedetto Croce, *Nuove pagine sparse, serie prima* (Naples: Riccardo Ricciardi, 1949), pp. 220–221. Here Croce assumed De Sanctis' point and developed it. See Francesco De Sanctis, *Saggio critico sul Petrarca* (Milan: Marzorati, 1971), pp. 125–127. For a critical comparison of De Sanctis and Croce on Petrarca, see my article, "Petrarca and Modern Criticism," *Rivista Rosminiana*, Fasc. I (Jan.-Mar., 1977): 35–42.

54. E. Cione, *Benedetto Croce* (Milan: Longanesi, 1935), pp. 63–64; Cosimo Gancitano, *Critica dell'estetica crociana* (Mazara: società editrice siciliana, 1948), p. 36.

55. G. Castellano, *Benedetto Croce* (Bari: Gius. Laterza & Figli, 1936), p. 37.

56. See Gancitano, *Critica dell'estetica crociana*, p. 36.

57. Orsini, *Croce*, pp. 210ff.

58. *Ibid.*, pp. 224–225.

59. *Ibid.*, p. 36.

60. *Ibid.*, pp. 213, 215–216.

61. Benedetto Croce, *Ultimi saggi* (Bari: Laterza & Figli, 1963), pp. 54–57.

62. Croce, *Nuovi saggi*, p. 124.

63. Croce's position on this point differed thus from René Wellek's interpretation of Crocean theory as holding that "Things could be settled for good." See René Wellek, *History of Modern Criticism, 1750–1950* (New Haven: Yale University Press, 1986), vol. 5, *English Criticism, 1900–1950*, p. xxiii.

64. *Nuovi saggi*, p. 79. Cf. Croce, *Guide to Aesthetics*, p. 73.

65. For a discussion of Croce's coherence theory see my "Benedetto Croce's Coherence Theory of Truth: A Critical Evaluation," *Filosofia* 19 (1968): 107–116. Also see Croce, *Logic*, pp. 391ff.

66. See Moss, *Benedetto Croce Reconsidered*, ch. 5.

67. See Croce, *Logic*, pp. 180ff.

68. See p. 120 below.

69. See pp. 121, 123 below.

70. See p. 28 below.

71. See pp. 55, 56 below.

72. See p. 75 below.

73. See p. 121 below.

74. Benedetto Croce, *La poesia: introduzione alla critica e storia della poesia e della letteratura* (Bari: Laterza, 1963). For an English translation, see Benedetto Croce, *Poetry and Literature*, trans. Giovanni Gullace (Carbondale: Southern Illinois University Press, 1981).

75. See Wimsatt and Brooks, *Literary Criticism: A Short History*, p. 519; René Wellek, *History of Modern Criticism*, vol. 5, p. xiii; and G. N. G. Orsini, "Theory and Practice in Croce's Aesthetic," *Journal of Aesthetics and Art Criticism*, 13 (1954–55): 308.

76. For a critical bibliography of treatments of Croce's thought in the United States from 1964–1984, see Ernesto Caserta's *Studi crociani negli stati uniti*.

77. T. D. B., "Modern Italian Critics," *The Nation*, 86, no. 2234 (April 23, 1908): 373. For a similar comment made more than thirty years later, see Thomas Munroe, "Aesthetics as Science: Its Development in America," *Journal of Aesthetics and Art Criticism*, 9 (1950–51): 162.

78. John Paul Pritchard, *Criticism in America*, p. 200. Also see René Wellek, *History of Modern Criticism*, vol. 5, p. viii. In the sixth volume of his *History of Modern Criticism*, entitled *American Criticism, 1900–1950*, p. 63, Wellek maintained that allusions to Spingarn were rare. Spingarn did draw attention to Croce, but Croce was also filtered through Ainslie's translation of the *Estetica*, while the bulk of his work was being ignored.

79. Joel Spingarn, *Literary Criticism in the Renaissance* (New York: Macmillan 1899). In a preface to the English second edition, written in 1924 and attached to the fourth and subsequent printings (the first printing of the second edition occurred in 1908), Spingarn remarked that the Italian translation of his book published in 1905 included much important material not present in the English editions.

80. Joel Spingarn, *La critica letteraria nel Rinascimento*, trans. Antonio Fusco with a preface by Benedetto Croce (Bari: Laterza, 1905).

81. See Joel Spingarn's review of Benedetto Croce's "Tesi fondamentali di un'Estetica come scienza dell'espressione e linguistica generale," *Atti dell'accademia pontaniana*, 30 (1900): p. 88, in *The Nation*, 71, no. 1846 (November 15, 1900): 386.

82. George Santayana, "Croce's Aesthetics," *Journal of Comparative Literature*, ed. G. E. Woodbury, J. Spingarn, J. B. Fletcher, 1 (1903): 191–195. This first and last issue included an essay on the concept of humor by Benedetto Croce. See B. Croce, *"L'umorismo,"* *ibid.*: 220–228.

83. George Santayana, "What is Aesthetics?" *Philosophical Review*, 13 (1904): 320. Also see Frederic S. Simoni's discussion of the harmful effect which Santayana's reviews had on subsequent U.S. philosophers in "Benedetto Croce: A Case of International Misunderstanding," *The Journal of Aesthetics and Art Criticism*, 11 (September 1952): 7–14; and James Steinman, "Santayana and Croce: An Aesthetic Reconciliation," *ibid.*, 30, no. 2 (Winter 1971): 251–253.

84. Benedetto Croce, *Estetica come scienza dell'espressione e linguistica generale* (Bari, 1902).

85. *The Nation*, 73, no. 1881 (July 18, 1901): 60.

86 Conrad Aiken, "Metaphysics and Art," *The New Republic*, 40, no. 520 (November 19, 1924): 301. Also see W. K. Wimsatt, Jr., and Cleanthe Brooks, *Literary Criticism: A Short History*, p. 504; W. K. Wimsatt, Jr., *Hateful Contraries: Studies in Literature and Criticism* (Kentucky: University of Kentucky Press, 1965), pp. 51, 69; and W. K. Wimsatt, Jr. with M. Beardsley, *The Verbal Icon* (Kentucky: University of Kentucky Press, 1954), pp. 257–258.

87. For an argument for the necessity of a philosophical foundation for aesthetics, see Ernesto Paolozzi, *I problemi dell'estetica italiana* (Naples: Società editrice napoletana, 1985).

88. *The Nation*, 75, no. 1943 (September 25, 1902): 252.

89. The erroneous belief that Croce advocated a complete dismissal of the literary genres, along with all other classifications of the arts, led to harsh criticism from aestheticians and historians. See for example, René Wellek, "The parallelism between Literature and the Arts, 1941," in *Literary Criticism: Idea and Act*, ed. W. K. Wimsatt (Berkeley: University of California Press, 1974), pp. 60–61; René Wellek, "Literary History," in N. Foerster, J. C. McGalliard, René Wellek, Austin Warren, Wilbur Schramm, *Literary Scholarship: Its Aims and Methods* (Chapel Hill: University of North Carolina Press, 1941), p. 127; Austin Warren, "Literary Criticism," *ibid.*, p. 142; and René Wellek, *History of Modern Criticism, 1750–1950*, vol. 2, *The Romantic Age*, p. 50.

90. W. K. Wimsatt, Jr., with M. Beardsley, *The Verbal Icon*, p. 283.

91. W. K. Wimsatt, Jr., and C. Brooks, *Literary Criticism: A Short History*, pp. 499–521.

92. This lecture delivered on March 9, 1910, was published first by Columbia University Press in 1911. Subsequently it was reprinted in *Criticism in America: Its Function and Status, op. cit.* and in J. E. Spingarn's *Creative Criticism and other Essays* (New York: Harcourt, Brace, 1931). There were no theoretical links

between Spingarn's lecture and John Crowe Ransom's *The New Criticism* (Norfolk: New Directions, 1941). According to René Wellek, the latter movement was anglocentric and provincial. Ransom criticized Croce for asserting that art is simple child's play and claimed that Crocean aesthetics denied him a criticism of art. (See René Wellek, *History of Modern Criticism,* vol. 6, p. 166). Perhaps Ransom's misinterpretation of Crocean aesthetics originated from Spingarn's identification of criticism with the creative act itself (see Spingarn, *Creative Criticism and other Essays,* pp. 36–37). On this point, also see Irving Babbitt, "Genius and Taste," *Criticism in America,* p. 175; and W. K. Wimsatt, Jr., and C. Brooks, *Literary Criticism: A Short History,* pp. 517ff.

93. Arthur James Balfour, *Criticism and Beauty: A Lecture Rewritten* (Oxford: Clarendon Press, 1910).

94. See *The Athenaeum,* 2, no. 4284 (December 4, 1909): 690–691.

95. Balfour, *Criticism and Beauty,* pp. 5, 12, 13, 46–48.

96. Spingarn, *Creative Criticism,* pp. 19–20.

97. *Ibid.,* pp. 16–17.

98. Henry Mencken, *Prejudices,* 1st series (New York: Knopf, 1919), pp. 10ff.

99. *Ibid.,* pp. 12–13.

100. *Ibid.,* p. 17.

101. Spingarn, *Creative Criticism,* p. 163.

102. *Ibid.,* p. 174.

103. *Ibid.,* p. 168–169.

104. Wimsatt with Beardsley, *The Verbal Icon,* p. 281.

105. Spingarn, *Creative Criticism,* pp. 20–37.

106. See, for instance, Norman Foerster, "The Esthetic Judgment and the Ethical Judgment," *The Intent of the Critic,* pp. 65–68.

107. During the 1920's, Raffaello Piccoli introduced Croce's literary criticism and philosophy to the American public through reviews and an Italian letter to *The Dial,* a journal devoted to literary criticism, discussion and information.

108. Conrad Aiken, "Metaphysics and Art," *The New Republic,* 40, no. 520 (November 19, 1924): 301.

109. Roy Kenneth Hack, "The Doctrine of Literary Forms," *Harvard Studies in Classical Philology,* ed. Committee of the Classical Instructors of Harvard University (Cambridge: Harvard University Press, 1916), 38: 1–65. Also see Sir

Henry Newbolt, *New Study of English Poetry* (London: Constable and Co., Ltd., 1917). See W. K. Wimsatt, Jr., and C. Brooks, *Literary Criticism: A Short History,* p. 519, for a description of the diffusion of Croce's thought.

110. John Dewey, *Art as Experience* (Carbondale: Southern Illinois University Press, 1987).

111. Croce's Italian review of Dewey's *Art as Experience* was translated by Katherine Gilbert into English. See Benedetto Croce, "On the Aesthetics of Dewey," *Journal of Aesthetics and Art Criticism,* 6, no. 3 (March 1958): 203–207. Also see Dewey's reply "A Comment on the foregoing Criticisms," *ibid.,* pp. 207–209; Croce's further comment "Dewey's Aesthetics and Theory of Knowledge," *ibid,* 11, no. 1 (September 1952): 1–6; and Stephen Pepper's essay "Some Questions on Dewey's Esthetics," in *The Philosophy of John Dewey,* ed. Paul Arthur Schilpp (New York: Tudor, 1951), pp. 369–389. Also see George H. Douglas, "A Reconsideration of the Dewey-Croce Exchange," *Journal of Aesthetics and Art Criticism,* 28 (1969–70): 497–504; and Patrick Romanell, "A Comment on Croce's and Dewey's Aesthetic," *ibid.,* 8 (1949–50): 125–128.

112. See Stephen Pepper, "Some Questions on Dewey's Esthetics."

113. During the decades of the twentieth century, there have been a number of excellent American and Italo-American translators and commentators on Croce's thought. Among the scholars who have helped my own work were Raffaello Piccoli, Patrick Romanell, Maurice Mandelbaum, Gian Orsini, Angelo De Gennaro, A. Robert Caponigri, H. Stuart Hughes, and Giovanni Gullace.

114. On our side Gian Orsini, and on the Italian Raffaello Franchini, emphasized the importance of understanding Croce's theory of judgment for a comprehension of his aesthetics and literary criticism.

Chapter 1: Homer

1. This essay was translated from "Omero: interpretazione moderna di taluni giudizî antichi," in *Poesia antica e moderna* (Bari: Gius. Laterza & Figli, 1966), pp. 31–89; published earlier under the title "Studî su poesie antiche e moderne. 26. Omero: interpretazione moderna di taluni giudizî antichi," in *La critica,* 38 (1940): 129–134.

2. See Aristotle, "De Poetica," trans. Ingram Bywater in *The Works of Aristotle,* ed. W. D. Ross (Oxford: Clarendon Press, 1959), vol. 11, ch. 26, 1461b.

Chapter 2: Terence

1. This essay was translated from "Terenzio," in *Poesia antica e moderna* (Bari: Guis. Laterza & Figli, 1966), pp. 1–30. It was published earlier under the title "Studî su poesie antiche e moderne. 1. Intorno alle commedie di Terenzio," *La critica,* 34 (1936): 401–423.

2. Recently these verses have been attributed instead to Cicero; see Hermann, in *Musée belge*, 34:243 ff.; G. de Sanctis in *Riv. di filol. classica*, n. s. 10 (1932): 330–331; Ferrarino, in *Studî ital. di filol. classica* (Florence, 1939): 51–58; but for a contrary position with good arguments, see G. Perrotta in the same volume of *Studî:* 111–125. [Croce's note]

3. Whether one places a comma after *vis* as in modern editions and *comica* becomes joined with *virtus* is not important. For here the sense would still be to deny Terence's power as a writer of comedies. I would exclude the interpretation that Terence generally lacked power and "did not strongly stir the emotion" (Tamagni-D'Ovidio, *Storia della letter. latina*, p. 331), or as Leo says (*Gesch d. röm. Liter.*, I [Berlin, 1913], pp. 253–254), "Terence is a half-Menander: he loves good language, but his gentle style lacks power. His expressive quality, thus, remains inferior to that of Greek comedy." I confess my reluctance to attribute to Caesar so many obviously contradictory statements (Terence is a simple cultivator of good language; a poet who touches the soul, but without poetic force, etc.). [Croce's note]

4. I do not understand how Prof. Edw. E. Rand, of Harvard University ("Térence et l'esprit comique," in *Revue des cours et conférences* [15 June 1935]: 393), can write: "Jules César . . . l'appelle un autre Ménandre, si j'interprète correctement cette fameuse phrase: 'dimidiate Menander.' " [Croce's note]

5. Benedetto Croce, *Poesia popolare e poesia d'arte*, 4th ed. (Bari, 1957), pp. 247 ff. [Croce's note]

6. Among others, there is one by Pichon, *Hist. de la littér. latine*, 3d ed. (Paris, 1903), p. 81. [Croce's note]

7. Pietro Napoli Signorelli, *Storia critica dei teatri antichi e moderni* (Naples: Orsini, 1813; the first and more succinct edition appeared in 1771), III, pp. 154 ff. [Croce's note]

8. The proper names "Macci," "Pappi," "Bucconi," and "Dossenni" refer to types of character represented in the *fabula Atellana*. "Maccus" played the fool; "Pappus" played the foolish old man, the dotard who was easily deceived; "Bucco" played the glutton or braggart; and "Dossennus" played the cunning swindler.

9. "Permit me a smile when one says: 'Racine did a great thing! He created *Phèdre!* But he confessed that he took it from Euripides.' Admit this, and admit even more: that he took more from Seneca than from Euripides; that the third scene, first act, derives almost entirely from Euripides; that Phèdre's declaration of love was lifted from Seneca; that the jealousy episode was inspired by Seneca. What more? Admit that he borrowed not only the situations, but also the images, thoughts, and sentiments. And then? Then you will have proven nothing. The distance between a collaborative patchwork and Racine remains infinite. You, who accuse Racine, have before you all of nature, all the works of art. I give you license

to imitate, to take from any source: take up your pen. Match Racine. And the pen falls from your hand." De Sanctis wrote thus in his 1856 essay on *Phèdre*. [Croce's note]

10. For this reason I am dissatisfied with Jachmann's twofold criteria for judging the artistic value of translations: first, the degree of difficulty which the original, its content, language, and meter present; and second, the degree of enrichment and refinement which popular language receives through the translator's work. (See Jachmann's article on Terence in the new edition of Pauly-Wissowa, *Encykl. der Klass. Altertumswissenschaft* [1934], p. 625). These criteria are indeed meritorious and culturally interesting. They are valuable for the history of the international circulation of literary works and of language, but not in respect to art. The fundamental condition for a beautiful translation is that the translator be himself a poetic spirit, who brings his own feeling-tone to the original, substituting it for what remains untranslatable in its fullness and individuality. See my *Poesia*, pp. 100–104. [Croce's note]

11. *Vorlesungen über dramatische literatur*, ed. Amoretti, I, p. 171. More inflexible, more acute and learned than anyone else among recent writers who present Terence as a mere translator, displaying the inevitable deterioration that obtains between the original and the translation is Jachmann. In the article just cited, he restricts Terence's originality exclusively to his technical ability of the "contaminatio" (p. 629). ["Contamination," consisted of the process of interweaving parts of two or more Greek comedies to form one Latin play. In three of the Menanderian plays, Terence supposedly practiced "contamination." M.M.] He acknowledges, indeed, the beauty of Terence's style, but as "atticism," as the result of his being "tief eingefühlt" in the Menanderian drama. But in truth this is not enough to explain his result. To experience sensitively the work of a poet, to relive it in its character, tone, and shading is the necessary condition for literary judgment. But to transplant poetry in a living way into another language, or into another form, requires something quite different. It requires a proper poetic disposition, which to some extent will always alter the original work, as we have already noted. Beautiful translations are "belle infedeli." I permit myself, besides, to doubt the concept of the "nachschaffen" or the "nachbilden" which are customarily used (even by Jachmann). The prefix *nach*, it seems to me, precludes *schaffen* and *bilden*. The distinction between "gestaltende" and "reproduzierende Dichter," even if it serves in ordinary conversation, will not stand rigorous scrutiny; because the poet, supposing he is a poet, is always, in some tone or other, *gestaltend* or *produzierend*. [Croce's note]

12. See my other observations on the tedious and futile disputes about the crypto-author of the Shakespearean plays (in *Ariosto, Shakespeare e Corneille*, 5th ed., pp. 75 ff.). [Croce's note]

13. See F. Nencini, *De Terentio eiusque fontibus* (Liburni: Giusti, 1891), p. 5: "Terenti aetatis tale fuisse ingenium, ut ad captandum spectatorum favorem poetae Graecorum fidos faterentur interpretes." [Croce's note]

14. For Terence, see Leo, *op. cit.*, pp. 238–248. [Croce's note]

15. G. Capovilla, *Menandro* (Milan, 1924), pp. 338–339, comparing the *Hecyra* with the *Epitrepontes,* criticizes Terence for the "make-shift of a very poor technique." G. Coppola, in his edition of *Le commedie di Menandro,* critical text and commentary (Turin, 1927), p. 163, adopting the same comparison, judges that the Roman author "emphasizes a most banal and unpleasant point in order to move the somewhat lame plot of the play" all of which "lead to an ineffective third act." Hence Terence or the Greek epigone whom he takes as a model "has imitated Menander very poorly, succeeding in suppressing the truly dramatic parts and unnecessarily coloring scenes devoid of value." The already cited Napoli Signorelli, an old "theatrical technician," very knowledgeable about the theater of every period, and himself the writer of comedies, judges the *Hecyra* quite differently: "the point at which the action begins is felicitously chosen, and the passions are handled in a masterly way. There are no mix-ups, no servile rogueries or buffooneries, but this shows that truly pleasant scenes can consist in other things. All the characters are good, not with the imaginary goodness of the morality schools, nor of the heroic sort that takes place in tragedies, but with a civil goodness that keeps us from guilt, without precluding us from weaknesses" (*Storia critica,* III, pp. 176 ff.). [Croce's note]

16. *Essais,* II, c. 10. [Croce's note]

17. Suetonius, in the *Vita P. Terentii,* recalls that: "Adelphorum principium Varro etiam praefert principio Menandri." Donatus, in his commentary, notes that Terence did "melius quam Menander," and elsewhere that he composed εὑρητικῶς, inventively, and so forth. Cupaiuolo believes that in general Terence aimed at a more "exact life-likeness." See his edition of the *Adelphoe* (Rome-Milan, 1904), p. LXXXI. [Croce's note]

18. See the most authoritative of these authors, Jachmann, *op. cit.,* p. 632. He writes that the first scene of the *Andria,* which does not occur in the two Menanderian comedies adopted by Terence, must have rested on "an irgendein attisches Muster." On pp. 635–637, Jachmann says that the scene with Antiphon in the *Eunuchus* could not have been invented and stylized so admirably by Terence, as Donatus holds, for Terence was a simple translator and not an original talent. To restore the authority of Donatus' text, which here too displays sound judgment, Pasquali (*Studî italiani di filol. classica,* vol. XIII, 1936, fasc. II, pp. 117–127), disagreeing with Jachmann, takes pains to prove that artistically the addition, after all, is no great thing and that even a poor wretch like Terence, gleaning here and there, could have written it. [Croce's note]

19. Montaigne, in the essay cited earlier, states: "J'estime que les anciens avoient encore plus à se plaindre de ceulx qui apparioient Plaute à Térence (celui-ci sent bien mieulx son gentilhomme), que Lucrèce à Virgile." (Montaigne, let it be noted in passing, cherished the belief that "Terence" was a pseudonym for Scipio and for Laelius: *Essais,* I, c. 39). Abhorring parallels, I will guard against comparing the two Roman comic writers and making one superior to the other, or one superior in certain matters and the other in other things. The passage that follows is typical of such current judgments and occurs in a good encyclopedia: "Von Plautus

zeichnet sich Terentius durch kunstgerechte Anlage und Eleganz der Sprache aus, steht ihm aber an Kraft und Witz nach, wie er auch hinter der lebendigen Komik seines Vorbildes Menanders zurückblieb." But I do not believe that it can be denied that Plautus concentrates principally on caricature, on the grotesque and the laughable; and everything, the many serious reflections that he introduces, even more the humanity that he shows himself to possess, is consistent with that interpretation; although he also composed a few comedies for "white nights," like the *Capitivi*, or comedies of pathetic adventures like the *Rudens.* "He makes all emotions ridiculous, without offending their nature," as Gravina says very well in his *Ragion poetica* (1709), ch. 24. In any case, the character of the two authors is conspicuously different; and entirely different is their treatment of the Greek originals. This fact is generally recognized: see Leo, *op. cit.*, pp. 246–248, 250–251. [Croce's note]

20. In the epistle LVIII *ad Paulinum* (Migne's edition, I, pp. 322–323: "Romani duces imitentur Camillos, Fabricios, Regulos, Scipiones. Philosophi proponant sibi Pythagoram, Socratem, Platonem, Ariostotelem. Poetae aemulentur Homerum, Vergilium, Menandrum, Terentium. Historici etc. etc." [Croce's note]

21. See the *Vita Terentii excerpta de dictis F. P.* (reprinted in the Hague edition, 1726). [Croce's note]

22. The difference between the two authors as formulated here is not the same as that put forward with the usual prejudice against Terence by Croiset ("Ménandre," *Revue des deux mondes* [15 April 1909]: 817), "Une comédie de Ménandre n'est pas du tout une simple série de dialogues finement nuancés où se refléteraient des sentiments toujours tempérés, etc." [Croce's note]

23. Many have admitted that the recent Menander discoveries do not support the belief that Terence's comedies are simple translations of Menander's work, yet they draw the already stated conclusions that if Terence did not copy from Menander, he must have copied from other Greeks. "Grâce aux papyres récemment découverts, nous voyons aujourd'hui s'accentuer les différences qui, d'après les témoignages des anciens eux-mêmes, distinguaient Térence de Ménandre. Mais en quelles proportions les caractères que nous croyons lui être propres ont-ils été développés par la lecture des poètes secondaires, de Diphile et d'Apollodore en particulier?": G. Lafaye, "Le modèle de Térence dans l'*Hecyra*," *Revue de philologie* 40 (1916): 30. [Croce's note]

24. K. Stavenhagen, "Menandros *Epitrepontes* und Apollodoros *Hecyra*," *Hermes* 45 (1910): 564–582. [Croce's note]

25. Thus Pasquali, "Perché s'intenda l'arte di Menandro," *Atene e Roma* 20 (1917): 178 n. [Croce's note]

26. "Die Freude am technischen Problem hat zur Umgestaltung der *Epitrepontes* geführt" (Stavenhagen, *op. cit.*, p. 581). [Croce's note]

27. G. Pasquali, *op. cit.*, 20 (1917): 177 ff.; 21 (1918): 21 ff. [Croce's note]

28. *Ibid.*, 21:15. [Croce's note]

29. *Ibid.*, 20:184–185. [Croce's note]

30. "A general solution of that problem, as long as society remains as it is, is impossible, for the only theoretically (?) acceptable one, which is that both sexes are obliged to remain absolutely chaste until marriage, conflicts too strongly with the nature of the male" (*op. cit.*, 20:185). [Croce's note]

31. *Op. cit.*, 20:185–186. [Croce's note]

32. All this should sound elementary; but since it always needs recalling, I will do so this time by quoting a passage written by the poet Grillparzer in 1816: "No poet on earth has ever, in creating a masterpiece, started from a general idea" (*Werke*, 4th ed., vol. 14, p. 7). [Croce's note]

33. "You will not endure the involuntary disgrace of a woman; I will show you how you have fallen into a similar one" (Coppola's edition, see ll. 608–609; Jensen's edition, see ll. 530–531. [Croce's note]

34. What happiness my visit has secured to Pamphilus, what blessings it has brought and what troubles cleared away! I give him back a child who by the women's doing and his own was within an ace of destruction; I restore him a wife with whom he never expected to live again; I have freed him from what made his father and Phidippus look askance at him . . .

From: Terence, "The Mother-in-law," vol. 2 of *Terence*, trans. John Sargeaunt (London: William Heinemann; New York: G. P. Putnam's Sons, 1931), p. 205. All subsequent English translations of Terence's plays are from this source.

35. Capovilla, *op. cit.*, p. 339. [Croce's note]

36. O Bacchis, oh my dear Bacchis, my preserver.

Terence, "The Mother-in-law," *Terence*, p. 209.

37. You were quite right to love your wife, Pamphilus.

Ibid.

38. And make no exception?

Ibid., p. 133.

39. Still I vow it's wrong to treat all alike.

Ibid.

40. Why, you profit by your goodness: *we* can't be good, the men we have to do with won't let us.

Terence, "The Self-tormentor," *Terence*, vol. 1, p. 155.

41. Article cited, p. 19: But the stress upon the ἑταῖραι χρησταί of Menander based on Plutarch, *Quaest. conviv.*, 8, 3, does not demonstrate that Menander treated the character of the courtesan with feeling. It says only that the *hetairai* and mistresses either are impudent and insolent, and are punished and abandoned by the young men; or they are honest and loving, and a legitimate father is found for them, or the young men are allowed to prolong their relationship with them for some time. [Croce's note]

42. Ha, that's the secret, that's the source of his tears, that's his compassion.

Terence, "The Lady of Andros," *Terence*, vol. 1, p. 15.

43. He darted forward, caught the girl round the waist, and cried "Oh my Glycerium, what are you thinking of? Why try to destroy yourself?" Then you might easily see they were no new lovers: bursting into tears she fell back in his arms, oh so trustingly!

Ibid., p. 17.

44. This stupendous scene has inspired scholars to observe merely the following: According to an inference from Donatus's commentary, here Terence has changed the original Greek dialogue between an old man and his wife into one between an old man and a freed man, who was once his servant. This alteration has disturbed the technical order of the comedy (see, among others, Leo, *op. cit.*, 1:338–339). With an acumen which I usually define as "perverse acumen," another scholar, Jacobi, discovered (and was praised for his discovery) that Terence "made use of the character of the slave to express his gratitude (as a freed slave) to his masters" (P. Fossataro, in *Riv. di filol. classica*, 43 [1914]: 453). [Croce's note]

45. What I, I bring myself to dream of such a thing? I be so selfish as to let the poor girl be deceived when she has trusted me with her heart, with all her life, when I have made her my heart's darling and treated her as the wife of my bosom? Trained and reared as she has been in virtue and purity, shall I allow her to be corrupted under the pressure of beggary?

Ibid., pp. 29, 31.

46. But *I* do. Ransom yourself from captivity as cheaply as you can; if you can't do it for a small sum, make the best bargain you can, and don't worry yourself to death.

Terrence, "The Eunuch," *Terence*, vol. 1, p. 243.

47. Don't torture yourself, don't for heaven's sake, my life, my dearest Phaedria. I swear it was not loving anyone more or valuing anyone more made me do it. Circumstances were such that I had to do it.

Ibid., p. 245.

48. Lord! what a strange disease it is! Think of men changing so much under love that you wouldn't know one for the same man! There was a time when there was no one less foolish, more grave, or more temperate.

Ibid., p. 255.

49. "The action of the *Hecyra* develops in its own way, even if somewhat forced, with the parallel relations between Sostrata-Laches and Myrrhina-Phidippus. We note too much symmetry between the grumbling of Laches to Sostrata and that of Phidippus to Myrrhina. It is true, nevertheless, that the characters of the two matrons are diverse, and in their differences, there are not a few points of contact." Capovilla, *op. cit.*, pp. 339–340). [Croce's note]

50. Why shouldn't I, if Hercules became slave to Omphale?
    A satisfactory precedent!

Terence, "The Eunuch," *Terence*, vol. 1, p. 343.

51. Unless this be the Thais to whom Propertius alludes (IV, 5, lines 43–44), and who does not seem to be remarkably charming: "mundi Thais pretiosa Menandri. Cum ferit astutos comica moecha Getas": here "pretiosa" means that she sells herself at a high price. [Croce's note]

52. In the above cited *Studî ital. di filol. classica*, p. 129. [Croce's note]

53. According to Leo, Terence's success was almost that of a writer's writer: "Doch gab es Kreise, denen das feine terenzische Wesen zusagte; es waren die literarische Interessierten, und diese waren zahlreich geworden, auch in die obersten Schichten der römischen Gesellschaft. Hier dauerte seine Wirkung fort, und wurde stärker mit dem Wachsen des literarischen Interesses" (*op. cit.*, p. 257). Varro's judgment of the three Roman comic writers has been interpreted too superficially by Leo (p. 237). He understands Varro's statement as meaning that Terence had adopted not only the "inventions" of Menander, but also his "determinations of the characters." The words of this passage in Varro (where no reference is made to Menander) would, in the light of good sense, seem to mean that Caecilius excels in structure or action ("in argumentis"), Plautus in lively dialogue ("in sermonibus"), and Terence in presentation of characters ("in ethesin"), or better as we say today, in portrayal of feelings. [Croce's note]

Chapter 3: Lucretius and Virgil

1. This essay was translated from "Lucrezio e Virgilio. Il 'De rerum natura' e i 'Georgica,' " in *Poesia antica e moderna* (Bari: Gius. Laterza & Figli, 1966), pp. 39–54. It appeared earlier under the title "Studî su poesie antiche e moderne. 19. Poesia latina. Intorno a due carmi didascalici. Il 'De rerum natura' e i 'Georgica,' " in *La critica*, 37 (1939): 241–252.

2. See note 10 below.

3. In the preface to a translation (1731) of *Sifilis* by Fracastoro (in *Opere*, VII, *Scritti varî*, ed. Nicolini, p. 46). [Croce's note]

4.   Thou, father, art
the discoverer of truths, thou dost supply us with a
father's precepts, from thy pages, illustrious man,
as bees in the flowery glades sip all the sweets,
so we likewise feed on thy golden words, thy
words of gold, ever most worthy of life eternal. For
as soon as thy reasoning born of a divine intelligence
begins to proclaim the nature of things, away flee
the mind's terrors, the walls of the heavens open
out, I see action going on throughout the whole
void: before me appear the gods in their majesty,
and their peaceful abodes, which no winds ever
shake nor clouds besprinkle with rain, which no
snow congealed by the bitter frost mars with its
white fall, but the air ever cloudless encompasses
them and laughs with its light spread wide abroad.

From Lucretius, *De Rerum Natura*, trans. W. H. D. Rouse, 3d ed. rev. (Cambridge: Harvard University Press; London: William Heinemann, 1964), p. 171. All subsequent English translations of the *De Rerum Natura* are taken from this source.

5. But nothing is more delightful than to possess well
fortified sanctuaries serene, built up by the teachings
of the wise . . .

Ibid., p. 85.

6.   . . . they cling
greedily close together and join their watering mouths
and draw deep breaths pressing teeth on lips; but all
is vanity, for they can rub nothing off thence, nor
can they penetrate and be absorbed body in body:
for this they seem sometimes to wish and to strive
for; so eagerly do they cling in the couplings of
Venus, while their limbs slacken and melt under
the power of delight. At length when the gathered
desire has been all exhausted, there is a short pause
for a while in the furious burning. Then the same
frenzy returns, and once more the madness comes;
when they are at fault themselves what it is they
want to reach, and can find no device to master the
trouble, in such uncertainty do they pine with their
secret wound.

Ibid., p. 327.

7. *Storia della letteratura latina*, vol. 1, pp. 187–188. [Croce's note]

8. *De Rerum Natura,* p. 9.

9. *Scienza nuova,* l. I, *Degli elementi,* XL. [Croce's note]

10. See page 53 above for Croce's reference to Vico's inexact reversal of Lucretius' description.

11. For often in front of the nobel shrines of the gods a
    calf falls slain beside the incense-burning altars,
    breathing up a hot stream of blood from his breast;
    but the mother bereaved wanders through the green
    glens, and knows the prints marked on the ground by
    the cloven hooves, as she surveys all the regions if she
    may espy somewhere her lost offspring, and coming to
    a stand fills the leafy woods with her moaning, and
    often revisits the stall pierced with yearning for her
    young calf; nor can tender willow-growths, and grass
    growing rich in the dew, and those rivers flowing
    level with their banks, give delight to her mind and
    rebuff that care which has entered there, nor can the
    sight of other calves in the happy pastures divert
    her mind and lighten her load of care: so persistently
    she seeks for something of her own that she knows
    well.

Ibid., pp. 109, 111.

12.   . . . from thee, O goddess, from thee,
    the winds flee away, the clouds of heaven from
    thee and thy coming; for thee the wonder-working
    earth puts forth sweet flowers, for thee the wide
    stretches of ocean laugh, and heaven grown peaceful
    glows with outpoured light. For as soon as the
    vernal face of day is made manifest, and the
    breeze of the teeming south wind blows fresh and
    free, thee first the fowls of the air proclaim, thee
    divine one, and thy advent, pierced to the heart by
    thy might: next the herds go wild and dance over
    the rich pastures and swim across rapid rivers, so
    greedily does each one follow thee, held captive
    by thy charm, whither thou goest on to lead them.
    Aye, throughout seas and mountains and sweeping
    torrents and the leafy dwellings of birds and verdant
    plains, striking soft love into the breasts of all
    creatures, thou dost cause them greedily to beget
    their generations after their kind.

Ibid., pp. 3, 5.

13.   For the very
nature of divinity must necessarily enjoy immortal
life in the deepest peace, far removed and separated from our troubles; for without any pain,
without danger, itself mighty by its own resources,
needing us not at all, it is neither propitiated with
services nor touched by wrath.

Ibid., p. 131. Perhaps for the reason given on page 55, Croce did not cite a loca-
tion for this passage. The translation cited above places it in Book II, lines 646–
651.

14. See the note appended here in the Giussani edition. [Croce's note]

15. See Bignone, "Nuove ricerche sul proemio del poema di Lucrezio" (in
Rivista di filologia classica, 47 [1919]: 423–433). [Croce's note]

16. Citation found in *Storia della letteratura romana* by Teuffel. [Croce's
note] "Virgil's *Georgics* are so far from being a poem absolute in all respects that
they are rather a poem altogether repugnant to true and genuine poetry." Title translated by Dr. John Steadman.

17. Fornari, *Arte del dire*, II, p. 279. [Croce's note]

18.   Need I tell of him who
flings the seed, then, hoe in hand, closes with the
soil, and lays low the hillocks of barren sand? next
brings to his crops the rills of the stream he guides,
and when the scorched land swelters, the green
blades dying, lo! from the brow of the hill-side
channel decoys the water? This, as it falls, wakes
a hoarse murmur amid the smooth stones, and with
its gushing streams slakes the thirsty fields.

From: Virgil, "The Georgics," vol. 1 of *Virgil*, trans. H. Rushton Fairclough, rev.
ed. (Cambridge: Harvard University Press, 1942), p. 89. All subsequent English
translations of "The Georgics" are taken from this source.

19.   Then
came iron's stiffness and the shrill saw-blade—for
early man cleft the splitting wood with wedges;
then came divers arts.

Ibid., p. 91.

20.   In alternate seasons you will also let your fields
lie fallow after reaping, and the plain idly stiffen
with scurf; or, beneath another star, sow yellow
corn in lands whence you have first carried off the
pulse that rejoices in its quivering pods, or the fruits

of the slender vetch, or the brittle stalks and rattling
tangle of the bitter lupine. For a crop of flax
parches the ground; oats parch it, and poppies,
steeped in Lethe's slumber.

Ibid., pp. 85, 87.

21.   Often under the
ground the tiny mouse sets up a home and builds his
storehouses, or sightless moles dig out chambers; in
holes may be found the toad, and all the countless
pests born of the earth; or the weevil ravages a
huge heap of grain, or the ant, anxious for a destitute
old age.

Ibid., p. 93.

22.   Then the rooks, with
narrowed throat, thrice or four times repeat their
soft cries, and oft in their high nests, joyous with some
strange, unwonted delight, chatter to each other
amid the leaves. Glad are they, the rains over, to
see once more their little brood and their sweet nests.

Ibid., p. 109.

23.   One I know spends wake-
ful hours by the late blaze of a winter-fire, and with
sharp knife points torches; his wife the while solaces
with song her long toil, runs the shrill shuttle through
the web, or on the fire boils down the sweet juice of
must, and skims with leaves the wave of the bubbling
cauldron.

Ibid., p. 101.

24. G. Mestica, *Istituzioni di Letteratura* (Florence: 1882), II, pp. 660–661.

Chapter 4: Aeneas Facing Dido

1. This essay was translated from "Virgilio: Enea di fronte a Didone," in
Poesia antica e moderna (Bari: Gius. Laterza & Figli, 1966), pp. 55–65. It was
published earlier under the title "Studî su poesie antiche e moderne. 13. Virgilio.
Enea di fronte a Didone," *La critica*, 36 (1938): 401–408.

2. I will not hide the fact that in 1882, at the age of sixteen, I too hurled
my pebble at Aeneas in a school essay, subsequently published in a literary journal,
that I now, with sweet amazement, see included in the body of "Virgilian literature." It is cited and discussed, for instance, in C. Buscaroli's rich anthology of

criticism, *Il libro di Didone.* The text, with facing translation, is followed by an ample interpretative and aesthetic commentary (Milan: 1932), *passim.* [Croce's note]

3. Publius Vergilius Maro, "Aeneid," vol. 1 of *Virgil,* trans. H. Rushton Fairclough, rev. ed. (Cambridge: Harvard University Press; London: William Heinemann LTD, 1967), p. 397. All subsequent translations of the "Aeneid" are taken from this source.

4.   Ah, what to do? With what
speech now dare he approach the frenzied queen?
What opening words choose first?

Ibid., p. 415.

5.   And now hither,
now thither he swiftly throws his mind, casting it in
diverse ways, and turns to every shift.

Ibid.

6.   But the queen—who may deceive a lover?—
divined his guile . . ,

Ibid.

7. *Ibid.,* p. 419.

8.   For why hide my feelings?
or for what greater wrongs do I hold me back? Did
he sigh while I wept? Did he turn on me a glance?
Did he yield and shed tears or pity her who loved
him?

Ibid., p. 421.

9.   But good Aeneas, though longing to soothe
and assuage her grief and by his words turn aside her
sorrow, with many a sigh, his soul shaken by his
mighty love, yet fulfils Heaven's bidding and returns
to the fleet.

Ibid., p. 423.

10. *Ibid.,* p. 427.

11.   I have lived, I have finished the course that
Fortune gave; and now in majesty my shade shall
pass beneath the earth.

Ibid., p. 441.

12. Anyone who wishes to determine from what depths the criticism of classical literature has risen in the last twenty years, ought to read an essay on Dido, published in the *Rivista di filologia classica,* 25 (1897), by Valmaggi, who was a professor in the University of Turin, written, as the author declares (p. 51), according "to the standard of scientific and experimental aesthetics." There it is asserted that the inspiration of the episode is "something quite different from amorous passion"; that it is "political and religious"; that the passionate figure is Aeneas and not Dido, who is "introduced exclusively to give him greater prominence"; that in Dido there is no love and not even "the delicate and unadulterated feeling of love"; that she "is not enamored of Aeneas for any notable physical (!) and moral quality in him . . . rather only by virtue of the will and immediate intervention of the divinity"; and to confirm all this, that in her encounter with Aeneas in hell she does not demonstrate that she still loves him, as she should notwithstanding all the offenses suffered, "since the poets have always imagined love as eternal"! [Croce's note]

13. "Aeneid," p. 419.

14. See "Aeneid," pp. 537, 539.

15.　　　With such speech amid springing tears Aeneas
would soothe the wrath of the fiery, fierce-eyed queen.
She, turning away, kept her looks fixed on the ground
and no more changes her countenance as he essays
to speak than if she were set in hard flint or Mar-
pesian rock. At length she flung herself away and,
still his foe, fled back to the shady grove, where
Sychaeus, her lord of former days, responds to her
sorrows and gives her love for love.

Ibid., p. 539.

16. A. Cartault, *L'art de Virgile dans l'Éneide* (Paris: 1926), pp. 456–457. [Croce's note]

Chapter 5: The Character and Unity of Dante's Poetry

1. This essay was translated from "Carattere e unità della poesia di Dante," in *La poesia di Dante* (Bari: Gius. Laterza & Figli, 1966), pp. 163–172. Portions of it were included in Croce's lecture, "Il sesto centenario dantesco e il carattere della poesia di Dante" (Florence: Sansoni, 1920).

2. "I who write this heard Dante say that never for the sake of rhyme did he say something different from what he meant to say, but that very often in his verses he used words in a very different sense than was the practice among other poets."

3. In reference to this point see my essay on Shakespeare in *Ariosto, Shakespeare e Corneille* (Bari: Gius. Laterza & Figli, 1968), pp. 83 ff. [Croce's note]

Chapter 6: Dante's Concluding Canto

1. This essay was translated from "Dante: L'ultimo canto della 'Commedia,' " in *Poesia antica e moderna* (Bari: Gius. Laterza & Figli, 1966), pp. 153–163. It was published earlier under the title "Studî su poesie antiche e moderne. 9. Dante. L'ultimo canto della 'Commedia,' " in *La critica*, 36 (1938): 81–88.

2. At times Croce used the "editorial we" to refer to the humanistic tradition that he presupposed in his critique. Here I have preserved Croce's use.

3. *Canto XXXIII of the Paradiso* (Florence: 1913), p. 24. [Croce's note]

4. *Canto XXXIII of the Paradiso* (new edition revised, 1922), p. 9; cf. p. 45. [Croce's note]

5. There you see Nothing—vacant gaping farness,
   Mark not your own step as you stride,
   Nor point of rest where you abide.

From Johann Wolfgang von Goethe, *Faust*, trans. Walter Arndt (New York: W. W. Norton & Co., 1976), p. 157. All subsequent English translations of *Faust* are taken from this source.

6. And by its light you will behold the Mothers;
   Some may be seated, upright, walking others,
   As it may chance. Formation, transformation,
   The eternal mind's eternal recreation,
   Enswathed in likenesses of manifold entity;
   They see you not, for only wraiths they see.

(Arnt, p. 158). Compare lines 6222ff, 6246ff, 6256, 6285ff. [Croce's note]

7. *L'ultima ascesa*, an introduction to the *Paradiso* (Bari: 1936), pp. 399–407. [Croce's note]

8.   As is he who
   dreaming sees, and after the dream the passion remains imprinted and the rest returns
   not to the mind; such am I, for my vision
   almost wholly fades away, yet does the sweetness that was born of it still drop within my
   heart. Thus is the snow unsealed by the sun;
   thus in the wind, on the light leaves, the
   Sibyl's oracle was lost.

From: Dante Alighieri, *The Divine Comedy: Paradiso*. 1. Italian text and translation, trans. with a commentary by Charles S. Singleton, vol. 3 (Princeton: Princeton University Press, 1975), p. 375. All subsequent English translations of the *Commedia* are taken from this source.

9.   The universal
form of this knot I believe that I saw, because, in telling this, I feel my joy increase.

Ibid., p. 377.

10. Behold Beatrice, with how many saints, for my
prayers clasping their hands to thee.

Ibid., p. 373.

11.   The eyes beloved and reverenced by God,
fixed upon him who prayed, showed us how
greatly devout prayers do please her . . .

Ibid.

12.   . . . then
they were turned to the Eternal Light,
wherein we may not believe that any creature's eye finds its way so clear.

Ibid.

13. Bernard was signing to me with a smile to
look upward . . .

Ibid., p. 375.

14.   A single moment makes for me greater ob-
livion that [sic] five and twenty centuries have
wrought upon the enterprise that made Neptune wonder at the shadow of the Argo.

Ibid., p. 377.

15. See the fragment in *Scaenicae Romanorum poësis fragmenta,* ed.
Ribbeck, I, pp. 187–188. [Croce's note]

16. Thus my mind, all rapt, was gazing, fixed, motionless and intent, ever enkindled by its gazing.

Dante, *Divine Comedy,* p. 377.

17. Giacomo Leopardi, "Amore e morte," *Canti* (Florence: Felice le monnier, 1967), canto 27, line 87, p. 270. This reference was provided by Dr. Jean-
Pierre Barricelli and by Dr. Ernesto Paolozzi.

Chapter 7: Petrarca

1. This essay was translated from "Petrarca: il sogno dell'amore sopravvivente alla passione" in *Poesia antica e moderna* (Bari: Guis. Laterza & Figli,

1966), pp. 164–172. It was published earlier under the title "Studî su poesie antiche e moderne. 4. Petrarca. Il sogno dell'amore sopravvivente alla passione," in *La critica*, 35 (1937): 161–167.

> 2. All my flowering, green age was passing, and I already felt the fire that burned my heart becoming cool, and I had reached the place from which life declines toward the end;
>
> my dear enemy was already beginning little by little to gain confidence against her fears, and her sweet chastity was turning into joys my bitter pains;
>
> the time was near when Love can be reconciled with Chastity and lovers may sit down together and say what occurs to them.
>
> Death envied my happy state, rather my hope, and she attacked it in the middle of the way like an armed enemy.

From: *Petrarch's Lyric Poems: The Rime Sparse and other Lyrics*, translated and edited by Robert M. Durling (Cambridge: Harvard University Press, 1976), p. 494. All subsequent English translations of Petrarca's poetry are taken from this source.

> 3. *Ibid.*, p. 46.

> 4. *Ibid.*

> 5. Worse than this interpretation is the one given by commentators, who compare the two sonnets of Boccaccio ("L'alta speranza," and "S'egli advien mai") to a more superficial one by Bembo ("O superba, o crudele"). [Croce's note]

> 6. R. Giani, *L'amore nel "Canzoniere" di Francesco Petrarca* (Turin: Bocca, 1917), pp. 230–233. [Croce's note]

> 7. It was by then time to find peace or truce from so much war, and it was perhaps under way, except that those glad steps were turned back by Death, who evens out all our inequalities;
>
> for as a cloud is dissolved in the wind, so quickly did her life pass away, hers who used to guide me with her lovely eyes, and whom I now must follow with my thoughts.
>
> She only needed to wait a little, for years and gray hair were changing my habits, so that she would not have needed to fear my speaking to her of my ills;

Petrarch's Lyric Poems, p. 494.

> 8. with what virtuous sighs I would have told her of my long labors! which now from Heaven she sees, I am certain, and, what is more, is sorry for them with me.

Ibid.

9. Love had shown me a tranquil harbor from my long and turbid storm—the years of virtuous maturity that divests itself of vice and puts on virtue and honor.

My heart and my high faithfulness were now visible to her lovely eyes and no longer displeasing to them. Ah, cruel Death, how quick you are to shatter in so few hours the fruit of many years!

If only she had lived, we would have come to where, speaking, I could have put down in those chaste ears the ancient burden of my sweet thoughts,

And she would perhaps have answered me with some holy word, sighing, though our faces were changed, and the hair of both.

Ibid., p. 496.

10. On this point, see De Sanctis, *Saggio sul Petrarca*, ed. Croce, pp. 286–288. [Croce's note]

11. *Ibid.*, pp. 237–238. [Croce's note]

12. This essay was translated from part II of Benedetto Croce's "Petrarca" in *Poesia antica e moderna, op. cit.*, pp. 172–178. It was published earlier under the title "Studî su poesie antiche e moderne. 22. Petrarca. Canzone 'Quell'antiquo mio dolce empio signore,' " in *La critica*, 37 (1939): 414–419.

13. Critics have also said that the design of this canzone was anticipated in a sonnet by Cino da Pistoia: "Mille dubbî in un dí, mille querele," which is not, however, by Cino (see edition of Zaccagnini [Geneva: 1925], p. 24), but by some sixteenth century Petrarchist, and perhaps, as Muratori, (*Perfetta poesia*, II, p. 246), supposes, by Gandolfo Porrino, who first sent it to Castelvetro. [Croce's note]

14.   He has made me love God less than I ought and be less concerned for myself; for a lady I have equally disregarded all cares. In that, he alone has been my counselor, always sharpening my youthful desire with his wicked whetstone, and I hoped for rest under his harsh fierce yoke.
          Wretch! Why were that dear high intellect and the other gifts given to me by Heaven? For my hair is turning, but I cannot turn from my obstinate will: thus this cruel one whom I accuse despoils me of all liberty . . .

Petrarch's Lyric Poems, p. 562.

15.   Since I have been his I have not had a tranquil hour, nor do I expect any, and my nights have banished sleep and cannot draw it back to themselves by herbs or by charms; by treachery and force he has made himself master of my spirits, and since then no bell has struck, when I have been in some town, that I have not heard.

Ibid., p. 564.

16.   for no worm ever gnawed old wood as he gnaws my heart, where he makes his nest . . .

Ibid.

17.   . . . and I gave her such sweet speech and such soft singing, that no low or heavy thought could ever endure in her presence.

Ibid., p. 566.

18. I had so carried him under my wings that his speech pleased ladies and knights; and I made him rise so high that among brilliant wits his name shines, and in some places collections are made of his poems; who now would perhaps be a hoarse murmurer of the courts, one of the mob!

Ibid.

19. At this I raise a tearful cry, and shout: "He gave her to me indeed, but he soon took her back!"

Ibid., p. 568.

20. He replies: "Not I, but One who desired her for Himself."

Ibid.

20.   Finally, both turning to the seat of justice, I with trembling, he with high and cruel voice, each of us concludes for himself: "Noble Lady, I await your sentence." She then, smiling: "It pleases me to have heard your pleas, but more time is needed for so great a lawsuit."

Ibid.

22. "Though I was present at the Creation I still do not understand it fully." [Croce's note]

23. See his *Salmodia metafisicale.* [Croce's note]

Chapter 8: Ludovico Ariosto: The Realization of Harmony

1. This essay was translated from "L'attuazione dell'Armonia," in *Ariosto, Shakespeare, e Corneille* (Bari: Laterza, 1961, pp. 43–57). It was published earlier under the same title in *La critica*, 16 (1918): 92–103.

2. "Il primo cangiamento ch'essi soffersero. . . . " The pronoun "essi" refers to "sentimenti" (sentiments), which were discussed in the preceding chapter of *Ariosto, Shakespeare, e Corneille,* under the heading of "material" for Ariosto's harmony *(la materia per l'armonia).*

3. "Armonia" (Harmony) is capitalized in the text.

4. "Aria confidenziale."

5. The fear and late sea-sorrow, which had weighed
    So long upon the dame and broke her rest,
    The finding herself safe in greenwood shade
    Removed from noise, and, for her tranquil breast
    (Knowing her lover was beside her laid)
    No further thoughts, no further cares molest,
    Olympia lay [?] in slumber so profound,
    No sheltered bear or dormouse sleeps more sound.

From Ludovico Ariosto, *Orlando Furiosos,* trans. William Stewart Rose (New York: Bobbs-Merrill, 1968), canto 10:18, p. 83. All subsequent English translations of *Orlando Furioso* are taken from this source.

6. As two fair generous pards, that from some crag
    Together dart, and stretch across the plain;
    When they perceive that vigorous goat or stag,
    Their nimble quarry, is pursued in vain,
    As if ashamed they in that chase did lag,
    Return repentant and in high disdain:
    So, with a sigh, return those damsels two,
    When they the paynim king in safety view . . .

Ibid., canto 39:69, p. 418.

7. Julia Gonzaga, she that wheresoe'er
    She moves, where'er she turns her lucid eyes,
    Not only is in charms without a peer,
    But seems a goddess lighted from the skies . . .

Ibid., canto 46:8, p. 496.

8. And those, yet living or of earlier day,
    Mantegna, Leonardo, Gian Belline,
    The Dossi, and, skilled to carve or to pourtray,
    Michael, less man than angel and divine . . .

Ibid., canto 33:2, p. 347.

9. OH! mighty springs of war in youthful breast,
    Impetuous force of love, and thirst of praise!
    Nor yet which most avails is known aright:
    For each by turns its opposite outweighs.

Ibid., canto 25:1, p. 257.

10. Neither the rattling drum nor trumpet's ring
    Initiate the amorous assault,

But kisses like the dove's to war we bring,
And these give signal to advance or halt.

Ibid., canto 25:68, p. 264.

11. For a discussion of Croce's views on the concept of humor in literary criticism, see Benedetto Croce, "L'umorismo. Del vario significato della parola e del suo uso nella critica letteraria," *Journal of Comparative Literature*, 1 (1903): 220–228.

12. Crimson his waistcoat was, and white his pall;
Vermillion seemed the mantle, milk the vest:
White was that ancient's hair, and white withal
The bushy beard descending to his breast . . .

Orlando Furioso, canto 34:54, p. 367.

13. Olympia's beauties are of those most rare,
Nor is the forehead's beauteous curve alone
Excellent, and her eyes and cheeks and hair,
Mouth, nose, and throat, and shoulders . . .

Ibid., canto 11:67, p. 100.

14. A cheek of white, suffused with crimson grain,
Medoro had, in youth a pleasing grace.

Ibid., canto 18:166, p. 186.

15. Here Croce is referring to a passage in Dante's *Commedia:*

As through smooth and transparent glass,
or through clear and tranquil waters, yet not
so deep that the bottom be lost, the outlines
of our faces return so faint that a pearl on a
white brow comes not less boldly to our eyes . . .

From *The Divine Comedy: Paradiso, op. cit.*, canto 3, lines 10–15, p. 27. This reference was provided by Dr. Daniel J. Donno.

16. And this new sense of fear increased her trouble,
And made the trembling lady's heart beat double.

Orlando Furioso, canto 41:33, p. 432.

17. When they are entered, and she sees no show
Of joyful triumph, she, without a word,
Without a hint to indicate that woe,
Knows that no longer living is her lord.

Ibid., canto 43:157, p. 467.

18. Upon the paladin's return the cry
Redoubled, and the mourning louder grew.

Ibid., canto 43:169, p. 468.

Chapter 9: Shakespeare's Poetic Sentiment

1. This essay was translated from "Il sentimento shakespeariano," *Ariosto, Shakespeare e Corneille* (Bari: Gius. Laterza & Figli, 1968), pp. 83–96. It was published earlier in *La critica,* 17 (1919): 138–148. Croce uses the term "sentiment" *(sentimento)* in a sense which has no exact equivalent in English usage. He recognizes that its meaning poses difficulties in Italian as well. See pp. 111–112 where he discusses it.

Chapter 10: Shakespeare's Art

1. This essay was translated from "L'arte dello Shakespeare," in *Ariosto, Shakespeare e Corneille* (Bari: Gius. Laterza & Figli, 1968), pp. 159–172; earlier published as "Shakespeare e la critica shakespeariana. 4. L'arte dello Shakespeare," in *La critica,* 17 (1919): 197–207.

2. In the preceding chapter Croce discusses various motifs of Shakespearean "poetry," that is, art. These themes include the tragedy of good and evil, the tragedy of will, justice and clemency.

3. See Otto Ludwig, *Shakespeare-Studien,* intro. Moritz Heydrich, 2nd ed. (Leipzig: Verlag von C. Cnobloch, 1874), p. 9.

4. *Macbeth,* act 1, sc. 6, lines 3–4, 8, 10.

5. *Ibid.,* act 5, sc. 8, line 22.

6. *Othello,* act 5, sc. 2, lines 82, 84, 86–87.

7. *A Midsummer-Night's Dream,* act 5, sc. 1, lines 12–22.

8. *Hamlet,* act 3, sc. 2, lines 6–8.

9. Recent scholarship proposes that this passage was the fourth addition to the original play, placed between scenes 12 and 13, act 3, i.e., Thomas Kyd, *The Spanish Tragedy,* ed. Philip Edwards (Manchester: Manchester U. P., 1981). However, Hieronimo's doubt is shown as occurring earlier in the passage than where Croce's commentary suggests.

10. August von Platen-Hallermünde (1796–1835) was a poet and dramatist who opposed romanticism.

11. See Frank Harris, *The Man Shakespeare and his Tragic Life-story* (New York: M. Kennerley, 1909).

Chapter 11: Corneille's Ideal

1. This essay was translated from "L'ideale del Corneille," *Ariosto, Shakespeare e Corneille* (Bari: Gius. Laterza & Figli, 1968), pp. 209–224; earlier published in part in the *Giornale d'Italia*, 20 (16 January, 1920); and then in its entirety in *La critica*, 18 (1920): 1–42.

2. In the preceding chapter Croce reviews various critiques of Corneille's plays. He concludes that most of these critiques have not treated the central problem of literary criticism, that is, of the presence or absence of art. They have evaluated Corneille's work instead in terms, so he believes, of their prejudices and have found it defective. See *ibid*, pp. 195–208.

Chapter 12: Wagner, the Pedant

1. This essay was translated from "Il pedante Wagner," in *Goethe; con una scelta delle liriche nuovamente tradotte*, part 1 (Bari: Gius. Laterza & Figli, 1959), pp. 24–32; earlier published in *La critica*, 16 (1918): 163–168.

2. Jean Paul Friedrich Richter (1763–1825), one of the great German humorists. Dr. Richard Lillard supplied Jean Paul's last name, omitted from the Italian text.

3.   Hedda. My dear Judge, Tesman is—a specialist.
       Brack. Undeniably.
       Hedda. And specialists aren't at all amusing to travel with. Not
in the long run, anyway.
       Brack. Not even—the specialist that one *loves*.
       Hedda. Ugh—don't use that syrupy word!

From Henrik Ibsen, *The Complete Major Prose Plays*, trans. Rolf Fjelde (New York: New American Library, 1978), *Hedda Gabler*, act 2, p. 724.

[Croce's note]

4.   O Tod! ich kenn's—das ist mein Famulus—
       Es wird mein schönstes Glück zu nichte!
       Dass diese Fülle der Gesichte
       Der trockne Schleicher stören muss!

[Croce's note]

       Death! It's my famulus—I know that knock;
       My fairest hour of luck is spoiled.
       Oh, must this wealth of visions then be fouled
       By that dry sneaking cluck?

From Johann Wolfgang Von Goethe, *Faust: A Tragedy*, trans. by Walter Arndt and ed. by Cyrus Hamlin (New York: W. W. Norton & Co., 1976), p. 14. All subsequent English translations of *Faust* will be taken from this source.

5. Ambrogio Calepino (c. 1440–1510) was one of the earliest European lexicographers. He became an Augustinian monk and compiled a dictionary of Latin languages (1502).

6. Nizzolio (a.k.a. Nizolio, Mario; Nizzoli; Nizolius; Nizzolius) was an Italian humanist-philosopher chiefly interested in Ciceronianism (1498–1576).

7. Compare the mind's delights which wing us poring
   From book to book, from leaf to leaf!
   Then nights of winter bloom with grace and zest,
   Your limbs glow with a blissful warming leaven,
   And, ah! should you unroll a worthy palimpset,
   Then there descends on you the whole of heaven.

Ibid., p. 27.

8. How difficult the means are to be found
   By which the primal sources may be breached;
   And long before the halfway point is reached,
   They bury a poor devil in the ground.

Ibid., p. 15.

9. What sentiments, great man, must swell your breast
   Upon the homage of this multitude!
   Ah, he who can derive such good
   From his own gifts indeed is blessed!
   Fathers lift boys up as you go,
   All push and run and ask the cause,
   The fiddle rests, the dancers pause.
   You pass, they stand there, row on row,
   And all the caps go flying high:
   They all but genuflect and bend down low
   As if the Sacrament came by.

Ibid., p. 25.

10. A dog, if ably trained and clever,
    Will even gain a wise man's favor.
    Yes, he deserves your good will without scruple,
    The undergraduate's accomplished pupil.

Ibid., p. 29.

11.   Farewell! my heart is sore, alack!
        I fear I may not ever see you back.

Ibid., p. 176.

Chapter 13: Marcel Proust

1. This essay was translated from "Un caso di storicismo decadentistico," *Discorsi di varia filosofia*, vol. 2 (Bari: Gius. Laterza & Figli, 1959), pp. 138–145; earlier published under the title "Conversazioni filosofiche. 15. Note d'istorica. 4. Un caso di storicismo decadentistico," *La critica*, 42 (1944): 53–58.

2. In the *Oeuvres complètes* (Paris: 1929–1936), in the part entitled: *Le temps retrouvé*, II, pp. 252–253. [Croce's note]

3. In the part entitled *La prisonnière*, vol. 1, pp. 247–248. [Croce's note]

4. *Le temps retrouvé, loc. cit.*, p. 253. [Croce's note]

5. *Albertine disparue*, vol. 1, p. 102. [Croce's note]

6. *Le temps retrouvé*, II, p. 253. [Croce's note]

7. *Ibid.*, p. 251. [Croce's note]

8. *La vie littéraire, Deuxième serie* (Paris: Calman Lévy, s. a.), pp. 115–124. [Croce's note]

Chapter 14: Poe's Essays on Poetry

1. This essay was translated from "Intorno ai saggi del Poe sulla poesia" in *Letture di poeti e riflessioni sulla teoria e la critica della poesia* (1950; Bari: Laterza, 1966), pp. 197–203. Croce dated it with the year 1947.

2. Yvor Winters, *Aspects de la littérature américaine: Hawthorne, Cooper, Melville, Poe, Emerson, Jones Very, Emily Dickinson, Henry James*, trans. into French by Georges Belmont (Paris: du Chêne, 1947). The French edition is a translation of Yvor Winters, *Maule's Curse: Seven Studies in the History of American Obscurantism* (Norfolk, Conn.: New Directions, 1938).

3. See Yvor Winters, "Edgar Allan Poe: A Crisis in the History of American Obscurantism," *In Defense of Reason* (Denver: University of Denver Press, c. 1949), pp. 234–261. All subsequent references to Winters' criticism of Edgar Allan Poe as writer and theorist are from this source.

4. Edgar Allan Poe, "The Poetic Principle," *The Works of Edgar Allan Poe*, ed. with a memoir, critical introductions, and notes by Edmund Clarence Stedman and George Edward Woodbury (Chicago: Stone and Kimball, 1895), vol. 6, *Criticism*, pp. 8–9. All subsequent references to Poe's writings on literary criticism are from this source.

5. *Ibid.*, p. 11.

6. *Ibid.*, p. 9.

7. *Ibid.*, pp. 3–6.

8. *Ibid.*, pp. 4–5.

9. Winters, "Poe," *op. cit.*, pp. 237–241.

10. *Ibid.*, p. 246.

11. *Ibid.*, p. 240.

12. Poe, *op. cit.*, pp. 31–46.

13. *Ibid.*, pp. 47–104.

14. Winters, "Poe," *op. cit.*, pp. 251ff.

Chapter 15: Ibsen

1. This essay was translated from "Ibsen," *Poesia e non-poesia* (Bari: Gius. Laterza & Figli, 1964), pp. 292–307; published earlier under the title "Note sulla poesia italiana e straniera del secolo decimonono. 10. Ibsen," *La critica*, 19 (1921): 1–11.

2. Henrik Ibsen, *Peer Gynt*, trans. Michael Meyer (New York: Anchor, 1963), p. 74.

3. Henrik Ibsen, *Brand*, trans. G. M. Gathorne-Hardy (Seattle: University of Washington Press, 1966), p. 205.

4. *Ibid.*, p. 209.

5. Henrik Ibsen, *The Complete Major Prose Plays*, trans. Rolf Fjelde (New York: Farrar Straus Giroux, 1978), p. 908.

6. *Ibid.*

7. *Ibid.*, p. 934.

8. *Ibid.*, pp. 928–929.

9. *Ibid.*, p. 762.

10. *Ibid.*, p. 1055.

11. *Ibid.*, p. 985.

12. *Ibid.*, p. 702.

13. *Ibid.*, p. 697.

Chapter 16: Gerard Manley Hopkins

1. This essay was translated from "Un gesuita inglese poeta, Gerard Manley Hopkins," *Poesia antica e moderna* (Bari: Gius. Laterza & Figli, 1966), pp.

423–448. Croce dated it 1936. However, it was published a year later under the title "Studî su poesie antiche e moderne. 3. Un gesuita inglese poeta. Gerard Manley Hopkins," *La critica*, 35 (1937): 81–100.

2. Richard Watson Dixon, *History of the Church of England, from the Abolition of the Roman Jurisdiction* (Oxford: Oxford University Press, 1891–1902).

3. Hopkins's letter of Dec. 1, 1881, to Dixon, in the *Correspondence of Gerard Manley Hopkins and Richard Watson Dixon*, ed. C. C. Abbott (London: Oxford University Press, 1935), pp. 93–96. [Croce's note] Although Hopkins chose not to hyphenate "Jesuit poet," Croce's Italian term reads "gesuita-poeta."

4. G. M. Hopkins "To. R. B." in *Poems of G. M. Hopkins*, edited by W. H. Gardner and N. H. Mackenzie (London: Oxford University Press, 1967, 4th ed.), p. 108. Although Croce himself cited an earlier second edition, 1935, I have consistently drawn from the fourth edition for Hopkins's poetry.

5. *Confess.*, pt. I, l. VI. [Croce's note]

6. To judge from the biography of Hopkins, which was written by his Jesuit brother G. F. Lahey, *G. M. H.* (London: Humphrey Milford, 1930) and in which Hopkins the poet dominates. [Croce's note]

7. See Hopkins's *Correspondence of Hopkins and Dixon*, 1878, p. 14. [Croce's note]

8. Croce's footnote directs us to Hopkins's correspondence with Bridges (*The Letters of G. M. H. to Robert Bridges*, ed. C. Colleer Abbott, London, 1935), letter of 1881, p. 88. However Hopkins wrote of torment and vacillation to Dixon, see *Correspondence of Hopkins and Dixon*, 1881, p. 88.

9. See *The Letters of G. M. H. to Robert Bridges*, ed. C. Colleer Abbott (London: Oxford U. P., 1935), letter of 1883, pp. 174–175.

10. Croce's footnote again directs us to Hopkins's correspondence with Bridges, *op. cit.*, p. 75 (letter of 1881), but he actually takes this statement from an 1881 letter to Dixon (see *Correspondence of Hopkins to Dixon*, pp. 75–76), omitting the quotation marks that I have supplied.

11. *Poems of Gerard Manley Hopkins*, edited with notes by Robert Bridges, 2nd edition with an Appendix of additional poems and a critical introduction by Charles Williams (4th printing, Oxford U. P., 1935). [Croce's note]

12. Of the critical works on this point, I know only the one by E. E. Phare, *The Poetry of G. M. H., a Survey and Commentary* (Cambridge: U. P., 1933), and the excellent study by C. Abbott in his edition of Hopkins's letters to Bridges, which has been cited. In Italy, Olivero, *Correnti mistiche della letteratura inglese moderna (Mystical Currents in Modern English Literature)* (Turin: Bocca, 1932), pp. 73–100, has interpreted Hopkins's lyrical poems in terms of their religious aspect. With a quite different understanding of their character and artistic value,

Giuseppe de Luca has discussed them in *Nuova antologia,* 16 April 1934, pp. 635–638. See in the *Frontespizio,* Florence, Oct. 1936, p. 23, the translation of *"Rosa Mystica,"* contributed by M. Escobar (and subsequently the translation of "The Wreck of the 'Deutschland,' " by S. Baldi, *ibid.,* March 1939 and, by the same person, of five other lyrical poems in *Letteratura,* Florence, April–June 1940). [Croce's note]

13. *Poems of G. M. H.,* pp. 67–68.

14. *Ibid.,* p. 68.

15. *Ibid.,* p. 79.

16. *Ibid.*

17. *Ibid.,* pp. 69–70.

18. *Ibid.,* pp. 82–83.

19. *Ibid.,* p. 106.

20. *Ibid.*

21. *Ibid.,* p. 19.

22. In order somewhat to reduce the inevitable disadvantage [of translations], we have provided and will continue to provide readers with some strophes in the original language, so that those who can may enjoy the full flavor and beauty of the poems. [Croce's note]

23. *Correspondence of Hopkins and Dixon,* pp. 65, 135. [Croce's note]

24. *The Poems of G. M. H.,* p. 89.

25. *Ibid.,* p. 68.

26. *Ibid.,* p. 66.

27. *Ibid.,* pp. 66–67.

28. *Ibid.,* p. 71.

29. Elsie E. Phare, *The Poetry of Gerard Manley Hopkins* (London: Cambridge University Press, 1933), pp. 130–150. [Croce's note]

30. *The Poems of G. M. H.,* p. 69.

31. *Ibid.,* p. 86.

32. *Ibid.,* p. 84–85.

33. *Ibid.,* pp. 88–89.

34. *Ibid.,* pp. 97–98.

35. *Ibid.,* p. 98.

36. *Ibid.*, no. 65, untitled, p. 100.

37. *Ibid.*, no. 67, untitled, p. 101.

38. "Carrion-comfort": the comfort sought in despair, which amounts to seeking nourishment in carrion. [Croce's note]

39. *Poems of G. M. H.*, no. 64, untitled, pp. 99–100.

40. *Ibid.*, no. 69, untitled, pp. 102–103.

41. *Ibid.*, no. 74, untitled, pp. 106–107.

42. *Ibid.*, p. 85.

43. *Ibid.*, no. 68, untitled, p. 102.

44. *Ibid.*, pp. 184–185.

45. *Correspondence of Hopkins and Dixon* of 1881, p. 74. [Croce's note]

46. My translation. See the *Letters to Bridges,* pp. 85, 146, 182, 225, and *Correspondence of Hopkins and Dixon,* pp. 8, 11, 13, 17, 71, 121, which refer merely to some of the many passages that could be cited with regard to this point. [Croce's note]

47. *Correspondence of Hopkins and Dixon,* pp. 31, 39, 43. [Croce's note]

48. *Letters to Bridges,* pp. 37–38. [Croce's note]

49. Recently there has been published a new volume of Hopkins's writings: *The Note-books and Papers of Gerard Manley Hopkins,* edited with Notes and Preface by Humphrey House (London: Oxford U. P., 1937). See the *Times Literary Supplement,* 23 (January 1937): 57; where there is a journal of the years 1868–1875, from which one sees how "the changing faces of sky and sea and land were the writer's great stimulants, which left the busy world of men excluded from his interest." [Croce's note]

SELECTED BIBLIOGRAPHY

The most complete bibliography of Benedetto Croce's works has been compiled by Silvano Borsari in *L'opera di Benedetto Croce* (Naples: Istituto Italiano per gli Studi Storici, 1963). An excellent but less detailed bibliography is given in Fausto Nicolini's *L'* "editio ne varietur" *delle opere di B. Croce: Saggio bibliografico con taluni riassunti o passi testuali e ventinove fuori testo* (Naples: Biblioteca del "Bollettino" dell'archivio storico del Banco di Napoli, 1960). For secondary works and articles written from 1960 through 1972, see the bibliography appended to *Thought, Action and Intuition*, edited by L. M. Palmer and H. S. Harris (New York: George Olms, 1975). Ernesto G. Caserta's *Studi crociani negli stati uniti* (Naples: Loffredo, 1988) provides a critical bibliography of Croce studies in the United States from 1964 to 1984. The bibliography appended to Giovanni Gullace's translation of Benedetto Croce's *La poesia: Introduzione alla critica e storia della poesia*, contains a detailed bibliography of writings in English on Croce's aesthetics.

The bibliography that follows has been selected mostly from Croce's writings on aesthetics and literary criticism. The English and Italian secondary sources listed treat of Crocean aesthetics, literary criticism, and other related subjects. The dates of the works are of the editions cited in the introduction and text, in order to help the reader to more easily locate the references. Because some of the Italian texts and their translations are difficult to locate outside of Italy, whenever possible I cited more than one source for the reference.

CROCE'S WRITINGS

1. Books and Articles

"Aesthetics." In *Encyclopaedia Britannica*, 14th ed., 1929. Pp. 263–272. Reprinted in English in *Philosophy, Poetry, History*, pp. 215–247, and in Italian under the title "Aesthetica in nuce," in *Ultimi saggi*, pp. 3–43.

"Antiestetica ed antifilosofia." *La critica: Rivista di letteratura, storia e filosofia*, I (1903): 316–320. Reprinted in *Problemi di estetica*, pp. 471–477.

Ariosto, Shakespeare e Corneille, 1st economic reprint of 5th ed. Bari: Laterza, 1968. Translated by D. Ainslie under the title *Ariosto, Shakespeare and Corneille*. 1920. Reissue. New York: Russell & Russell, 1966. The essays "Persona pratica e persona poetica" and "La tragedia della volontà" were translated also by C. Sprigge in *Philosophy, Poetry, History*, pp. 886–899.

Breviario di estetica: Quattro lezioni. Bari: Laterza, 1913. Translated by D. Ainslie and published first in English under the title "The Breviary of Aesthetic." *The Book of the Opening of the Rice Institute*. Houston: The Rice Institute, 2 (1912): pp. 450–517. This translation was subsequently revised and republished under the title *The Essence of Aesthetic*. London: Heinemann, 1921. More recently the *Breviario* was retranslated by Patrick Romanell under the title *Guide to Aesthetics*. Indianapolis: Bobbs-Merrill, 1965.

"Il carattere di totalità della espressione artistica." *La critica: Rivista di letteratura, storia e filosofia*, 16 (1918): 129–140. Reprinted in *Nuovi saggi di estetica*, pp. 117–146. This essay was translated by C. Sprigge under the title "The Totality of Artistic Expression" in *Philosophy, Poetry, History*, pp. 261–273.

"Contributo alla critica di me stesso." In *Etica e politica*, pp. 375–423. This essay was translated into English by R. G. Collingwood, with a preface by J. A. Smith, under the title *Benedetto Croce: An Autobiography*. Oxford: Clarendon Press, 1927.

Conversazioni critiche, 4th rev. ed. of 1st and 2nd series. Bari: Laterza, 1950.

Conversazioni critiche, 2nd ed. rev. of 3rd, 4th, and 5th series. Bari: Laterza, 1951.

"La critica e la storia delle arti figurative e le sue condizioni presenti." *La critica: Rivista di letteratura, storia e filosofia*, 17 (1919): 265–278. Reprinted in *Nuovi saggi di estetica*, pp. 259–285.

La critica letteraria: Questioni teoriche. Rome: Loescher, 1894. Reprinted in *Primi saggi*, pp. 73–168.

"Dewey's Aesthetics and Theory of Knowledge." *Journal of Aesthetics and Art Criticism*, 11 (1952): 1–6.

"Difesa della poesia." *La critica: Rivista di letteratura, storia e filosofia*, 32 (1934): 1–15. Reprinted in *Ultimi saggi*, pp. 61–81. This essay was published first in English under the title *The Defence of Poetry: Variations on the Theme of Shelley*, trans. E. F. Carritt. Oxford: Clarendon Press, 1933.

Discorsi di varia filosofia. 2nd ed., 2 vols. Bari: Laterza, 1959.

Estetica come scienza dell'espressione e linguistica generale, 10th ed. Bari: Laterza, 1958. This work was translated into English under the title *Aesthetic as Science of Expression and General Linguistic*, trans. D. Ainslie. London: Macmillan & Co., 1909. The *Aesthetic* (1909) was revised in the 2nd edition (1922), but did not include the essay "Pure Intuition and the Lyrical Character of Art." See *Aesthetic as Science of Expression and General Linguistic*. New York: Noonday Press, 1958.

"Estetica e psicologia del linguaggio." *La critica: Rivista di letteratura, storia e filosofia*, 5 (1907): 411–413. Reprinted in *Problemi di estetica*, pp. 186–190.

"Fantasia e immaginazione." Quaderni della "critica," 15 (1949): 117. Reprinted in *Terze pagine sparse*, 2: pp. 163–164.

La filosofia di G. B. Vico. 3rd economic reprint of 6th ed. Bari: Laterza, 1973. Translated by R. G. Collingwood under the title *The Philosophy of Giambattista Vico*. 1913. Reissue. New York: Russell and Russell, 1964.

Filosofia, poesia, storia. Milan, Naples: Ricciardi, 1951. Translated by C. Sprigge under the title *Philosophy, Poetry, History*. London: Oxford University Press, 1966.

"Giambattista Vico, primo scopritore della scienza estetica." *Flegrea*, 3rd year, 2 (1901): 1–26, 97–116. Translated in *Aesthetic* (1958), pp. 220–234.

Goethe con una scelta delle liriche nuovamente tradotte, 5th ed. 2 parts. Bari: Laterza, 1959. Part I was translated into English by E. Anderson with an introduction by D. Ainslie under the title *Goethe.* New York: Kennikat Press, 1970.

"L'intuizione pura e il carattere lirico dell'arte." *La critica: Rivista di letteratura, storia e filosofia,* 6 (1908): 248–250. Reprinted in *Problemi di estetica,* pp. 3–30. This article was translated by D. Ainslie in the first edition (1909) of the *Aesthetic* but did not appear in the revised edition (1922).

"Intuizione, sentimento, liricità." *La Critica: Rivista di letteratura, storia e filosofia,* 5 (1907): 248–250. Reprinted in *Pagine sparse* I: 211–217.

La Letteratura della nuova Italia. 4 vols. Bari: Laterza, 1914–1915; vol. 5 and 6, 1939–1940.

La letteratura italiana del settecento. Note critiche. Bari: Laterza, 1949.

Letture di poeti. 3d economic reprint of 1st ed. Bari: Laterza, 1966.

"Lineamenti di una Logica come scienza del concetto puro." *Atti dell'accademia pontaniana,* 35 (1905): 1–140. Croce considered this essay as the first edition of the *Logica.* Reprinted in *La prima forma dell'Estetica,* pp. 119–312.

Logica come scienza del concetto puro, 9th ed. Bari: Laterza, 1963. The 2nd edition (1909) was translated into English by D. Ainslie under the title *Logic as the Science of the Pure Concept.* London: Macmillan, 1917.

Memorie della mia vita. Verona: Valdonega, 1966.

My Philosophy and Other Essays on the Moral and Political Problems of Our Time. Selected by R. Klibansky and translated by E. F. Carritt. London: George Allen & Unwin, 1951.

Nuove pagine sparse. 1st series, *Vita, pensiero, letteratura.* 2nd series, *Metodologia, storiografica, osservazioni su libri nuovi—varietà.* Naples: Riccardo Ricciardi, 1949.

Nuovi saggi di estetica, 4th ed. Bari: Laterza, 1958.

"On the Aesthetics of Dewey." *Journal of Aesthetics and Art Criticism,* 6 (1948): 203–207.

Pagine sparse, 2nd ed. Vol. 1, *Letteratura e cultura.* Vol. 2, *Biografie; storia napoletana; schermaglie per varia occasione; ricordi di vita ministeriale; questioni del giorno; documenti storici.* Vol. 3, *Postille; osservazioni su libri nuovi.* Bari: Laterza, 1960.

La poesia: Introduzione alla critica e storia della poesia e della letteratura, 6th ed. Bari: Laterza, 1963. Translated with an introduction and notes by Giovanni Gullace under the title *Benedetto Croce's Poetry and Literature: An Introduction to its Criticism and History.* Carbondale: Southern Illinois University Press, 1981.

Poesia antica e moderna: Interpretazioni, 5th ed. Bari: Laterza, 1966.

La poesia di Dante, 11th ed. Bari: Laterza, 1966. Translated by D. Ainslie under the title *The Poetry of Dante.* New York: Paul P. Appel, 1971.

Poesia e non poesia: Note sulla letteratura europea del secolo decimonono, 7th ed. Bari: Laterza, 1964. Translated by D. Ainslie under the title *European Literature in the Nineteenth Century.* London: Chapman & Hall, 1925.

Poesia popolare e poesia d'arte: Studi sulla poesia italiana dal tre al cinquecento, 5th ed. Bari: Laterza, 1967.

Poeti e scrittori del pieno e del tardo Rinascimento, vols. 1 and 2, 1945; vol. 3, 1952 (Bari: Laterza).

La prima forma della "Estetica" e della "Logica." Messina-Rome: Principato, 1924.

Primi saggi, 3rd ed. Bari: Laterza, 1951.

Problemi di estetica e contributi alla storia dell'estetica italiana, 5th ed. Bari: Laterza, 1951.

"Il programma della Critica." *La critica: Rivista di letteratura, storia e filosofia,* 1 (1903): 1–5. Reprinted in *Conversazioni critiche,* 2d series, pp. 353–357.

Saggi sulla letteratura italiana del seicento. Bari: Laterza, 1911.

Terze pagine sparse. 2 vols. Bari: Laterza, 1955.

"Tesi fondamentali di un'Estetica come scienza dell'espressione e linguistica generale." *Atti dell'accademia pontaniana,* 30 (1900): 1–88. Reprinted in *La prima forma dell'Estetica,* pp. 1–118.

Ultimi saggi, 3rd ed. Bari; Laterza, 1963.

"L'umorismo: Del vario significato della parola e del suo uso nella critica letteraria." *Journal of Comparative Literature,* 1 (1903): 220–228. Reprinted in *Problemi di estetica,* pp. 275–286.

2. Correspondence

Croce, Benedetto. *Epistolario: scelta di lettere curata dall'autore, 1914–1935.* Naples: Istituto Italiano per gli Studi Storici, 1967.

——— . *Lettere a Giovanni Gentile, 1896–1924.* A cura di Alda Croce with an introduction by Gennaro Sasso. Milan: Arnoldo Mondadori, 1981.

Gentile, Giovanni. *Lettere a Benedetto Croce.* 4 vols., a cura di Simona Giannantoni. Florence: Sansoni, 1972–1980.

CRITICAL TREATMENTS OF CROCE'S THOUGHT

1. Books

Abbate, M. *La filosofia di B. Croce e la crisi della società italiana.* Turin: Einaudi, 1966.

Albeggiani, F. *Inizio e svolgimento della filosofia dello spirito di Benedetto Croce.* Palermo: Gino, 1960.

Aliotta, A. *La conoscenza intuitiva nell'estetica del Croce.* Piacenza: Bertola, 1904.

——— . *L'estetica del Croce e la crisi dell'idealismo moderno.* Naples: Perrella, 1917.

Antoni, Carlo. *Commento a Croce.* Venice: Pozzi, 1955.

——— . *Il tempo e le idee.* Naples: Edizioni Scientifiche Italiane, 1968.

Balfour, Arthur James, *Criticism and Beauty: A Lecture Rewritten.* Oxford: Clarendon Press, 1910.

Bartolomei, T. *Idealismo e realismo*. Turin: Marietti, 1938.

Bausola, A. *Filosofia e storia nel pensiero crociano*. Milan: Società Editrice Vita e Pensiero, 1965.

Borgese, G. A. *La poetica dell'unità*. Milan: Treves, 1934.

Bosanquet, B. *Three Lectures on Aesthetic*. London: Macmillan & Co., 1915.

Brescia, Giuseppe. *Il tempo e la libertà: teorie e sistema della costruttività umana*. Manduria: Lacaita editore, 1984.

Brown, M. E. *Neo-Idealistic Aesthetics: Croce-Gentile-Collingwood*. Detroit: Wayne State University Press, 1966.

Bruno, Antonino, ed. *Benedetto Croce trent'anni dopo*. Bari: Laterza, 1983.

————. *La crisi dell'idealismo nell'ultimo Croce*. Bari: Laterza, 1964.

————. *Metologia e metafisica nel pensiero crociano*. Bologna: Leonardi, 1964.

Calogero, G. *La conclusione della filosofia del conoscere*. Florence: Le Monnier, 1938; rev. ed. Florence: Sansoni, 1960.

————. *Estetica, semantica, istorica*. Turin: Einaudi, 1947.

————. *Studi crociani*. Rieti: Biblioteca, 1930.

Caracciolo, Alberto. *L'estetica e la religione di Benedetto Croce*. Azona: Plaideia, 1958.

Carbonara, C. *Sviluppo e problemi dell'estetica crociana*. Naples: Humus, 1947.

Carr, H. W. *The Philosophy of Benedetto Croce*. New York: Russell & Russell, 1969.

Carritt, E. F. *The Theory of Beauty*. London: Methuen, 1914.

Caruso, E. G. *Per la critica dell'estetica e dell'idealismo crociano*. Syracuse: Artigrafiche Santoro, 1949.

Caserta, Ernesto G. *Croce and Marxism*. Naples: Morano, 1987.

————. *Croce critico letterario, 1882–1921*. Naples: Giannini, 1972.

————. *Studi crociani negli stati uniti: bibliografia critica (1964–1984)*. Naples: Loffredo, 1988.

Castellano, Giovanni. *Benedetto Croce*. Bari: Laterza, 1936.

————. *Introduzione allo studio delle opere di Benedetto Croce*. Bari: Laterza, 1920.

Cione, E. *Benedetto Croce e il pensiero contemporaneo*. Milan: Longanesi, 1963.

————. *Bibliografia crociana*. Rome: Fratelli Bocca, 1956.

Collingwood, R. G. *The Principles of Art*. New York: Oxford University Press, 1958.

Colonnello, Pio. *Croce e i Vociani*. Genoa: Studio Editoriale di Cultura, 1984.

Colorni, E. *L'estetica di B. Croce*. Milan: La Cultura, 1932.

Contini, Gianfranco. *L'influenza culturale di Benedetto Croce*. Milan and Naples: Ricciardi, 1967.

Corsi, M. *Le origini del pensiero di Benedetto Croce*. Florence: La Nuova Italia, 1951.

Crespi, Angelo. *Contemporary Thought of Italy*. New York: Knopf, 1926.

Croce, Elena. *L'infanzia dorata e recordi familiari*. Milan: Adelphi, 1970.

De Feo, Italo. *Benedetto Croce e il suo mondo*. Turin: Edizioni Rai Radiotelevisione Italiana, 1966.

De Gennaro, Angelo A. *The Philosophy of Benedetto Croce*. New York: Citadel Press, 1961.

De Gennaro, Giovanni. *Il concetto della unità delle arti nella estetica di Benedetto Croce*. Molfetta: Messina, 1969.

De Ruggiero, Guido. *Modern Philosophy*, trans. A. H. Hannay and R. G. Collingwood. New York: Macmillan, 1921.

Dewey, John. *Art as Experience*. Carbondale: Southern Illinois University Press, 1987.

Faucci, D. *Storicismo e metafisica nel pensiero crociano*. Florence: La Nuova Italia, 1950.

Flora, F., ed. *Benedetto Croce*. Milan: Malfasi, 1953.

Franchini, R. *Croce interprete di Hegel: e altri saggi filosofici*. Naples: Giannini, 1964.

———. *Esperienza dello storicismo*, 4th ed. rev. Naples: Giannini, 1971.

———. *Interpretazioni: da Bruno a Jaspers*. Naples: Giannini, 1975.

———. *Intervista su Croce*. Naples: Società Editrice Napoletana, 1978.

———. *L'oggetto della filosofia*. Naples: Giannini, 1967.

———. *Le origini della dialettica*. Naples: Giannini, 1965.

———. *La teoria della storia di Benedetto Croce*. Naples: Morano, 1966.

Gancitano, Cosimo. *Critica dell'estetica crociana*. Marzara: Società editrice siciliana, 1948.

Garibaldi, Rinaldo. *Genesi e svolgimento storico delle prime tesi estetiche di B. Croce*. Florence: Fussi, 1949.

Gentile, G. *Filosofia dell'arte*. Milan: Treves, 1931. Translated and with an introduction by Giovanni Gullace under the title *The Philosophy of Art*. Ithaca and London: Cornell University Press, 1972.

———. *La filosofia italiana contemporanea*. Florence: Sansoni, 1941.

———. *Frammenti di estetica e letteratura*. Lanciano: Carabba, 1920.

Giammattei, Emma. *Retorica e idealismo*. Bologna: Il Mulino, 1987.

Jacobitti, Edmund E. *Revolutionary Humanism and Historicism in Modern Italy*. New Haven: Yale University Press, 1981.

Lamanna, E. Paolo. *Introduzione alla lettura di Croce*. A cura di D. Pesce. Florence: Felice Le Monnier, 1969.

Lanza, Adriano. *Benedetto Croce: Breviario d'estetica*. Rome: Le Muse, 1969.

Levi, G. *Studi estetici*. Lapi: Città di Castello, 1967.

Lombardi, A. *La filosofia di Benedetto Croce*. Rome: Bardi, 1946.

Melillo, Rita. *Tra Hegelismo e neoempirismo: Saggio su G. R. G. Mure*. Naples: Società Editrice Napoletana, 1986.

Mencken, Henry. *Prejudices*, first series. New York: Knopf, 1919.

Montano, Rocco. *Miti della critica postcrociana*. Naples: G. B. Vico Editrice, 1975.

Moss, M. E. *Benedetto Croce Reconsidered: Truth and Error in Theories of Art, Literature and History*. Hanover: University Press of New England, 1987.

Murray, G.; Brosio, M.; and Calogero, G. *Benedetto Croce*. London: Westerham Press, 1953.

Nicolini, F. *Benedetto Croce*. Turin: Unione Tipografico-Editrice Torinese, 1962.

———. *Benedetto Croce; vita intelletuale*. Naples: Cacciavillani, 1944.

Orsini, Gian N. G. *Benedetto Croce: Philosopher of Art and Literary Critic*. Carbondale: Southern Illinois University Press, 1961.

Palmer, L. M., and Harris, H. S., eds. *Thought, Action and Intuition: A Symposium on the Philosophy of Benedetto Croce.* Hildesheim-New York: George Olms, 1975.

Paolozzi, Ernesto. *I problemi dell'estetica italiana: dal secondo dopoguerra al 1985.* Naples: Società Editrice Napoletana, 1985.

————. *Vicende dell'estetica fra vecchio e nuovo positivismo.* Naples: Loffredo, 1985.

Pardo, F. *La filosofia teoretica di B. Croce.* Naples: Perrella, 1928.

Parente, A. *Croce per lumi sparsi. Problemi e ricordi.* Florence: La Nuova Italia, 1975.

Pesce, Domenico. *L'estetica dopo Croce.* Florence: Philosophia, 1962.

Petruzzellis, N. *Il problema della storia nell'idealismo moderno,* 2d ed. Florence: Sansoni, 1940.

————. *Sistema e problema.* Bari: Laterza, 1954.

Piccoli, Raffaello. *Benedetto Croce: An Introduction to His Philosophy.* New York: Harcourt, Brace & Co., 1922.

Pritchard, John Paul. *Criticism in America to 1956.* Norman: University of Oklahoma Press, 1956.

Puppo, M. *Benedetto Croce e la critica letteraria.* Florence: Sansoni, 1974.

————. *Il metodo e la critica di Benedetto Croce.* Milan: Murcia, 1964.

Roberts, David D. *Benedetto Croce and the Uses of Historicism.* Berkeley: University of California Press, 1987.

Robertson, John M. *Croce as Shakespearean Critic.* London: George Routledge and Sons, 1922.

Roggerone, G. *Prospettive Crociane.* Lecce: Milella, 1968.

Romano, P. *Infussi del pensiero Kantiano nell'estetica di B. Croce.* Bari: Accolti, 1938.

Rossani, W. *Croce e l'estetica.* Milan: Pan, 1976.

Russo, L. *La critica letteraria contemporanea.* Bari: Adriatica, 1942.

Saragat, G. *On the Centenary of the Birth of Benedetto Croce.* New York: Istituto Italiano di Cultura, 1966.

Sasso, G. *Benedetto Croce: La ricerca della dialettica.* Naples: Morano, 1975.

Seervelt, C. G. *Benedetto Croce's Earlier Aesthetic Theories and Literary Criticism: A Critical Philosophical Look at the Development during his Rationalistic Years.* Kampen, Netherlands: J. H. Kok, 1958.

Sgroi, G. *Gli studi estetici in Italia.* Florence: La Nuova Italia, 1932.

————. *Benedetto Croce: svolgimento storico della sua estetica.* Messina: D'Anna, 1947.

Spingarn, J. *Creative Criticism: Essays on the Unity of Genius and Taste.* New York: Henry Holt and Co., 1917. *Creative Criticism and Other Essays.* New York: Harcourt Brace, 1931.

————. *La critica letteraria nel rinascimento,* translated by Antonio Fusco with a preface by Benedetto Croce. Bari: Laterza, 1905.

————. *Literary Criticism in the Renaissance.* New York: Macmillan, 1899.

Spirito, U. *L'idealismo italiano e i suoi critici.* Florence: Le Monnier, 1930.

————. *Il nuovo idealismo italiano.* Rome: Alberti, 1923.

Sprigge, C. *Benedetto Croce: Man and Thinker.* Cambridge: Bowes & Bowes, 1952.

Struckmeyer, O. K. *Croce and Literary Criticism.* Cambridge: Cambridge University Press, 1921.

Tanga, Iginio. *L'estetica di Benedetto Croce.* Rome: Copa, 1959.

Valentini, F. *La controriforma della dialettica.* Rome: Editori Riuniti, 1966.

Walkley, A. *Dramatic Criticism.* London: John Murray, 1903.

Wellek, René. *Four Critics: Croce, Valéry, Lukács, and Ingarden.* Seattle: University of Washington Press, 1981.

————. *History of Modern Criticism, 1750–1950. The Romantic Age,* vol. 2. New Haven: Yale University Press, 1955.

————. *History of Modern Criticism, 1750–1950. English Criticism, 1900–1950,* vol. 5. New Haven: Yale University Press, 1986.

————. *History of Modern Criticism, 1750–1950. American Criticism, 1900–1950,* vol. 6. New Haven: Yale University Press, 1986.

Zacchi, A. *Il nuovo idealismo di B. Croce e G. Gentile.* Rome: Ferrari, 1925.

2. Articles

Arisato, Hiroshi. "Pensiero del De Sanctis e del Croce sull'Ariosto." *Studi italici* (Kyoto), 15 (Dec. 1966): 45–56.

Assunto, Rosario. "La revisione critica del pensiero crociano e il problema della categoria estetica." In *Interpretazioni crociane,* pp. 5–106. Bari: Adriatica Editrice, 1965.

Attisani, Adelchi. "Introduzione all'Estetica di Benedetto Croce." *Letterature moderne,* 2 (1961): 440–460.

————. "Gli studi di estetica." In *Cinquant' anni di vita intellettuale italiana, 1896–1946.* Naples: Edizioni Scientifiche Italiane, 1950. Pp. 290ff.

————. "Svolgimento del pensiero estetico di B. Croce, III." *Letterature moderne,* 2 (1961): 569–585.

Battaglia, Felice. "Rassegna di studi crociani." *Giornale di metafisica,* 19 (1964): 718–736.

Bausola, Adriano. "Immanenza e individualità in Benedetto Croce." *Studium,* 62 (1966): 494–505.

Bertocci, A. P. "The Development of Croce's Aesthetic." *Boston University Graduate Journal,* 10 (1962): 86–95, 127–139.

Biondolillo, Francesco. "Benedetto Croce: Nel centenario della sua nascità." *Ausonia,* 21 (1) (1966): 47–52.

Blocker, H. Gene. "Another Look at Aesthetic Imagination." *Journal of Aesthetics and Art Criticism,* 30 (1972): 529–536.

Brescia, Giuseppe. "I primi scritti di Benedetto Croce." *Cultura,* 9 (1971): 279–281.

Brown, Merle E. "Croce's Early Aesthetics: 1894–1912." *Journal of Aesthetics and Art Criticism,* 22 (1963): 29–41.

Bruno, Raffaelle, "Benedetto Croce. L'estetica e il problema della legittimità dell'arte." *Pensiero e società,* 23–24 (1986): 31–48.

Calogero, G. "Postilla ai ricordi crociani." *Cultura,* 5 (1967): 166–179.

————. "Ricordi e riflessioni: Benedetto Croce." *Cultura,* 4 (1966): 145–179.

Caponigri, A. Robert. "Croce, Benedetto." In *Encyclopaedia Britannica*, 15th ed., 1974.

Carus, P. "Croce's Use of the Word 'Intuition.' " *The Monist*, 26 (1916): 312–315.

Caserta, Ernesto. "Croce, Benedetto." In *Dictionary of Italian Literature*, co-edited by Peter Bondanella and Julia Conaway Bondanella. Westport: Greenwood Press, 1979. Pp. 131–134.

————. "Croce critico di Dante," *Dante Studies*, 89 (1971): 217–233.

————. "Croce e D'Annunzio," *Romance Notes*, 14 (1973): 430–438.

————. "Croce e la linguistica." *Rivista di studi italiani*, 1 (1985): 105–115.

————. "Croce, Pirandello e il concetto d'umorismo." *The Canadian Journal of Italian Studies*, 2–3 (1983): 103–110.

————. "Croce, Pirandello e il problema estetico," *Italica* (1974): 20–42.

Colonnello, Pio. "Pensiero e linguaggio: l'influenza di Croce su G. de Robertis al tempo della 'Voce.' " *Rivista di studi crociani*, 3 (1976): 1–7.

De Mauro, Tullio. "La letteratura critica più recente sull'estetica e la linguistica crociana." *De homine*, 11–12 (1964): 273–286.

Dewey, John. "A Comment on the Foregoing Criticisms." *Journal of Aesthetics and Art Criticism*, 6 (1948): 207–209.

Dimler, G. R., S. J. "Creative Intuition in the Aesthetic Theories of Croce and Maritain." *The New Scholasticism*, 37 (1963): 472–492.

Donagan, A. H. "Collingwood's Debt to Croce." *Mind*, 81 (1972): 265–266.

Douglas, George H. "Croce's Early Aesthetic and American Critical Theory." *Comparative Literature Studies*, 7 (1970): 204–215.

————. "Croce's Expression Theory of Art Revisited." *The Personalist*, 54 (1973): 60–70.

————. "A Reconsideration of the Dewey-Croce Exchange." *Journal of Aesthetics and Art Criticism*, 28 (1970): 497–504.

Fisch, Max H. "Croce e Vico." *Rivista di studi crociani*, 5 (1968): 9–30, 151–171.

Flora, Francesco. "Occasioni e aperture: De Sanctis, Croce e la critica contemporanea." *Letterature moderne*, 11 (1961): 5–33.

Foerster, Norman. "The Esthetic Judgment and the Ethical Judgment." In *The Intent of the Critic*, edited by D. A. Stauffer. Massachusetts: Peter Smith, 1963. Pp. 65–88.

Franchini, R. "Croce e la metodologia storiografica." In *Interpretazioni crociane*. Bari: Adriatica Editrice, 1965. Pp. 171–195.

————. "La dialettica 'negativa.' " *Rivista di studi crociani*, 8 (1971): 253–259.

Gullace, Giovanni. "An American Symposium on Benedetto Croce." *International Studies in Philosophy*, 9 (1977): 127–134.

————. "Benedetto Croce." In *Critical Survey of Literary Theory*, edited by Magill. Pasadena: Salem Press, 1988. Pp. 326–333.

————. "Benedetto Croce and the Problem of Translation." *Italian Quarterly*, 25 (1984): 15–27.

————. "Benedetto Croce et la Critique Cornélienne." *Les Lettres Romanes*, 29 (1975): 2–42.

————. "Poetry and Literature in Croce's *La poesia*." *Journal of Aesthetics and Art Criticism*, 19 (1961): 453–461.

————. "Gentile versus Croce: A Comparison of two Rival Aesthetic Systems."
    Symposium, 11 (1957): 75–91.

Guzzo, Augusto. "Itinerario estetico." *Filosofia,* 23 (1972): 349–374.

Hack, R. "The Doctrine of Literary Forms." *Harvard Studies in Classical Philol-
    ogy,* edited by The Committee of the Classical Instructors of Harvard Uni-
    versity, 27 (1916): 1–65.

Harris, H. S. "Croce, Benedetto." In *Encyclopedia of Philosophy,* edited by Paul
    Edwards, 2:263–267. New York: Macmillan, 1972.

Mandelbaum, Maurice. "The History of Philosophy: Some Methodological Issues."
    Journal of Philosophy, 74 (1977): 561–572.

Montale, Eugenio, "L'estetica e la critica." *Mondo,* 14 (1962): 3–4.

————. "Lesson on Croce: Esthetics and Criticism." *Italian Quarterly,* 7 (1963):
    48–65.

Moss, M. E. "Benedetto Croce's Sphere of the Aesthetic: Pure Intuition and Art."
    Claremont Journal of Philosophy, 6 (1986): 1–13.

————. "The Crocean Concept of the Pure Concept." *Idealistic Studies,* 17
    (1987): 39–52.

————. "Croce's Theory of Intuition Reconsidered." *Rivista di studi crociani,* 15
    (1978): 292–306.

————. "The Enduring Values in the Philosophy of Benedetto Croce." *Idealistic
    Studies,* 10 (1980): 46–66.

————. "Petrarch and Modern Criticism: De Sanctis and Croce." *Rivista rosmin-
    iana di filosofia e di cultura,* (1977): 35–42.

Oberti, Elisa. "Valore storico e teoretico delle proposte estetiche di Croce." *Vita e
    pensiero,* 49 (1966): 507–514.

Orsini, Gian N. G. "Coleridge e Croce: Note di estetica e di critica della poesia."
    Rivista di studi crociani, 4 (1964): 444–453.

————. "Recent Accounts of Croce." *Italian Quarterly,* 5 (1961): 61–64.

————. "Theory and Practice in Croce's Aesthetic." *Journal of Aesthetics and Art
    Criticism,* 13 (1954–55): 300–313.

Paolozzi, Ernesto. "L'estetica di B. Croce fra realismo e idealismo." *Forum Itali-
    cum,* 22 (1988): 187–203.

Parente, A. "Estetica e gusto nell'opera critica di Croce." *Rivista di studi crociani,*
    3 (1966): 283–294.

Patanker, R. B. "What Does Croce Mean by 'Expression'?" *British Journal of Aes-
    thetics,* 2 (1962): 112–125.

Pepper, Stephen. "Some Questions on Dewey's Esthetics." In *The Philosophy
    of John Dewey,* edited by P. A. Schilpp. New York: Macmillan, 1951.
    Pp. 369–389.

Perricone Jr., Cristopher. "The Place of Idiom in Benedetto Croce's Theory of Aes-
    thetic." *Rivista di studi crociani,* 20 (1983): 41–49.

Pesce, Domenico. "L'estetica di B. Croce." In E. Paolo Lamanna. *Introduzione
    alla lettura di Croce.* Pp. 191–248.

Puppo, Mario. "La metodologia del Croce e le tendenze della recente critica letter-
    aria." *Studium,* 62 (1966): 520–527.

Read, Sir Herbert. "The Essence of Beauty." *John O'London's Weekly,* July 6,
    1961, p. 3.

Reynolds, Barbara. "Benedetto Croce." *Times,* London, Oct. 3, 1963, p. 15.
Rossani, Wolfango. "La critica figurativa e l'estetica crociana." *Osservatore politico letterario,* 7 (1961): 84–102.
Russo, Luigi, and Alfredo Parente. "La polemica fra Croce e Dewey e l'arte come esperienza." *Rivista di studi crociani,* 5 (1968): 201–227.
Santayana, George. "Croce's Aesthetics." *Journal of Comparative Literature,* 1 (1903): 191–195.
Santoli, V. "Benedetto Croce, *Filosofia poesia storia.*" *Rivista di letterature moderne,* 1 (1952): 60.
Sasso, Gennaro. "Due variazioni polemiche sull'interpretazione di Croce." *Cultura,* 6 (1968): 260–276.
Simoni, Frederic S. "Benedetto Croce: A Case of International Misunderstanding," *The Journal of Aesthetics and Art Criticism,* 11 (1952): 7–14.
Steinman, James F. "Santayana and Croce: An Aesthetic Reconciliation." *Journal of Aesthetics and Art Criticism,* 30 (1971): 251–253.
Tertulian, Nicolas, "Introduzione all'estetica di Croce." *Rivista di studi crociani,* 8 (1971): 138–153, 378–394.
Wellek, René. "Literary History." In *Literary Scholarship: Its Aims and Methods.* Chapel Hill: University of North Carolina Press: 1941.
———. "The Parallelism between Literature and the Arts, 1941." In *Literary Criticism: Idea and Act.* Berkeley: University of California Press, 1974.
White, Hayden V. "What Is Living and What Is Dead in Croce's Criticism of Vico." In *Giambattista Vico: An International Symposium,* edited by Giorgio Tagliacozzo and Hayden V. White. Baltimore: Johns Hopkins University Press, 1969. Pp. 379–389.

INDEX